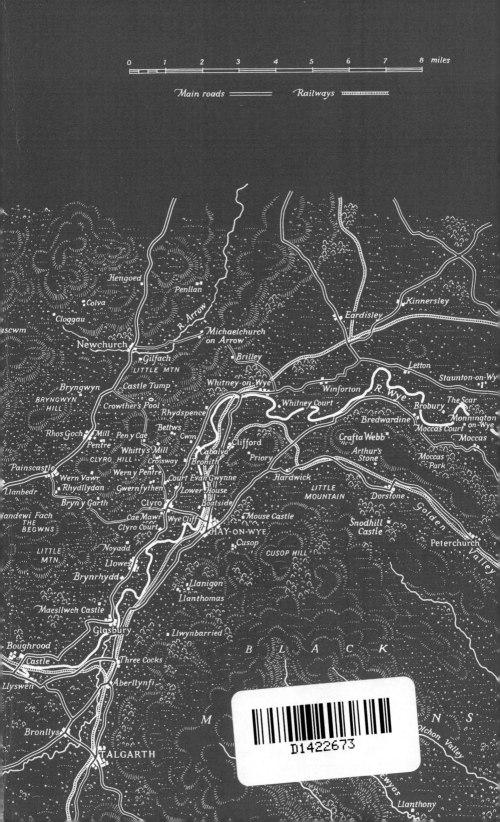

0   1   2   3   4   5   6   7   8 *miles*

Main roads ═══════   *Railways* ┅┅┅┅┅┅

Hengoed

Penllan

•Colva

•Cloggau

•scwm

R. Arrow

•Michaelchurch
on Arrow

Newchurch

Gilfach

Brilley

LITTLE MTN

Kinnersley

•Eardisley

Letton

Staunton-on-Wy

Bryngwyn

Castle Tump

Whitney-on-Wye

Winforton

R. Wye

BRYNGWYN
HILL

Crowther's Pool

Rhydspence

Whitney Court

Brobury

The Scar

Rhos Goch•

Mill
Pentre

Pen y Cae

Bettws

Cwm

Bredwardine

Monnington
on-Wye

Moccas Court

Moccas

Crafta Webb

Moccas
Park

CLYRO HILL

Whitty's Mill

Cabalva

Clifford

Priory

Arthur's
Stone

Painscastle

Crossway

Bronith

Wern Vawr

Wern y Pentre

Court Evan Gwynne

Hardwick

Llanbedr

Rhydllydan

Gwernfythen

Lower House

Bryn y Garth

Clyro

Boatside

LITTLE
MOUNTAIN

Dorstone

andewi Fach

Cae Mawr

Wye Cliff

HAY-ON-WYE

Golden

THE
BEGWNS

Clyro Court

Cusop

Snodhill
Castle

Peterchurch

LITTLE
MTN.

Noyadd

Llowes

CUSOP HILL

Valley

Brynrhydd

Llanigon

Maeslwch Castle

Llanthomas

Glasbury

Llwynbarried

B   L   A   C   K

Boughrood

•Castle

Three Cocks

Llyswen

Aberllynfi

M

N   S

Bronllys

TALGARTH

olchon Valley

ewas

Llanthony

JOURNAL OF A COUNTRY CURATE
Selections from the Diary of Francis Kilvert
1870–79

Selected and with an introduction by Peter Wait
Photographic re-creations by Tim Stephens

The Folio Society, London, 1977

PRINTED IN GREAT BRITAIN
by Shenval Press Limited, Harlow

CONTENTS

ILLUSTRATIONS

The illustrations, which have been specially prepared for this edition by Tim Stephens, are partly from contemporary material, kindly loaned by the Secretary of the Kilvert Society, and partly from new photographs. Sometimes old and new have been combined on one plate to evoke the changes between Kilvert's time and today, particularly having regard to the disappearance or decay of buildings he mentions frequently.

INTRODUCTION

Why do I keep this voluminous journal? I can hardly tell. Partly because life appears to me such a curious and wonderful thing that it almost seems a pity that even such a humble and uneventful life as mine should pass altogether away without some such record as this, and partly too because I think the record may amuse and interest some who come after me.

(3 November 1874)

The case of Kilvert is strange. Eminent critics have hailed his diary as a classic, ranking with Pepys, comparable with but more vivid and more human than Dorothy Wordsworth. Yet many people who would regard as an insult the suggestion that they are not acquainted with Pepys, have never even heard of Kilvert. On the other hand he has a passionately addicted following and a flourishing society devoted to the study of his life and writing.

So the writer of an introduction faces a difficulty. How much does the reader need to be told? In what follows I hope I may be forgiven for stating what may be all too familiar to many. I hope, too, I may be excused an excursion into literary criticism and psychological analysis. As for the first, as an eminent critic has said, 'Literary, unlike divine, masterpieces do not need prophets or scientists to reveal their essences', and this may be taken to apply even more so to diaries, where personal enjoyment is the main criterion. As for the second, however much one may be tempted to discuss Kilvert's character, it hardly needs it. He is as self-revealing as Pepys. What some readers may need, perhaps, is some information about the diary itself, and what this edition of part of it consists of; about the diarist's family and social background; and about the people and places where he worked.

As to the diary. It is the diary of a country parson, and it covers, with gaps, the years 1870 to 1879. Only a portion survives and the present edition – as I shall explain later – prints only a part of this portion.

In 1937 there came into the hands of William Plomer, the poet, novelist and critic, twenty-two notebooks of various shapes and sizes written in a 'sloping angular hand'. Between 1938 and 1940 he published, with the firm of Jonathan Cape, three volumes of selections amounting to about a third of their total contents. He had made a typed transcript of all the notebooks. Being pressed for space during the war he destroyed this, confident that the original notebooks would be preserved. Unfortunately they were not, and only two have survived out of the original twenty-two; the remainder, for reasons shrouded in mystery, were destroyed by their final owner, a daughter of the diarist's sister. Plomer says that in his selection he was as careful as possible 'to retain everything that seemed most worth preserving', and on another occasion, 'I can assure you that the best and most essential parts of the Diary are in print. I left out what seemed to me commonplace and trivial'. Unfortunately not everyone has the same notion of the commonplace and trivial. Professor Garrod thought much of Dorothy Wordsworth's journals 'prolix and trivial'. So one can only regard the destruction as disastrous.

The diary starts at the beginning of the year 1870 when Kilvert, then in his thirtieth year, had already been a curate in the parish of Clyro, in Radnorshire, for some five years, and continues to 1879, the year in which he married, and died. Some of these years he spends working in his father's Wiltshire parish as a curate, and the remainder on the Welsh border, in the Wye valley, first as curate and later as a vicar. The present volume is a selection taken from the portion which records the years in Wales and Herefordshire, for there the combination of a unique social scene and a magical countryside seems to have had an emotional effect on the diarist that gives this part of his record a vivid unity which sets it apart from the rest. Kilvert loved the Welsh. 'I believe I must have Welsh blood. I always feel so happy and at home among the kindly Welsh.' The omission of his more placid life in Wiltshire, and some splendid descriptive writing, is regrettable, but he is always at the top of his form in Wales – as writer, person and parish priest.

The diarist's background and family connections were what today might be described as modestly 'county'. He was born in 1840 in the small Wiltshire village of Hardenhuish (also known as 'Harnish'), where his father, the Rev. Robert Kilvert, was rector. Robert and his brothers had had a fairly hard upbringing owing to the early death of their father and loss of money through a bank failure. However, he had managed to gain an exhibition to Oriel College, where Keble was at that time a tutor, and shortly after leaving Oxford he was ordained. While he was at Harnish he married Thermuthis Coleman, the daughter of Walter Coleman of Langley Fitzurse and first cousin to Squire Ashe of Langley Burrell, both old Wiltshire families. In 1855 he became the rector of Langley Burrell. Francis Kilvert had thus spent his entire childhood at Harnish, and perhaps had been taught at the little school his father, like Trollope's Dr Wortle, had kept there. He finished his schooling at his uncle Francis Kilvert's school at Claverton Lodge, near Bath. He then went up to Oxford, to Wadham College, where he was a contemporary of Lewis Carroll, whose affectionate interest in little girls he shared. He was ordained in 1863, and worked as a curate in his father's parish until he went, also as a curate, to Clyro, close to the English border. There he remained until 1872, when he returned to Langley to help his father, paying occasional short visits to Wales. In 1876 he was presented to the living of St Harmon's, Rhayader, and in 1877 became the vicar of Bredwardine. All these three parishes are in the valley of the Wye. Descriptions of landscape figure so largely in the diary that there is no need for any here. Suffice it to say that Clyro lies between the rich undulating pastoral countryside of Herefordshire and the wild, rugged, remote and mountainous country of Wales. The area is now known as the 'Kilvert country', and a good deal of descriptive writing has been lavished on it. The reader is strongly recommended to refer to the map provided in this edition, which helps to give an idea of the diarist's perambulations and to understand what lies beneath this typical utterance:

It is a fine thing to be out on the hills alone. A man can hardly be a beast or a fool alone on a great mountain. There is no company like the grand solemn beautiful hills. They fascinate and grow upon us and one has a feeling and a love for them which one has for nothing else. I don't wonder that our Saviour went out into a mountain to pray and continued all night praying to God there.

No record exists of his life at St Harmon's. He went to Bredwardine in November 1877; the diary recommences in December of the same year and ends finally in March 1879; in August he married Elizabeth Rowland, and in September he died of peritonitis.

Such are the bare outlines of the diarist's life. More needs to be said about his family, to whom there are constant references. Francis had a brother and four sisters; Edward (called either Teddy or Perch), Thermuthis (Thersie), Emily (Emmie), Frances (Fanny) and Sarah Dorothea Anne (Dora). Emmie is married to Col. Samuel Wyndowe, a surgeon general in the Indian Army, and is not mentioned in this part of the diary. In 1871 Thersie marries the Rev. William Smith, who becomes rector of Monnington-on-Wye and a close neighbour of the diarist when he goes to Bredwardine. In 1878 Perch marries Nellie Pitcairn. Dora appears frequently in the diary and keeps house for Kilvert at Bredwardine. On the last page of the diary she receives a proposal of marriage from Nellie Pitcairn's brother, James.

A bewildering number of people pass through the pages of the diary, for Kilvert was not only a diligent visitor of his poorer parishioners, but a welcome guest in the houses of the local gentry. One of the principal characters in the chronicle is 'Mr V.', the Reverend Richard Lister Venables, the vicar of Clyro. He appears in the diary as a kind, hospitable, liberal-minded and conscientious priest. From other sources he is known to have been very comfortably off, well connected, active in county affairs. Country curates could lead obscure lives, and though Kilvert was of gentle birth and moved with assurance in all social circles, Mr V.'s support must have been of considerable value. During much of the diary Mr V. is taken up with his family home at Llysdinam between Builth and Rhayader, and his rebuilding operations there. Kilvert is his frequent guest and Mrs V., a youngish woman, Mr V.'s second wife, is the confidante of his problems in courting Daisy Thomas. There are, too, the Baskervilles of Clyro Court (Mr Baskerville was the squire of Clyro), the Bevans of Hay Castle, the Thomases of Llanthomas, the Crichtons of Wye Cliff, the Dews, the de Wintons, the Vaughans; mostly clergy, some landed gentry, some a combina-

tion of both. There are, too, his vividly described parishioners:
the 'old soldier', John Morgan, a veteran of the Napoleonic
wars, Emma Griffiths, Hannah Whitney, the notable Priscilla
Price, with her reminiscences of George IV. I have provided a
brief guide to the most frequently mentioned names and places.
While I am on the subject of people I think it worth mentioning
that *in toto* they were very thin on the ground. The total population of Radnorshire in 1871 was only 25,000 (53 persons to the
square mile). What is implicit in the whole background of the
diary, though far from obtrusive, is the extreme poverty and
squalor in which so many of Kilvert's parishioners live. Dirt,
disease and death are bravely accepted. Hardly a family but
loses one or more children, mainly it would seem from consumption. Kilvert was deeply compassionate. He loved mankind, and
it is transparently clear that mankind loved him. Although he
ate the pheasants and drank the champagne of the wealthy with
enthusiasm, there are signs that he was not happy about the
glaring contrasts in the social scene, or the artificial manners
and modes of the upper classes.

What was going on in the outside world during the nine years
covered by the diary? Apparently not much that affected the life
of a country clergyman in such a remote district. The slow decay
of British agriculture seems barely perceptible. There had been
no foreign war since 1856. Yet it was a period of intense political
and legislative activity: the second Reform Bill had recently
added a million voters to the electoral roll. The Education Act
of 1870 was to revolutionize public education. Girton College
for women had been founded in the same year. In 1872 Joseph
Arch launched his agricultural trade union movement, and there
was much agrarian unrest in the country. In 1875 fifty thousand
Welsh miners went on strike for four months. Prince Albert was
dead and the queen was living in absolute seclusion. Her name
is never mentioned, though the Prince of Wales's recovery from
illness is greeted with feverish enthusiasm. The Franco-Prussian
war began in 1870. Such were a few of the social and political
questions which occupied men's minds during the years of the
diary and which might have been expected to interest Kilvert.

As for the intellectual background: the heyday of Victorian

literature had passed. Thackeray, Dickens, Mrs Gaskell, the Brontës, were dead, though Browning and Tennyson were flourishing. 1871 saw the publication of three widely differing works, George Eliot's *Middlemarch*, Hardy's *Far from the Madding Crowd*, and Lewis Carroll's *Alice through the Looking Glass*. In 1878 Kilvert was reading Trollope's *Is he Popenjoy?*, which prompts speculation about his views on that great genre painter of the country clergyman. But he is never mentioned again. Wordsworth was a great favourite of Kilvert's – 'dear old Wordsworth'. The diaries have been compared with those of Dorothy Wordsworth, and there are certainly extraordinary similarities in their descriptions of scenery. One may be tempted to think that he was influenced by her writing from the fact that we see he was given a copy of her Journal for his birthday in 1874. This was, however, almost certainly *Recollections of a Tour made in Scotland* published that same year; for the Alfoxden and Grasmere *Journals*, which alone of her writings were in many ways Kilvertian, were not published until after Kilvert's death. He is fond of Tennyson: the reader may discover two unacknowledged quotations. He mentions, too, Browning, Sterne, Burns, Shakespeare, Coleridge, Kingsley, but none of the classic Victorian novelists. In all his descriptions of nature one feels above all the presence of Wordsworth, who, only a few miles from Clyro, on the river Wye, had

> *learned*
> *To look on nature, not as in the hour*
> *Of thoughtless youth; but hearing oftentimes*
> *The still, sad music of humanity.*

So far as religion was concerned, the Tractarian movement was now a thing of the past, though many of its protagonists were still alive. Although *The Origin of Species* had been in circulation for over ten years when the diary began, *The Descent of Man* was published only in 1871. Darwin and Lyell had destroyed *Genesis*. But the theory of evolution did not take long to become respectable; much more serious was the blow to received ideas about the absolute truth and divine inspiration of the Bible delivered by the authors of *Essays and Reviews*, and the general movement for the historical criticism of ancient texts, sacred or otherwise. We do not know what Kilvert's views were on these matters, though on one occasion he says, 'If I had children I should teach them to believe all the dear old Bible stories.' One thing is certain – and this divides him from the modern world more surely than anything else – his, and the almost universal, belief in an after-life; so that where education was concerned 'it was natural for a clergyman to think that a child's most urgent need was to be fitted, not so much for this life, as for eternity'.*

It is not obvious to the reader that Kilvert was working, at least in Clyro and St Harmon's, in a part of the country where dissent was strong. He says little about it, and when he does it is often to express dislike. He speaks of church v. chapel antagonisms, and there is an amusingly deleterious description of non-conformist influence at an election. At St Harmon's, where he was vicar for about eighteen months, probably at least half the locals were non-conformists. There is evidence that Kilvert was very friendly with them.† Clyro was too near the English border for dissent to have been so strong there (and Bredwardine was actually in England); but there was a chapel at Rhos Goch, two in Painscastle, and another in the Bronith near Clyro. There was, of course, a connection between dissent and the Welsh language, and 40 per cent of the population were Welsh speakers. Very few of the Anglican clergy could speak Welsh: 'Anglican clergy were expected to be gentry. Welsh speakers were seldom gentry.' ‡No bishop in Wales had spoken Welsh *from birth* since the days of Queen Anne, and the first Welsh-speaking bishop in the century was Joshua Hughes, appointed to the see of St Asaph in 1870. ‡Did Kilvert speak Welsh? Long before he was appointed to St Harmon's he referred to it as 'the only Welsh speaking parish in Radnorshire', and it would be surprising if with his interest in folklore and poetry he did not have some Welsh. But there is no positive evidence. Certainly very many people in St

*From *Churchmen and the Condition of England, 1832–1885*, G. Kitson Clark, Methuen.
†From *A Kilvert Miscellanea*, Kilvert Society; June 1969.
‡The source of these two pieces of information is *The Victorian Church* (Vol. II), Owen Chadwick, Cambridge University Press.

Harmon's spoke English. The language situation was to change; the Education Act of 1870 made English compulsory in schools.

How much was a country parson paid? Professor Chadwick tells us that, admittedly rather earlier in the century, in the diocese of St Davids there were eighty-six livings paying less than £75 a year, and the average was £137. A curate would have been paid much less. Stipends depended on tithe, and Welsh agriculture was poor. When Kilvert's father entered on his first curacy at Keevil in Wiltshire he received £70 a year and (by grace of an absentee vicar) the use of an unfurnished house. When Kilvert gives notice to leave Clyro, his vicar, Mr Venables, offers him £160 a year to stay on. As vicar at St Harmon's he earned between £300 and £400 a year, but had no vicarage; at Bredwardine nearly £400 and an extremely pleasant house. His expenses were not high: when he hired a housekeeper for Bredwardine vicarage he paid her £14 a year – £2 more than her previous employer. He charges £80 for boarding and tutoring Sam Cole. He is to inherit £2,700 when his parents die. When, as a young curate, he sought the hand of Daisy Thomas his prospects were too poor for her father to consider the idea. (Only a few years earlier Bella Wilfer had married Our Mutual Friend on £150.) Daisy, as we now know, died unwed. One entry in the diary gives an idea of local views on a farmer's wealth. On 26 October 1870 he notes that the Gores of Whitty's Mill 'are very well-off, make at least £200 a year, the schoolmistress says, and have a matter of £300 in the bank'.

Confining this edition to Kilvert's life in the Wye country has, as I said earlier, meant sacrificing some splendid passages. There has also been the risk of giving a lop-sided view of his character, tastes and the general course of his life. I have tried to compensate for this by providing occasional linking notes between breaks in his life on the Wye. He goes to his home in Wiltshire very often (by means of a railway system which no longer exists); he has trips to the sea, to Oxford, to Bath for church congresses (and the dentist), jaunts with his father: not all have been recorded. There are too his love affairs. No portrait of the diarist can be complete that does not show his very strong feelings for the opposite sex, of whatever age. Two of his strongest attachments, for 'Kathleen Mavourneen' and Ettie Meredith Brown, occur during the Wiltshire period of his existence, but I have not omitted them entirely. His description of Ettie at their first meeting is such a splendid piece of Victorian romantic painting that it has to be included. There is no lack of pretty girls in the Wye country, from the pretty schoolgirls Gipsy Lizzie and Florence Hill to the maturer beauty of Daisy Thomas. Kilvert's feelings for little girls may seem rather overheated; his taste for (to quote William Plomer) 'paintings representing distressed and scantily dressed women caught in precarious but romantic situations' peculiar for a respectable clergyman. But when he is faced with reality the eye of the painter takes over. To quote – from the other part of the diary, when he is at Shanklin:

I stopped to watch some children bathing from the beach directly below. One beautiful girl stood entirely naked on the sand, and there as she half sat, half reclined sideways, leaning upon her elbow with her knees bent and her legs and feet partly drawn back and up, she was a model for a sculptor, there was the tender supple waist, the gentle dawn and tender swell of the bosom and the budding breasts, the graceful rounding of the delicately beautiful limbs and above all the soft and exquisite curves of the rosy dimpled bottom and broad white thigh. Her dark hair fell in thick masses on her white shoulders as she threw her head back and looked out to sea. She seemed a Venus Anadyomene fresh risen from the waves.

One may enjoy without the slightest feeling of distaste his behaviour towards the opposite sex. In an age when relations between the young of the middle classes were riddled with taboo, Kilvert's happy sublimations seem refreshingly free of humbug. Besides he badly wanted children of his own. From the same part of the diary: 'It came over me like a storm and I turned away hungry at heart and half envying the parents as they sat upon the sand watching their children at play.'

Obviously those who enjoy the diary and want to know more of the diarist must read Plomer's three-volume edition and his Introductions. Since its last printing many new facts about Kilvert and his family have been discovered through the efforts of the Kilvert Society. It was thought that Kilvert met his wife, Elizabeth Rowland, only a few months before their wedding. In fact he had met her in 1876, probably shortly after the Ettie episode. Mrs Kilvert inherited the diary, and it has been said by her niece, Miss Rowland, that before handing it down she decided to remove all those parts that referred to her. It will be seen that Kilvert went to St Harmon's in 1876, and that there is no diary for his time there. Presumably there were references to the future Mrs Kilvert, who seems to have visited him there. The same reason may account for the brevity of the Bredwardine portion, though there are others: his extreme assiduity as vicar, his increasing ill-health.

It seems likely, too, that she destroyed the Wiltshire sections with their history of his affair with Ettie. If so, her censorship was not confined to tearing out single pages, but involved the destruction of whole notebooks, perhaps ten altogether. Another fact that gives rise to speculation is that the diary begins with no introductory remarks on 1 January 1870, when Kilvert had already been in Clyro for five years. Had he started much earlier? Evidence from the existing notebooks appears to make this unlikely. Two only of the notebooks survive, and from these it seems that Kilvert wrote up his diary daily, with an average entry of 800 words. Plomer calculated that, in all he had written at least three quarters of a million words. So, we shall never know how much Mrs Kilvert removed. We can only be thankful she let so much remain. Her photograph shows a handsome, good-humoured, kind, strong face. She was only married for five weeks, and never married again. She died in 1911.

Few impressions of Kilvert's appearence survive. A cousin who remembered him from childhood describes him as 'very sleek and glossy and gentle – rather like a nice Newfoundland dog', and an old man in Rhayader – 'Ah, a real nice gentleman . . . quiet gentleman. Great black beard. Like a foreign gentleman. No we don't see such gentlemen today. Nor such beards. 'E was a great walker, sir. Many a pair of boots my father soled for Mr Kilbert [sic].'* His eye-sight was bad. He speaks of 'my poor disfigured eyes', and at Bredwardine in 1878 he is telling his parishioners of his 'blindness and difficulty in knowing my own sheep by sight'.

*From *A Kilvert Miscellanea*, Kilvert Society June 1969.

There are passing references in the diary to his poetry. He has pieces published in the *Hereford Times*; he contributes to joint collections; he offers a volume to Mr Longman who politely declines it, unseen. Shortly after his death some of his poems were published under the title *Musings in Verse*. Later, all were collected and published by the Kilvert Society. His other writings on folklore and antiquarian subjects were never published. He was not the only writer in his family. His father's elder brother Francis, also in holy orders, who kept a small school at Claverton near Bath, was a prolific writer, mainly of sermons and antiquarian articles; also, of course, of the memoir of Bishop Hurd, which so angered Maria Kilvert in Worcester (30 November 1870). Robert Kilvert wrote his own memoirs of the years 1803–32. These are rambling and repetitious, but contain much of interest about life in Bath, at school, the repercussions of the Napoleonic wars. The diarist's sister Emily also wrote some recollections of her childhood.*

In conclusion, I would urge all readers who have enjoyed the present volume to acquire William Plomer's splendid edition of the entire surviving part of the Diary. That will provide a feast to which what follows is a delicious hors d'œuvre. The next step is to join the Kilvert Society, to whose devoted secretary, Mr C. T. O. Prosser,† I offer grateful thanks for the information and help he has given me. I am also grateful to Mr Frederick Grice, to whose recently published *Francis Kilvert, Priest and Diarist* I owe much of the information about the fate of the Diary, and about some of the characters in it. He also kindly sent me a copy of his even more recently published *Who's Who in Kilvert's Diary* just in time for me to use it in compiling 'People and Houses' (overleaf). Information about Kilvert and his background is slowly accumulating, and Mr Grice's book provides a useful bibliography.

PETER WAIT

*Both the Rev. Robert Kilvert's and his daughter's memoirs have been published by the Kilvert Society.
†Enquiries about the publications of the Society and its membership should be addressed to him at 8 Prince Edward Road, Broomy Hill, Hereford.

PEOPLE AND HOUSES

This list is far from complete and includes only the people and their houses most frequently referred to in the diary. Where families are concerned the names of individuals are not listed.

Alford, Rev., curate of Glasbury
Baskerville, squire of Clyro, and family, *Clyro Court*
Bevan, Rev. R. L., vicar of Hay, and family, *Hay Castle* (Mrs Bevan was sister of Rev. Henry Dew)
Bold, Mr and Mrs, *Boughrood Castle*
Bridge, Capt. and Mrs, *Pont Vaen*
Bynon, Miss, well-to-do Clyro parishioner, *Pentwyn*
Chaloner, Mrs, Kilvert's landlady in Clyro
Clouston, Dr, Clyro doctor
Cornewall, Rev. Sir George, rector of Moccas, *Moccas Court*
Crichton, Mr and Mrs (called by F. K. The 'Flower of Glamorgan'), and family, *Wye Cliff*
De Winton, Rev. Henry, rector of Boughrood, Mrs, and family, *Boughrood Rectory*
De Winton, Walter, and Mrs, *Maesllwch Castle*
Dew, Rev. Henry and Mrs, Rector of Whitney, and numerous family, *Whitney Rectory*, also Henry Dew junior and Mrs
Dew, Tomkyns, *Whitney Court*
Dyke, Mr and Mrs, and family, farmer, Upper Cabalva
Evans, Mr and Mrs, and family, schoolmaster in Clyro
Giles, Dr, Staunton doctor
'Gipsy Lizzie' (Elizabeth Jones) lived at Pen-y-Cae in the family of John Harris, farmer; was 10 in 1871
Gores, of the *Holly House*, and family
Gores of *Whitty's Mill*, and family; Mr Gore is a miller
Haigh Allen, Mr and Mrs, and family, also brother, Major Allen, *Clifford Priory*
Hill, Mr and Mrs, farmer of Upper Noyadd (family of 'Florence' who was aged 9 in 1871)

Hodgson Mr and Mrs and family, farmer, Lower Cabalva

Houseman, Rev., vicar of Bredwardine (succeeded by Kilvert after his death)

Jones the 'jockey', and Mrs, horsebreaker, Clyro

Kilvert, Rev. Robert and Mrs, rector of Langley Burrell, parents of the diarist; other children, Edward (Teddy, or Perch) marries Miss Nellie Pitcairn; Emily (Emmie) married to Col. Samuel Wyndowe, Indian Army; Frances (Fanny), Sarah Dorothea Anne (Dora), keeps house for F. K. at Bredwardine, marries James Pitcairn after end of diary; Thermuthis (Thersie), marries Rev. William Smith, rector of Monnington.

Lyne, Rev. J. L. 'Father Ignatius', the monk of Capel y Ffin

Meredith, R., land surveyor and amateur antiquarian

Morrell, Mr and Mrs and family, *Cae Mawr*

Newton, Miss, keen and helpful Bredwardine parishioner, *The Cottage*

Pope, Rev. Andrew, curate of Cusop; F. K. is best man at his marriage to Miss Mary Money Kyrle

Price, Rev. John, vicar of Llanbedr, the 'Solitary of Llanbedr'

Thomas, Mr and Mrs, and numerous family (including 'Daisy'), *Llanthomas*

Vaughan, Rev. David and Mrs, and family (including several pretty daughters), vicar of Newchurch, *Gilfach-y-rheol*

Venables, Rev. R. L. ('Mr V.') and Mrs, vicar of Clyro, to whom F. K. is curate; family home *Llysdinam Hall*

Wall, Mr and Mrs, and numerous family, farmer of Bettws

Webb, Rev. and Mrs, and family (parents of 'Helen of Troy') vicar of Hardwick, *Hardwick Vicarage*

Williams, Rev. Tom, vicar of Llowes, *Llowes Vicarage*

1870

[When the diary starts, in January 1870, Kilvert, aged 29, has already been in Clyro for nearly five years.]

Tuesday, 8 February

Called at Wye Cliff and took Mrs Crichton a large book I brought down for her from 11 Eaton Place. She came down from her room where she was busy painting the walls. It is a real pleasure to do anything for her. Crichton was at home too and I tried to describe to them the 'Good Shepherd' of Murillo.

[Kilvert has just returned from a visit to London during which he has been to an exhibition of old masters at the Royal Academy. His description of the Murillo is worth quoting as it exemplifies so much that is typical of his outlook.]

One of the finest pictures and the one which struck me most was a priceless Murillo, 'The Good Shepherd', a child with a crook walking between and guiding two lambs. One of the lambs walks meekly by the child's side. The other looks playfully up into his face. The child's eyes are uplifted and in them and over his whole face there is a marvellous beauty. An indescribable look of heavenly light and purity and an expression in which are blended sweetness and trust, resignation and love. The Good Shepherd whilst guiding his lambs looks upward for guidance himself. No words can do justice to or convey an adequate impression of this extraordinary picture. Nothing short of inspiration could have enabled the painter to conceive and execute that face and its gentle, tender, almost mournful beauty. In the upraised eyes dwells a shade of melancholy prescient of future suffering and sorrow – but they are fixed with a touching look of perfect love and trust on heaven. It must be seen to be believed.

Wednesday, 9 February

A very cold night and a slight shower of snow fell early this morning. Then it froze all day. The mountains all white. Went up the Cwm to White Ash. Old Sarah Probert groaning and rolling about in bed. Read to her Mark vi and made sure she knew the Lord's Prayer by heart, making her repeat it. Hannah Jones smoking a short black pipe by the fire, and her daughter, a young mother with dark eyes and her hair hanging loose, nursing her baby and displaying her charms liberally. Thence went down to John Watkins to give him some good advice but could not talk to him much as the houseful of people was just sitting down to tea. Went with the Venables to dine at Whitney Court, driving in the mail phaeton and sitting behind with Charlie. Bitterly cold with a keen E. wind but we were well wrapped up and the hood kept the wind off us going. Miss Jane from the Rectory at dinner. Lent Miss Dew Robertson's Lectures on Corinthians. The Squire and his mother made the rest of the party. A grand night with stars glittering frosty keen and we came home at a rattling pace.

Friday, 11 February

Bought 4 valentines at Herthens after searching through a tumbled heap for a long time (2 Valentines to go to Cranmers) and ordered some cheese at Hadley's. Coming back the hills were lovely. The morning spread upon the mountains, beautiful Clyro rising from the valley and stretching away northward dotted with white houses and shining with gleams of green on hills and dingle sides, a tender blue haze over the village and woods in the valley and Clyro Court* a dim grey.

Baskerville in his brougham with the old bay cob came to the

*Home of Mr Baskerville, squire of Clyro.

door at 6.3. Very cold drive. Mrs Bevan, Mary, and the Crichtons arrived before us all in Mrs Allen's yellow chariot. The
Welfield (Edward) Thomases staying in the house. Mr and Capt.
Thomas from Llanthomas. Mrs and Miss Thomas of Llwyn
Madoc staying in the house. They came in last and we went
into dinner immediately. Miss Thomas looking very pretty and
nice in blue silk high dress, sat opposite me at dinner and afterwards when we came into the drawing-room she came up and
shook hands cordially and kindly, talked to me about Cranmers,
Llewellyn, Owen, Hugh, Llwyn Madoc, etc. till Baskerville's
carriage was announced. It was a very happy evening.

Septuagesima Sunday, St Valentine's Eve

Preached at Clyro in the morning (Matthew xiv, 30). Very few
people in Church, the weather fearful, violent deadly E. wind
and the hardest frost we have had yet. Went to Bettws in the
afternoon wrapped in two waistcoats, two coats, a muffler and a
mackintosh, and was not at all too warm. Heard the Chapel*
bell pealing strongly for the second time since I have been here
and when I got to the Chapel my beard moustaches and whiskers
were so stiff with ice that I could hardly open my mouth and my
beard was frozen on to my mackintosh. There was a large christ-
ening party from Llwyn Gwilym. The clerk (Wilding) thrust a
tallow candle between the bars of the stove grate lighted it and
set it upon the table that once probably did duty for a Communion table. I had it put out again as the daylight was suffi-
cient. The baby was baptized in ice which was broken and
swimming about in the Font. A sad day for mother and child to
come out. Dined at the Vicarage.

Monday, St Valentine's Day

A pretty flower Valentine from Incognito, but from the neighbourhood evidently as the Hay post mark was the only one.
Walked to Hay with Mr V. We went to Williams the drapers
and looked at blankets, sheets and coverlets, as we propose to

*The parish had a chapel in Bettws as well as the church in Clyro.

spend some of the surplus Communion Alms in bedding for the poor people who want it much this vigorous weather. Called at the castle.*

Tuesday, 15 February

Visited Edward Evans in the village. He was ill with cold from this vicious poisonous E. wind, and sitting before the fire. Finding they have no blankets but only sheets and a coverlet I gave him an order on Williams for a pair of blankets and I hope his wife will fetch them this afternoon. Coming back called on the Lewises at the Bronith and the old Peninsular veteran.† The red round moon hanging over Clifford Hill. Owls hooting in the dusk across the dingles and from the height of Cefn Cethin. Volunteer band in Hay playing across valley, a review in preparation for a Volunteer Concert tonight.

Thursday, 17 February

Edward Evans better and very thankful for wine and a pair of blankets. Visited Sackville Thomas, Jinny very funny and in good spirits. Polly saying hymns very fast. Sackville sitting hat on by a scorching fire and the venomous east wind blowing full in at the open door. Jinny says 'unhackle' for undress and 'to squeeze your ears against your head and say nothing' means to be discreetly silent and cautiously reticent. Market people passing by open door with shawls and handkerchiefs tied over hats and bonnets. A girl from Dol y canney came in for her apron she had left. Gave Jinny an order for a blanket a pair of sheets. Next to Mrs Bowen's Bird's Nest. Then to Lower Cwmbythog. Grand handsome Mrs Evans nursing her baby in the dark ruinous old hovel, a brave patient woman and practically religious. The children at tea. Black-eyed, black-haired Mary in her blue check pinafore growing so like her mother. Gave Mrs Evans an order for 2 pairs of sheets. Slithering down the steep rocky lane full of a torrent of ice. How this poisonous E. wind strains and weakens the eyes.

*Hay Castle, home of the Bevans. †John Morgan.

Saturday, 19 February

Rachel Williams and Sarah Williams came for Blankets. Mrs Evans of Cwmbythog for sheets. Writing sermon all the morning. Eyes still very bad but I hope they will be better by tomorrow or I don't know how I shall read the service. After lunch went up the Cwm. John Watkins standing in the middle of his cottage hat and stick in hand and shaking like the very palsy or ague. Harriet baking, heating the oven and very bashful about something. Next to Mrs Corfield's and she was deeply thankful for a blanket and pair of sheets, having only one blanket and a house full of children. Then to New Barn. Smith and Edward poking a turnip down a heifer's throat with a probe. The turnip had stuck in her gullet. Handsome Mrs Smith preparing tea for the family. Esther bashful in one room out of sight and Pussy very shy hiding in another. Sent by her mother for fun to get some hot water on purpose to make her appear. Pussy came into the kitchen in confusion of curls and blushes.

Sexagesima Sunday, 20 February

Drunk too much port after dinner at Cae Mawr* last night and a splitting headache all today in revenge. Eyes better but not much. Everything in a daze and dazzle and I could hardly see to read. Got through the services somehow, but in the afternoon came to a deadlock in the middle of the 1st Lesson. The people very attentive to the sermon in the Parable of the Sower from the Gospel for the day. A blessed change in the weather. Wind westerly and no longer deadly poison.

Friday, 25 February

Called on R. Meredith and as usual heard some antiquities and curiosities from him.

Saturday, 26 February

My Father's Birthday. Wrote to him and sent him the *Illustrated London Almanac*. A lovely warm morning so I set off to

*Home of the Morrells.

walk over the hills to Colva, taking my luncheon in my pocket, half a dozen biscuits, two apples and a small flask of wine. Took also a pocket book and opera glasses. . . . Called at Tymawr and promised Mrs Davies a pair of blankets as she has none. The baby very ill. Went on up the Green Lane. Very hot walking. At the Green Lane Cottage found Mrs Jones and a daughter at home sewing. Mrs Jones remembered me. Price Price sitting half hidden in the chimney corner but alas there was no Abiasula as the last time I was there. Price Price something like his sister Abiasula. A sturdy boy with a round rosy good-humoured face and big black eyes, volunteered to guide me to Colva Church. So he came out of his chimney corner in the ingle nook and we started at once, accompanied by a grey and black sheep-dog puppy. We were out on the open mountain at once. There was the brown withered heather, the elastic turf, the long green ride stretching over the hill like a green ribbon between the dark heather. There was the free fresh fragrant air of the hills, but, oh, for the gipsy lassie with her wild dark eyes under her black hood. We passed 'The Fforest' but she was not to be seen. Price Price recognized and named the Black Mountain, but did not know the Fan of Brecon. As we went down the Fuallt a grouse cock uttered his squirling crow and flew over the crest of the hill. I never heard a grouse crow before. 'What's that bird crying?' I said to the boy. 'A grouse', he said, adding, 'There he goes over the bank. They be real thick hereabout.'

Tried to get across the swift Arrow (swollen by the junction of the Glasnant just above) by climbing along a rail but we failed and had to go up a meadow till we got above the meeting of the waters, when we crossed the Glasnant on a hurdle laid flat over the stream and then we jumped the Arrow. Up the steep breast of the Reallt to Dol Reallt and along the road to the Wern and Bryntwyn from whence a field path leads to Colva Church. Here Price Price left me after showing me across one field. I asked him to have some bread and cheese and beer at the Sun Inn, Colva, but he would not and could scarcely be prevailed on to take sixpence. Tried the echo in the field against the belfry and west end of the poor humble dear little white-washed church sequestered among its large ancient yews. The echo was very clear sharp and perfect. Richard Meredith told me of this echo. Mrs Phillips, the landlady of the Sun, was much frightened when I asked for her husband, uneasy and nervous lest I should have come to apprehend him for having been in a row or doing something wrong. But when I said I wanted the words of an old song, she was greatly relieved and said at once, 'Oh I know who you are. You are the gentleman from Clyro.' I laughed and she began to smile. Mrs Phillips took me into the parlour where I sat down, tore a leaf out of my pocket book and wrote with my address a request that Phillips would send me by post 1. the song about our Saviour, 2. the song about Lazarus, 3. the song about King James and the Tinker. Mrs Phillips brought me a pint of excellent light bright beer, some hard sweet homebaked bread, and some hard cheese, carrying the bread and cheese in her arms as she ran in with it, as I was in a hurry to push on. . . . At Gilfach-y-rheol Vaughan* sitting on a sofa with a nose fearfully swollen with a carbuncle, but it is better and he hopes to be able to do duty at Bryngwyn, New-church and Bettws tomorrow. His son John from Llwyn Gwil-lim had come over and was sitting with him. They made me stay to tea and I was thirsty but could eat nothing at four o'clock after luncheon at the Sun at Colva so shortly before. John went home before tea. At tea there were Sarah, Emmeline with her Geneva brooch and fair curls and saucy Jinny with her dark eyes. She gave me a kiss at parting. I found Matilda and Willie in the kitchen, and I met Willie in the village. Went home by Llwyn Gwillim and reached Clyro just in time to dress for dinner at Cae Mawr. But as I was going out I was sent for to baptize Mrs Jones the jockey's baby opposite and I was only too thank-ful that it was so near and that I had not to right about face and march back up to the top of Clyro Hill again. The child was said to suffer from convulsions, so I baptized it, but it was prob-ably quite well. The name selected was as far as I could make out Mahalah which Mrs Jones declared to be the name of one of Cain's wives, on the authority of a book she had read called the Life of Abel. She called her elder girl Thirza, which she says was the name of Cain's other wife. Not a happy allusion.

*Vicar of Newchurch.

March Eve, Monday

Supper at Vicarage. Home after midnight in wind and rain, cheered by the solitary light in Hay looking towards the Moors. Wind rustling through trees at Peter's pool, branches creaking loud.

Ash Wednesday, 2 March

Rain all morning, very gloomy so that I could scarcely see to read the Lessons or Commination service in Church. Very few people at the service. Preached from Isaiah lviii, 6-7. Received by post through Kington from the clerk and publican of Colva two old songs, imperfect but very curious and of some merit. One about our Saviour has the true ballad swing, the other about Dives and Lazarus. The clerk had forgotten the song about King James and the Tinker but said 'he would try to think of him'.

Friday, 4 March

A wild stormy night. The Dulas, Clyro, roaring red, and the Wye surging broad yellow and stormy. Heaven pity the *Pilgrims of the Night* who had no shelter. Pussy had a new brass comb in her clustering light curly hair and her blue bright eyes looked up very archly. The Dingle Flower of fair Llandovery goes back to her home among the sweet Carmarthenshire hills tomorrow. I took her *Alone in London* as a Sunday School prize and wrote her name in it. Her delight was unbounded and she evidently felt much more than she said, for she was very shy and the English did not come readily. But she has much more 'Saesneg' than she had and is much improved by her visit at the school house. I think she was sorry to part and her clear soft eyes spoke volumes. Mrs Evans* said she (Annie) had been longing to take back a Sunday School prize as they are thought so much of in Wales. And as she came and goes in the middle of a quarter she has not had a chance of one in the ordinary course

*Wife of Josiah Evans, the Clyro schoolmaster.

of things. She will find it very quiet in her native dingle among the hills of Shire Carmarthen. But there's no place like home.

Saturday, 5 March

Very cold last night, and sharp frost and the day brilliant and the air exquisitely clear though the wind was East. The view from the banks lovely, the river winding down from Glasbury like a silver serpent, flowing beneath at the foot of the poplars. Hay in the distance bright in brilliant sunshine. Every water-course clear upon the mountains in the searching light. As the sun went down a pink and then a deep purple glow bathed the mountains and Cusop Hill and a keen frost set in. The rich pink and deep purple light very unusually splendid.

1 Sunday in Lent, 6 March

Last night there was a sharp frost, the crescent moon hung cold and keen, and the stars glittered and flashed gloriously. Orion all in a move of brilliance.

Wednesday, 9 March

Coming out of Church Mr V. asked me to luncheon. But then Morrell proposed an expedition to the Black Mountain and take luncheon with us. So I changed my clothes, got ready and went to Cae Mawr where I found Mrs Crichton. We started from Cae Mawr at 12.35. Mrs Morrell walked to Peter's Pool with us, then turned back. We went on with Mrs Crichton to the foot of Wye Cliff woods, across the woods. She turned up the steep winding path. . . .

Short of the New Fforest stopped to lunch by a gate and old ash and upset some sandwiches in the gateway mud. However there were plenty left and we had besides rissoles and bread and cheese and a soda water bottle full of sherry. Went on across some swampy meadow land and rough wood till we came to the Jack thus cutting off a corner. The Jack a desolate poor dirty cottage with a small farm yard. I went to the open door to ask about

A chapel in the Black Mountains

the path across the mountain. By the fire sat a fine peasant woman suckling her child.

[*Part of page cut out*.]

We asked if there were any shorter way across the mountain to Llanthony than the bridle road. She said there was one, a path that the shepherds used, but she thought that probably we should not find it and advised us to keep to the beaten track. Leaving the Jack we crossed a little wood and dingle and came out on the open mountain, at the mountain foot just below Twyn-y-beddau. Soon leaving the road we struck off to the left over some rough ground, banks and gullies and we struck a track with hoof marks winding up the steep mountain side, and soon we were at the top, which was covered with peat bog and black and yellow coarse rushy grass and reed. Here and there were pools and holes filled [with] black peat waters. The ground was frozen hard and icy-snow lay in the hollows and long icicles dripped from stones and little rock caves in the hillside. The mountains were very silent and desolate. No human being in sight, not a tree. No living thing moving except a few mountain sheep some of them with long curling horns. Not a bird to be heard or seen. The only sounds were the sighing of the wind through the rushes and the rushing of distant streams in the watercourses with which the mountain sides were seamed and scarred. . . .

The wind which had been very mild and almost still on the mountain top now freshened and we made the best of our way down, descending upon Hay by a new route past Cadwgan, and Upper Dan-y-fforest which we agreed to be the shortest way to and from the mountain. As we struck the road we met a young man coming down from Craswall where he had been hedging, carrying a huge bundle of hazel rods for garden sticking. His face was very handsome, swarthy as an Italian but with a fresh colour. His hair and eyes fine and black. The walking was capital in the mountain but the E. wind wrapped the country in a mist which spoilt the view. We got home soon after 6 pretty tired and at seven I dined at Cae Mawr. Hassie had made us three nosegays of snowdrops, violets and primroses in honour of his father's birthday.

Thursday, 10 March

A heavenly day, lovely and warm, real spring. People busy in their gardens planting and sowing. Every one rejoicing in the unclouded splendid weather, and congratulating each other on it in their greetings on the road. The roads lively with market women riding to the Hay. A woman on a cream coloured horse with black mane and tail riding past the school and alternately in sunshine and the shadow of the Castle clump over the hill. . . .

John Watkins in the Cwm no better, staggering round and round his house whirling his head round about like a mad man on a Polar bear, unable to sit down, he says, so kneeling on the floor sometimes to rest himself. He gets no rest in bed or at night, dreads the coming on of darkness and is haunted by evil thoughts and dreams. He seems to be suffering from despondency and remorse, and is plainly in a most miserable pitiable state of mind and body. Gwenny Williams shakes her head at his condition.

Saturday, 12 March

. . . went to Upper Cabalva where Mrs Dyke gave me a pocketful of golden pippins. Annie up at Llwyn Gwillim, but before she went she had gathered a glassfull of primroses from the rickyard hedge. On to Lower Cabalva. Women carrying home on their heads heavy burdens of wood from the dingle and fields where a fall of timber is going on. Mrs Collett with a new baby to be christened at Bettws Chapel tomorrow. Mary Collett proud to show me her Whitney School prizes and all her little treasures. She is a very good girl very fond of reading and going to school and devours books. I lent her Miss Edgeworth's *Parent's Assistant*. She has good eyes but she will never match her mother's beautiful noble face. Mrs Collett says they must have their turkey cock killed because he knocks the children down and stocks (pecks) them. Collett set one child to drive the turkey with a stick but the bird flew at her, knocked her down and stocked her too, so there were two children roaring at once and the turkey triumphant.

Sunday, 13 March

I looked out last night at 11.30 and was surprised to see snow on the ground. This morning showed a fall of 3 inches level and the snow fell straight and even as there was no wind. The mountains evidently deep in snow. Few children at school as the poor darlings could not come far through the snow. Very few people in Church. Mr Venables preached and I went to Bettws, a lovely walk in the glorious afternoon. At Cross Fordd the great dark stone standing in a sheet of dazzling snow a solitary silent witness of some dead covenant or boundary. The shady steep hill descending to the Mill covered with snow. The Chapel field, Bettws, deep in snow. The clerk and two other men lounging about the W. end of the Chapel till they saw me crossing the white waste when the clerk (Wilding) disappeared round the corner and immediately after the bell pealed out over the snow. Mrs Collett rode a pony up to Chapel on a man's saddle and was churched. The baby came in after the sermon and was baptized 'Alice Shelburne', an old name in Collett's family he says. The baby very good and quiet.

Climbed the ladder to see old Jones in bed who complained of a headache and nothing more. Read to him Mark ii out of his old fashioned Bible. Went into the old blind 'Simon's' house and read to him. At the bend of the Wye between Bronydd & Cabalva the mountain clad in deep snow and tinged with rose colour was reflected in the river like Mont Blanc in the Lake of Geneva. As the sun set a lovely rose tint stole over the snowy mountains, but paled and died leaving the mountain tops cold dim blue before I reached Clyro. The silent folk lying still in their winding sheets in the churchyard. Dined at the Vicarage and read to Mr V. the ballad of our Saviour and the Three Children* which interested him much.

Wednesday, 16 March

I ate so much hare that I could hardly walk and saw stars, but at 4 went up the hill by the Bron Penllan and Little Wern y Pentre. The lane between Little Wern y Pentre and the Tall Trees infamous, so deep and soft that it is almost impossible to feel bottom. Mrs Williams plunging down the lane through the mud and fording the pools with a sack of swedes on her back. In the meadow between the Tall Trees and Sunny Bank was singing the first lark I have noticed this year. He was coming down, his song stopped suddenly and he dropped to his nest.

Below Tybella a bird singing unseen reminded me how the words of a good man live after he is silent and out of sight 'He being dead yet speaketh'.†

Also the scent of an unseen flower seemed like the sweet and holy influence of a good kind deed which cannot be concealed though the deed itself may be hidden. On to Cefn y Blaen where a 'King' once lived. Alas for the pretty merry yellow haired

*See p. 29
†The words that were to be inscribed on his tombstone.

lassie who used to make this house so bright. Three rather nice
rosy black haired grey eyed girls. The men sitting at tea but they
had finished and went out as I came in. A tall spare old man
with a wild eye and a night cap rose from the chimney corner,
came forward and shook me by the hand respectfully, claiming
acquaintance as he had seen me at Wernnewydd. Round the
corner of the Vicar's Hill to Little Twyn y Grain, passing by the
Great Twyns which I am happy to see is falling into ruin, the
window frames falling in. How well I remember and how short
a time ago it seems though nearly five years. I never pass the
house without thinking of that afternoon when after neglecting
Margaret Thomas' dying son for a long time I went to call and
was inexpressibly shocked to find that he had died only ten minutes before . . .

Faint sunshine on Bryngwyn Hill and a cold cheery gleam of
water from the great peat bog below on the edge of which stands
the grey cluster of buildings and the tall dark yew of Llanshifr. I
went down there and waded across the yard to the house through
a sea of mud and water. The kitchen was very dark, the bank
rising steep in front of the window. Mrs Morgan gave me some
tea and cake. On the settle sat a man perfectly still, silent and in
such a dark corner that I could not see his face. On a stool in
the chimney corner sat little girl 'Ellen' holding a baby lately
vaccinated, both sound asleep, and Mrs Morgan very anxious
lest the girl should 'fall the baby'. Morgan anxious to get out to
his ewes and lambs and a tall girl strode into the kitchen crying
in a peculiar strident voice that 'a ewe was going up Cae Drws
alone' as if about to yean. Morgan went out with some hot milk
and showed me the remains of the moat, where the Scotch pedlar
was hidden after being murdered for the sake of his pack while
lodging in the house and where his skeleton was found when the
moat was cleared out. The moat that is left is a broad deep
formidable ditch and rather a long pond at one end of the house
and full of water. It extended once all round the house and had
to be crossed by a bridge. Llanshifr a fearfully wet swampy place,
almost under water and I should think very unhealthy. One of
the twin yews was lately blown down and cut up into gate posts
which will last twice as long as oak. The wood was so hard that

Morgan said it turned many of the axes as if they were made of lead. Other axes splintered and broke upon the wood and the old yew was a crucial test of the axes.

Thursday, 17 March

On leaving the school at 11, I went up to Cae Mawr to see Morrell and he proposed a walk to Aber Edw as the morning was so lovely. We started soon after noon diverging to Clyro Court to leave a message for Baskerville who was salmon fishing. We stopped for lunch under the shelter of a hedge near the beautiful Cwm of Llandewi, a sudden narrow break or cleft in the hill side forming the head of an abrupt, deep-wooded gorge, romantic and picturesque from above as fairy land and leaving room for play of the imagination. We were hungry and the sandwiches very good. While we were eating two people, a woman and a boy, hove in sight over a rise of the hill, bound for Hay under great press of canvas, that is with large umbrellas spread, though there was no rain. Asked them if it was raining on their side of the hedge, but they did not see the force of the remark and held on their course much puzzled. Down the hill side to Llan-bach-howey and forded the river over large stepping stones which reminded me of Collins' picture of the two barefooted gleaning girls fording the brook on stepping stones, 'Come Along'. Near the whitewashed ugly abject-looking farmhouse we heard a sweet voice singing, but the singer was nowhere to be seen. Presently on looking through the hedge we saw a crazy girl with a coarse ugly face under an old bonnet in the field sitting on the grass singing to herself something like a hymn tune in a rich mellow voice, the words indistinguishable, perhaps there were none. When she saw us through the hedge she suddenly stopped singing and saluted us in a sharp abrupt tone. She is said to be the illegitimate daughter of a gentleman in Bath who pays the people of one of these farms to keep her.

We went on till we came to a brow of a hill which fell away abruptly from our feet. Then we saw the Begwns behind us looking very near, much too near, and directly afterwards we spied a whitewashed church perched on a tump and shaded by a huge

yew in the valley below. I took the Church to be Aber Edw
Church, but coming to a shoemakers' house with a small farm
yard we found it was Llandeilo, and we looked blankly at each
other having completely lost our way. The handsome black-
haired and bearded shoemaker who said he was ill and therefore
idle for a day volunteered to show us the way. He was accompanied by a little wiry sandy knowing terrier and he told us
stories of fox hunting and badger baiting, the men he mentioned
as his associates being in the sporting not to say the poaching
line, known well to us, viz., James Pugh, now dead, of Llanbychllyn and Henry Warnell of Clyro Hill. The shoemaker, our
guide philosopher and friend, seemed to me an innocent kind of
man but from his dog and discourse Morrell thought him not
unacquainted with the art of poaching 'on a shining night in the
season of the year'. However he was a very good and civil guide.
He led us over the shoulder of another great rolling hill till we
saw Aber Edw lying below us, the famous rocky wooded gorge,
the Edw and the Wye and the meeting of the sweet waters. The
turf was firm and dry and elastic, splendid walking.

3 Sunday in Lent, 20 March

A beautiful morning and a good many people in Church. Spoke
to the people very seriously about coming to the Holy Communion, and the small number of Communicants. Baptized
Michael Thomas the blacksmith's baby in the name of Annie
Madelina. The first yappingale* I have heard this year was
laughing in the dingle close to the village this afternoon.

Monday, 21 March

While dressing this morning heard the first woodpigeon coo-ing
in the dingle. Standing at the window after breakfast reading
The Times, Morrell passing by, tapped on the railings with his
fishing rod. He was on his way to Cabalva, salmon fishing.
I threw up the window. 'Going to Cabalva?' – 'Yes.' 'How's
the river?' – 'First rate order.' 'Beautiful morning.' – 'Yes,

*Yaffle, or green woodpecker.

and a nice breeze.' – 'Wish you sport.' So he went on.

Evans the schoolmaster very much interested and rather anxious about the Education Bill. At 3 went to Wye Cliff by meadow and wood but the Crichtons not at home. The children playing in the sunshine in front of the house and just being hoisted on board their donkey by the two nursemaids, three riding at once in panniers, or basket saddles, one on each side and one at the top. The sun scalding hot as I came up the steep path through the Cliff Wood. Next to Pen y Maes, where the yellow crocuses and pink hepaticas were strikingly lovely. . . . Between Pen y Maes and Hay I heard clear and loud the solemn toll of the soul bell at Clyro booming across the valley and river from the sequestered unseen Church, and wondered who could be dead. No sooner had I crossed the bridge than the soul bell and funeral bell at Hay Church tolled out in answer.

Tuesday, 22 March

Called at John Watkins in the Cwm. He was just in the same abject wretched pitiable state, shaking from head to foot fancying himself unable to sit down or keep still, remorse gnawing at his mind. Neighbours say he is 'roguish' and shams, probably it is the cunning of insanity. Went on to White Ash and directly old Sarah Probert heard me come in she began to groan and roll about in the bed. Hannah in spectacles sitting by the fire working. Her daughter and the children gone to Llowes. I told Sarah to cheer up but she rolled and groaned all the more and said I was a 'rum un' and a 'Job's comfort'. When I came out of the White Ash house it was very cold, suddenly cold, as if there were snow in the air. And probably the cold rainstorms that lashed the windows this morning fell in snow showers upon the high hills. The Clyro women (Mary Phillips especially) stride about the village like storks. The industrious blacksmith chinks away at his forge night and morning late and early, and the maidens and mothers go up and down the water steps with their pitchers continually. Heavy loads of timber, large long trees on the timber carriages grinding through Clyro village every evening from Cross Ffordd and Cabalva.

Wednesday, 23 March

Looked in upon the old soldier* and stayed there reading and chatting to him an hour and a half. He told me of a cottage called 'Hell Hole' that used to stand in the Cwm near Sunny Bank. Talking of wolves he said he remembered when the English army was in Spain at Correa, every night soon after sunset he used to see the wolves come down to drink at the river. Then they would walk up the hill again into the coverts and vineyards, sometimes there were 4 or 5 of them at once. They were like mastiffs and as big. The soldiers used to scare them by snapping the locks of their flint muskets and making a flash in the pan.

Saturday, 26th March

A delicious day upon Clyro Hill. It was sunny and warm under the sheltering bank and woods of Wern Vawr and pleasant walking along the low road leading to the old farm house with its large projecting and highgabled porch. There was a stir about the house and yard. They had killed a fat stall-fed heifer yesterday and a party of people much interested in the matter, among them old Jones and his wife were busy cutting up the carcase in the barn. A man went to and fro from the barn to the house with huge joints of beef having first weighed them on the great steelyard which hangs at the barn door. In the house Mrs Jones of New Building an old daughter of the house was engaged in the great kitchen taking up the joints from the table where the man laid them and carrying them into an inner room or larder to put them in salt. By the fire sat a young woman who hid her face and did not look up. She had a baby lying across her lap.

I decided to explore the lane running parallel with the brook towards Painscastle and discover the old Rhos Goch Mill. There was a good deal of water and suddenly I came upon the mill pond and the picturesque old mill with an overshot wheel. A path went along the top of the bank of the mill pond and then passed between rows of larches planted in a strip of green sward by the waste waterside where some fine white ducks were

*John Morgan.

gobbling. I crossed one of the streams on a larch felled across the water for a bridge and came back round the front of the cosy old picturesque ivy-grown mill house with its tall chimney completely covered with ivy. A handsome young man with a fine open face, fresh complexion and dressed as a miller was having a romp with a little girl before the door. He said his name was Powell, his father was dead and he carried on the business and with the most perfect politeness and well bred courtesy asked me to come in and sit down. But I had not time to stop so after a few words of chat I went on glad to have seen the famous old Rhos Goch Mill under the most favourable aspects in the bright beautiful sunny evening. The mill was not going and there was a great quiet about the place broken only by the dripping of the water from the wheel, the rippling of the brook, and the subdued voices of the people in the house coming through the open door and the old porch. There is something very fascinating to me about an old fashioned flour mill on a brook. So this is the place that I have heard old Hannah Whitney talk of so often, the place where the old miller sleeping in the mill trough used to see the fairies dancing of nights upon the mill floor. Near the Mill I came upon the Rhos Goch Chapel which I have often heard of too, the place where Griffiths of Portway preaches. I was leaning over the wall reading the epitaphs on the tombstones in the Chapel yard when a woman who was sweeping out the Chapel appeared at the door and asked me if I would like to come in as the gate was open. So I went into the building which was very ugly, high and boxy-looking and of course whitewashed, the usual conventicle. Inside there were a number of dark coloured long wooden seats armed and moveable, benches with backs and arms in short, a fixed bench running all round the room against the wall, a pulpit between the two windows, a plain high box of dark wood with two brass sconces and a plain naked wooden table standing in front of all the benches and beside the pulpit. I asked the woman who said her name was Sheen if she were a communicant. She said 'Yes'. Then I asked how the Sacrament was administered and she said the people sat stiff in their seats while the 'deacon' carried round to them the bread and wine. On Sunday evenings she said, the Chapel is crowded and sometimes 200 people are present. I could hardly have believed the room would hold so many. Probably it will not.

At Rhos Goch Lane House no one was at home so I stuck an ivy leaf into the latch hole.

Round the corner of the Vicar's Hill to Cefn y Blaen where I found Davies, the new tenant of the Pentre. While talking to Davies outside I heard old William Pritchard within coughing violently. I went in and sat some time talking to him and his niece Mrs Evans. He remembers the old house of Cefn y Blaen and the large famous room which he says was 20 *yards* long and was used for holding a Court of Justice in for the country round in the time of Charles I. I asked him if he had ever heard any talk of Charles I ever having been about in this country. 'Oh yes', he said, 'I have a jug that the King once drunk out of at Blaen cerdi. He had breakfast that day in Brecon, dined at Gwernyfed and slept at Harpton, passing through Newchurch. His army was with him and riding two and two in the narrow lanes the line reached from Pen Vaen in Newchurch, through the village up to Blaen cerdi. At Blaen cerdi all the farm people, boys and girls ran out to see the King pass. The King was afoot. He stopped opposite the house and asked my ancestress Mary Bayliss to give him something to drink. She went to the house and fetched him milk and water in this jug which has been handed down with the tradition in my family. I have always heard that this Mary Bayliss was an extraordinarily fine beautiful woman. I never learnt that the King gave her anything in return for the draught. Before this jug came into my possession it was broken by some water being left to freeze in it, but it can easily be cemented, being in two large pieces, the bottom having been broken off. David Jones the auctioneer in Hay offered me a great deal of money for the jug.

'Charles II was in hiding for some time in this country and went about in disguise as a lady's servant. Once when he was in the pantry with the butler of the house where they were staying he asked the butler if he would give him a glass of wine. The butler said in a meaning way "You are able to command what wine you like".' So far W. Pritchard.

Monday, 28 March

Williams says the petty chief great landlords were called 'Normandy Kings'. One of them lived at Cefn y Blaen, one at Llanshifr, another at Great Gwernfydden. The one who lived at Painscastle was a giant. This giant carried off to Painscastle 'screaming and noising' Miss Phillips of the Screen Farm near Erwood whom he found disporting herself with her lover Arthur on or at Bychllyn Pool. Arthur sent for help to Old Radnor Castle and Cefn y Blaen. At Cefn y Blaen there were then 40 men each 7 feet high. The giant on the other hand sent for succour to Court Evan Gwynne where there was an 'army', also to Hay Castle and Lord Clifford of Clifford Castle. While these hostile forces were converging upon Painscastle, a woman in the castle favoured the girl's escape and dressed her in man's clothes to this end. Arthur watching for her outside and not knowing of the disguise seeing what he thought was a man and one of his enemies coming out of the castle shot his lover dead with an arrow. Arthur then furious stormed the castle with a battle axe: took it and killed the giant. Next day the opposing parties arrived at the Rhos Goch, there was a fearful battle near Rhyd Llyden and the Painscastle party was defeated with great slaughter by the forces from Old Radnor and Cefn y Blaen.

Thursday, April Eve

Read to old Price the keeper and then walked to Hay across the fields. Sun very hot. Found Capt. Thomas at home and he ordered in some sherry. He talked of his prospects, intention of selling out of the army, and wish to get a Queen's Messengership, seeming to think times hard and gloomy and openings few. . . .

In Hadley's shop I met Dewing who told me of a most extraordinary misfortune that befell Pope the curate of Cusop yesterday at the Whitney Confirmation. He had one candidate Miss Stokes a farmer's daughter and they went together by train. Pope went in a cutaway coat very short, with his dog, and took no gown. The train was very late. He came very late into church and sat down on a bench with the girl cheek by jowl. When it came to his turn to present his candidate he was told by the Rector (Henry Dew) or someone in authority to explain why he came so late. The Bishop of Hereford (Atlay) has a new fashion of confirming only two persons at a time, kneeling at the rails. The Bishop had marked two young people come in very late and when they came up to the rails thinking from Pope's youthful appearance and from his having no gown that he was a young farmer candidate and brother of the girl. He spoke to them severely and told them to come on and kneel down for they were extremely late. Pope tried to explain that he was a clergyman and that the girl was his candidate but the Bishop was overbearing and imperious and either did not hear or did not attend, seeming to think he was dealing with a refractory ill-conditioned youth. 'I know, I know,' he said. 'Come at once, kneel down, kneel down.' Poor Pope resisted a long time and had a long battle with the Bishop, but at last unhappily he was overborne in the struggle, lost his head, gave way, knelt down and was *confirmed* there and then, and no one seems to have interfered to save him, though Mr Palmer of Eardisley and others were sitting close by and the whole Church was in a titter. It is a most unfortunate thing and will never be forgotten and it will be unhappily a joke against Pope all his life. The Bishop was told of his mistake afterwards and apologized to Pope, though rather shortly and cavalierly. He said, what was quite true, that Pope ought to have come in his gown. But there was a little fault on all sides for if the Bishop had been a little less hasty, rough and overbearing in his manner things might have been explained, and the bystanding clergy were certainly very much to blame for not stepping forward and preventing such a farce. I fear poor Pope will be very much vexed, hurt and dispirited about it.

Tuesday, 5 April

The day broke cloudless after a sharp frost. Up early and went to Cae Mawr to breakfast, at 8 o'clock. Drove to Hay in Morrell's carriage. Drove on to Llanigon, the air fresh, cold driving. Alighted at Llanigon village and sent the carriage back. Walked up by the Church and took the field path to the Cilonw Farm. Fine dry walking on turf and road. We went leisurely up the beautiful deep wild gorge sometimes in the meadows sometimes walking in the lane by the side of the rushing brook foaming over pretty cascades, the hills and woods before us hazed with a gauzy veil of light tender blue under the cloudless blue sky and splendid sunshine.

Near the head of the gorge we met a cheery looking peasant woman coming down the meadows into the lane over a stile and she stayed to direct us very courteously. Indeed all the people up the road were most courteous and painstaking in telling us the way.

Down the pretty steep winding lane we went skirting the Honddu which had now developed from a mountain rill into a brook and brawled in its channel deep below the road. The road lined in many places with holly hedges and trees scarlet with berries. We met a handsome fairhaired rosy lad dressed like a miller's lad who told us it was only a mile on to Capel y Ffin. Across the valley at the mouth of a great dreadful dingle stood the ruins of the house which was swept away while the people were dancing, by an avalanche of snow or a torrent of snow water let loose by a sudden thaw. A young man who was coming up from Llanthony to join the party was saved by his greyhound unaccountably hanging behind, whining and running back so as to entice his master home again. I had not seen Capel y Ffin for 4 years (it is just 4 years ago this month that I was there), but I remembered the place perfectly, the old chapel short stout and boxy with its little bell turret, (the whole building reminded one of an owl) the quiet peaceful chapel yard shaded by the seven great solemn yews, the chapel house, a farm house over the way, and the Great Honddu brook crossing the road and crossed in turn by the stone foot bridge with its narrow gangway. Before the chapel house door by the brookside a buxom comely wholesome girl with fair hair rosy face blue eyes and fair clear skin stood washing at a tub in the sunshine, up to the elbows of her round white lusty arms in soapsuds. We asked her how far it was to the place where the monks were building their monastery. 'Oh,' she said, smiling kindly and stopping her washing for a moment to direct

us. 'Oh, none just. Please to go over the brook and up the lane.'
Two tramps were lounging against the bridge lighting their
pipes and said to each other when we had passed, 'They are only
going to see the monks'.

A few minutes walk up a lane now dry but which is probably
a watercourse in winter, and looking through the hedge we
exclaimed, 'There they are'. Two black figures were working in
a sloping patch of ground laid out as a garden, one digging and
the other wheeling earth to him in a barrow. They were dressed
in long black habits girt round the waist with scourge cords
knotted at the ends and dangling almost to the ground. The
black hoods or cowls were drawn over their heads leaving their
faces bare, and their naked feet were thrust into sandals with
which they went slip slop along as with slippers down at heel.
Father Philip was digging. Brother Serene or Cyrene was wheeling earth to him from a heap thrown out of the excavation dug
for the foundations of the monastery. He seemed very much
oppressed by his heavy black dress, for the sun was hot and he
stopped when he had wheeled his empty barrow back to the
heap and stood to rest and wipe his steaming brow. They both
seemed studiously unconscious of our presence, but I saw Brother
Serene glancing furtively at us from under his cowl when he
thought he was under cover of the heap of earth. We at first
thought of speaking to them but decided not to afterwards, fearing they might think our trespassing an intrusion on their priv-
acy, uncourteous and rude. We spoke to the masons of whom
there were two working at the foundations. They spoke with
great respect and some awe of the monks and did not seem the
least inclined to laugh at them. They answered all our questions
too very civilly. We saw the foundation stone which Father
Ignatius* came down to lay three weeks ago. Then he returned
to London and at present there are only these two monks in
residence. They have one servant a young man who was also
wheeling earth. They lodge at a farm house close by and live a
good deal on milk. They allow no woman to come near them and
do their own washing. Probably however there is little of that
to do. They may wear linen but they don't show any and

*The Rev. J. L. Lyne. See *Dictionary of National Biography*.

Llanthony Abbey

perhaps they did not take off their habits when at work because they had nothing under. They looked very much like old women at work in the garden. It does seem very odd at this age of the world in the latter part of the 19th century to see monks gravely wearing such dresses and at work in them in broad day. One could not help thinking how much more sensible and really religious was the dress and occupation of the masons and of the hearty healthy girl washing at the Chapel House, living naturally in the world and taking their share of its work, cares and pleasures, than the morbid unnatural life of these monks going back into the errors of the dark ages and shutting themselves up from the world to pray for the world. 'Laborare est Orare.' The masons had raised the foundation walls to the level of the ground and believed the house would be built by the end of May, which I doubt. The monks as usual had chosen a pretty and pleasant place on a fine slope at the foot of the mountain where there was good soil and plenty of good water, a trout stream and sand for mortar. The house which seemed from the ground plan as far as we could make it out, to be a long shallow building will look S.E. down the valley towards Llanthony Abbey. The monks have bought 32 acres. It is said they have collected £50,000 which may probably be divided by 10. Very few people came to the ceremony of laying the foundation stone.

We crossed a field and the fold of a farm house, scrambled down a narrow stony lane and struck the main road again. About a mile above Llanthony we described the Abbey ruins, the dim grey pile of building in the vale below standing by the little river side among its brilliant green meadows. What was our horror on entering the enclosure to see two tourists with staves and shoulder belts all complete postured among the ruins in an attitude of admiration, one of them of course discoursing learnedly to his gaping companion and pointing out objects of interest with his stick. If there is one thing more hateful than another it is being told what to admire and having objects pointed out to one with a stick. Of all noxious animals too the most noxious is a tourist. And of all tourists the most vulgar, illbred, offensive and loathsome is the British tourist. . . .

Morrell and I arrived at Clyro 7.50 and dined together comfortably at Cae Mawr sitting up talking afterwards till half past twelve. We were rather tired with our 25 miles walk, but not extraordinarily so.

Wednesday, 6 April

Villaging. Went to find William Pugh. Found him forking the rhubarb ground in the Vicarage garden and talked to him about coming to the Sacrament. Visited Morgan at the New Inn. He was much troubled in his mind about the sin against the Holy Ghost and could not reconcile that statement with other passages of Scripture, thinking the Bible contradicted itself. I tried to explain but he would not be comforted. As he was rather in a cantankerous carping unwilling mind (perhaps from pain) as he had one leg much swollen rested up on a chair, and as there were two men sitting in the inn kitchen listening it was not a very favourable opportunity for a pastoral visit.

Thursday, 7 April

Lunch at 12 and to Hay by the fields to take the Savings Bank.
Sat reading a Cheltenham paper and book of Religious Anecdotes for an hour and no one came. . . . At the top of Bridge St
met Richard Meredith and went in to his old smoky dusty dingy
room to have a crack with him. . . . I had the satisfaction of
managing to walk from Hay to Clyro by the fields without meeting a single person, always a great triumph to me and a subject
for warm self congratulation for I have a peculiar dislike to
meeting people, and a peculiar liking for a deserted road. When
I looked out between 11 and 12 before going to bed I saw one
of the magnificent sights of the world, the crescent moon setting.

> *When down the stormy crescent goes*
> *A light before me swims,*
> *Between dark stems the forest glows,*
> *I hear a noise of hymns.*

And the crescent moon was sinking low over the dingle behind
the poplars.

Friday, 8 April

In the green lane between York and Cefn y Fedwas I came upon
Smith of Wernwg hedging. He told me that a child had arrived
at Pen-y-wyrlod and wanted to know if something cannot be
done to separate Stephen Davies and Myra Rees. I said there
was no law to prevent people living in concubinage. People are
very indignant about this affair and think it a great scandal to
the parish, and rightly so. But what is to be done? The man's
family are mad with him especially Mrs Smith of New Barn,
but no one has any influence over him. He is infatuated with the
girl, whose tongue is so desperate and unscrupulous that everyone is afraid of her. Esther Gore openly acuses her of being 'a
liar, a thief, a whore, and a *murderer*' and offers to swear and
prove that Myra has made away with one infant, if not with
more.

Saturday, 9 April

Mr Brierley the curate of Presteign and Chaplain to the High Sheriff made two unfortunate mistakes. In going to Church he sat down *beside* the Judge with his hat *on*, and came to dinner with the Judge without his robes. Consulted Mr V. about Stephen Davies and Myra Rees but he does not see what can be done.

Across the wall and fields to Cwmbythog and the magnificent regal mistress* of the miserable shanty came to the rickety door with a brilliant smile in her deep grey eyes shadowed with long black lashes and over her grand richly browned face. She was preparing the clean clothes for Sunday. Black haired Mary nursing the baby, and brown haired Elizabeth feeding the roaring oven fire. The draught through the old hovel enough to blow one's hair about. From Cwmbythog I crossed the dingle and the brook and the little meadow and so up the path by the quarries along the hillside to John Morgan's the old soldier's. He and Mary his wife were cosily at tea. And after the veteran had done and pocketed his clasp knife he covered his face with his hand and whispered his long grace audibly. Talking of the Peninsular War he said he well remembered being in a reserve line at Vittoria when a soldier sitting close to him on the edge of a bank had his head carried off by a cannon ball which struck him in front on the throat. The head rolled along the ground, and when it ceased rolling John Morgan and the other soldiers saw it moving and 'playing' on the ground with a twitching of the features for five minutes after. They thought it so extraordinary that the subject was often talked over round the camp fires as an unprecedented marvel. There was one Lieutenant Bowen an Irishman who joined the regiment between the battles of Vittoria and the Pyrenees. He was very vicious to the men and much hated. Just before the battle of the Pyrenees (which John Morgan calls the Battle of the Pioneers) this Lieutenant Bowen became very mild and humble to the men fearing he should be shot on purpose by his own soldiers in the battle from revenge. He was not shot.

*Mrs Evans (see p.25).

Monday, 11 April

When I was leaving the Vicarage last night as we crossed the hill we heard the servants singing beautifully a hymn or an anthem. A bright calm night, the white rolling clouds lit up by the moon. I am reading with the school children this week the events of the Passion Week taken day by day.

Hay Fair and a large one. The roads thronged with men and droves of red white faced cattle hustling and pattering to the Fair, an unusual number of men returning drunk. . . .

A man was driving eight small white pigs back from Hay Fair to Llowes with the help of a sheep dog. The dog was very kind to the pigs, too tender the man said. He took a pig's ear or hind leg in his mouth and pressed it gently.

Wednesday, 13 April

6 p.m. A cavalcade of horses seven in number has just passed through the village at the trot, with four horsemen. They belong to Maesllwch and are just returning to the Castle* after exercising.

Dined at the Vicarage.

Thursday, 14 April. Maunday Thursday

Met Powell the relieving officer in Castle St and talked to him and Mr Trumper about John Watkins of the Cwm and the desirability of removing him to Abergavenny Asylum as he seems to have been a good deal more crazed lately wandering about the country and scarcely master of himself. Dr Clouston saw him this morning and thought him a case for the Asylum from the wildness of his talk. But when Mr Trumper as a magistrate went up with the relieving officer to see Watkins before giving the order for his removal, the cunning fellow probably saw what they were after and talked so sensibly and answered all questions so reasonably that the order could not be given. Powell came in when they returned passing through the village and told me all about it.

*Home of Walter de Winton.

Good Friday, 15 April

Up early and breakfast at 8. Writing Easter sermon afterwards
till 9.30, when I went to Hay. The walk across the fields in the
glowing hot sunshine, and the country basked lovely and peaceful. I saw one man ploughing on Ty-yr-mynarch and met no
one else till I came to Hay Bridge where the long empty sunny
white road stretched away straight over the river to the town,
the picturesque little border town with its slate-roofed houses
climbing and shining up the hill crested by the dark long mass
of the old ivy-grown castle with its huge warbroken tower. . . .
As I came up the town an unicorn* came out of the Rose and
Crown, the leader a chestnut, hobbling lame and no doubt about
to go a long journey. Poor beast. The turn-out, a long brake,
pulled up at the Blue Boar where a large party of '*gentlemen*' with
white waistcoats etc. were assembled evidently bent on a day's
pleasure such as it was. Good Friday has now become a holiday
& mere day of pleasure. . . . Took cross buns to Hannah Whitney, Sarah Williams, Margaret Griffiths, Catherine Ferris, Mary
Jones, five widows.

Saturday, Easter Eve, 16 April

I awoke at 4.30 and there was a glorious sight in the sky, one of
the grand spectacles of the Universe. There was not a cloud in
the deep wonderful blue of the heavens. Along the Eastern horizon there was a clear deep intense glow neither scarlet nor crimson but a mixture of both. This red glow was very narrow, almost
like a riband and it suddenly shaded off into the deep blue.
Opposite in the west the full moon shining in all its brilliance
was setting upon the hill beyond the church steeple. Thus the
glow in the east bathed the church in a warm rich tinted light,
while the moon from the west was casting strong shadows. The
moon dropped quickly down behind the hill bright to the last,
till only her rim could be seen sparkling among the tops of the
orchards on the hill. The sun rose quickly and his rays struck
red upon the white walls of Pen Llan, but not so brilliantly as
in the winter sunrisings. I got up soon after 5 and set to work on

*A carriage drawn by three horses.

my Easter sermon getting two hours for writing before breakfast. At ten Mr V. came in and we arranged that I should preach
tomorrow morning and go onto Bettws and go out driving with
him and his brother this afternoon.

At 11 I went to the school to see if the children were gathering
flowers and found they were out in the fields and woods collecting moss, leaving the primroses to be gathered later in the day
to give them a better chance of keeping fresh. Next I went to
Cae Mawr. Mrs Morrell had been very busy all the morning
preparing decorations for the Font, a round dish full of flowers
in water and just big enough to fit into the Font and upon this
large dish a pot filled and covered with flowers all wild, primroses, violets, wood anemones, wood sorrel, periwinkles, oxlips
and the first blue bells, rising in a gentle pyramid, ferns and
larch sprays drooping over the brim, a wreath of simple ivy to
go round the stem of the Font, and a bed of moss to encircle the
foot of the Font in a narrow band pointed at the corners and
angles of the stone with knots of primroses. At 2 o'clock Hetty
Gore of the Holly House came down from Cefn y Blaen and
upset all my arrangements for the afternoon saying that old
William Pritchard there was very ill not likely to live and wishes
to see me this afternoon that I might read to him and give him
the Sacrament. Hetty Gore thought he might not last many
days. So I was obliged to go to the Vicarage explain and give up
my drive. Found the schoolmaster and a friend staying with him
just going out to get moss and carrying the East window sill
board from the Church to the school to prepare it for tomorrow
with the text 'Christ is Risen' written in primroses upon moss.
Shall I ever forget that journey up the hill to Cefn y Blaen in
this burning Easter Eve, under the cloudless blue, the scorching
sun and over the country covered with a hot dim haze? I climbed
up the Bron panting in the sultry afternoon heat. Went up the
fields from Court Evan Gwynne to Little Wern y Pentre and
envied the sheep that were being washed in the brook below,
between the field and the lane, by Price of Great Wern y Pentre
and his excited boys. The peewits were sweeping rolling and tumbling in the hot blue air about the Tall Trees with a strange deep
mysterious hustling and quavering sound from their great wings.

When I started for Cefn y Blaen only two or three people were in the churchyard with flowers. Hetty Gore and Mrs Morgan of Cold Blow etc. But now the customary beautiful Easter Eve Idyll had fairly begun and people kept arriving from all parts with flowers to dress the graves. Children were coming from the town and from neighbouring villages with baskets of flowers and knives to cut holes in the turf. The roads were lively with people coming and going and the churchyard a busy scene with women and children and a few men moving about among the tombstones and kneeling down beside the green mounds flowering the graves. . . . I found Annie Dyke standing among the graves with her basket of flowers. A pretty picture she would have made as she stood there with her pure fair sweet grave face and clustering brown curls shaded by her straw hat and her flower basket hanging on her arm. It is her birthday to-day. I always tell her she and the cuckoos came together. So I went home and got a little birthday present I had been keeping for her, which I bought in the Crystal Palace in January, a small ivory brooch, with the carved figure of a stag. I took the little box which held it out into the churchyard and gave it to her as she was standing watching while the wife of one of her father's* workmen, the shepherd, flowered the grave that she came to dress, for her.

More and more people kept coming into the churchyard as they finished their day's work. The sun went down in glory behind the dingle, but still the work of love went on through the twilight and into the dusk until the moon rose full and splendid. The figures continued to move about among the graves and to bend over the green moulds in the calm clear moonlight and warm air of the balmy evening.

At 8 o'clock there was a gathering of the Choir in the Church to practise the two anthems for to-morrow, and the young people came flocking in from the graves where they had been at work or watching others working, or talking to their friends, for the Churchyard on Easter Eve is a place where a great many people meet. . . . The moonlight came streaming in broadly through the chancel windows. When the choir had gone and the lights were out and the church quiet again, as the schoolmaster and his

*The farmer of Upper Cabalva.

friend stood with me at the Church door in the moonlight we were remarking the curious fact that this year Good Friday like the Passover has fallen upon the 15th day of the month and the full moon. As I walked down the Churchyard alone the decked graves had a strange effect in the moonlight and looked as if the people had laid down to sleep for the night out of doors, ready dressed to rise early on Easter morning. I lingered in the verandah before going to bed. The air was as soft and warm as a summer night, and the broad moonlight made the quiet village almost as light as day. Everyone seemed to have gone to rest and there was not a sound except the clink and trickle of the brook.

Easter Day, 17 April

The happiest, brightest, most beautiful Easter I have ever spent. I woke early and looked out. As I had hoped the day was cloudless, a glorious morning. My first thought was 'Christ is Risen'. It is not well to lie in bed on Easter morning, indeed it is thought very unlucky. I got up between five and six and was out soon after six. There had been a frost and the air was rimy with a heavy thick white dew on hedge, bank and turf, but the morning was not cold. . . . The mill was silent except for the plash of the water from 'the dark round of the dripping wheel'. The mill pond was full, but I forgot to look at the sun in it to see if he was dancing as he is said to do on Easter morning. There was a heavy dew with a touch of hoar frost on the meadows, and as I leaned over the wicket gate by the mill pond looking to see if there were any primroses in the banks but not liking to venture into the dripping grass suddenly I heard the cuckoo for the first time this year. He was near Peter's Pool and he called three times quickly one after another. It is very well to hear the cuckoo for the first time on Easter Sunday morning. I loitered up the lane again gathering primroses where I could from among the thorn and bramble thickets and along the brook banks, not without a good many scratches. Some few grew by the mill pond edge and there was one plant growing on the trunk of a willow some way from the ground. The children have almost swept the lane clear of primroses for the same purpose for which I wanted them. However I got a good handful with plenty of green leaves and brought them home.

It was now 8 o'clock and Mrs Evans was down and just ready to set about finishing the moss crosses. She and Mary Jane went out to gather fresh primroses in the Castle Clump as last night's were rather withered. The moss had greatly improved and freshened into green during the night's soaking and when the crosses were pointed each with five small bunches of primroses they looked very nice and pretty because so very simple. Directly they were finished I carried them to the churchyard and placed them standing, leaning against the stone tombs of the two Mr Venables. People came up to look at the crosses and they were much admired. Then I ran home to dress and snatched a mouthful of breakfast.

There was a very large congregation at morning church the largest I have seen for some time, attracted by Easter and the splendour of the day, for they have here an immense reverence for Easter Sunday. The anthem went very well and Mr Baskerville complimented Mr Evans after church about it, saying that it was sung in good tune and time and had been a great treat. Mr V. read prayers and I preached from 1 John III.2, 3 about the Risen Body and Life. There were more communicants than usual: 29. This is the fifth time I have received the Sacrament within four days. After morning service I took Mr V. round the churchyard and showed him the crosses on his mother's, wife's, and brother's graves. He was quite taken by surprise and very much gratified. I am glad to see that our primrose crosses seem to be having some effect for I think I notice this Easter some attempt to copy them and an advance towards the form of the cross in some of the decorations of the graves. I wish we could get the people to adopt some little design in the disposition of the flowers upon the graves instead of sticking sprigs into the turf aimlessly anywhere, anyhow and with no meaning at all. But one does not like to interfere too much with their artless, natural way of showing their respect and love for the dead. I am thankful to find this beautiful custom on the increase, and observed more and more every year. Some years ago it was on the decline and nearly discontinued. On Easter Day all the young people come out in something new and bright like butterflies. It is almost part of their religion to wear something new on this day. It was an old saying that if you don't wear something new on Easter Day, the crows will spoil everything you have on. Mrs Chalmers tells me that if it is fine on Easter Day it is counted in Yorkshire a sign of a good harvest. If it rains before morning church is over it is a sign of a bad harvest.

The sweet suspicion of spring strengthens, deepens, and grows more sweet every day. Mrs Pring gave us lamb and asparagus at dinner.

Easter Tuesday, 19 April

Set off with Spencer and Leonard Cowper at 2 o'clock for Mouse Castle. By the fields to Hay, then to Llydiart-y-Wain. It is years since I have seen this house and I had quite forgotten how prettily it is situated. At least it looked very pretty today bosomed among its white blossoming fruit trees, the grey fruitful homestead with its two large gleaming ponds. Thence up a steep meadow to the left and by some quarries, over a stile in a wire fence and up a lovely winding path through the woods spangled with primroses and starred with wood anemones among trees and bushes thickening green. It was very hot in the shelter of the woods as we climbed up. The winding path led us round to the back of the hill till at last we emerged into a bold green brow in the middle of which stood a square steep rampart of grey crumbling sandstone rock with a flat top covered with grass bushes and trees, a sort of small wood. This rampart seemed about 15 feet high. The top of the hill round the base of the rampart undulated in uneven swells and knolls with little hillocks covered with short downy grass. One of the knolls overlooking the wooded side of the hill towards Hay was occupied by a wild group. A stout elderly man in a velveteen jacket with a walking stick sat or lay upon the dry turf. Beside him sat one or two young girls, while two or three more girls and boys climbed up and down an accessible point in the rampart like young wild goats, swarmed up into the hazel trees on the top of the rock and sat in the forks and swung. I could not make the party out at all.

They were not poor and they certainly were not rich. They did not look like farmers, cottagers or artizans. They were perfectly nondescript, seemed to have come from nowhere and to be going nowhere, but just to have fallen from the sky upon Mouse Castle, and to be just amusing themselves. The girls about 12 or 14 years old climbed up the steep rocks before and just above us quite regardless of the shortness of their petticoats and the elevating and inflating powers of the wind. We climbed up too and found no castle or ruin of one. Nothing but hazels and bushes. A boy was seated in the fork of one hazel and a girl swinging in the wind in another. We soon came down again covered with dust and went to repose upon an inviting knoll green sunny and dry, from which two girls jumped up and ran away with needless haste. The man lay down in the grass on his face and apparently went to sleep. The girls called him 'Father'. They were full of fun and larks as wild as hawks, and presently began a great romp on the grass which ended in their rolling and tumbling head over heels and throwing water over each other and pouring some cautiously on their father's head. Then they scattered primroses over him. Next the four girls danced away down the path to a spring in the wood with a pitcher to draw more water, leaving a little girl and little boy with their father. We heard the girls shrieking with laughter and screaming with fun down below at the spring in the wood as they romped and, no doubt, threw water over each other and pushed each other into the spring. Presently they re-appeared on the top with the pitcher, laughing and struggling, and again the romp began. They ran after each other flinging water in showers, throwing each other down and rolling over on the grass. Seeing us amused and laughing they became still more wild and excited. They were fine good looking spirited girls all of them. But there were one or two quite pretty and one in a red frock was the wildest and most reckless of the troop. In the romp her dress was torn open all down her back, but whilst one of her sisters was trying to fasten it for her she burst away and tore it all open again showing vast spaces of white, skin as well as linen. Meanwhile the water that had been ostensibly fetched up from the spring to drink had all been thrown wantonly away, some carefully poured over their father, the rest wildly dashed at each other, up the clothes, over the head down the neck and back, anywhere except down their own throats. Someone pretended to be thirsty and to lament that all the water was gone so the whole bevy trooped merrily off down to the spring again. I could not help envying the father his children especially his troop of lithe, lissome, high-spirited, romping girls with their young supple limbs, their white round arms, white shoulders and brows, their rosy flushed cheeks, their dark and fair curls tangled, tossed and blown back by the wind, their bright wild saucy eyes, their red sweet full lips and white laughing teeth, their motions as quick, graceful and active as young antelopes or as fawns, and their clear sweet merry laughing voices, ringing through the woods. Meanwhile the father began to roll down the hillockside to amuse his younger children who remained with him, laughing heartily. And from the spring below rose the same screaming and laughing as before. Then we heard the voices gradually coming near the top of the hill ascending through the wood, till the wild troop of girls appeared once more and the fun began again. Next the father went to hide himself in the wood for the girls to find him and play hide and seek. And in the midst of their game we were obliged to come away and leave them for it was nearly 4.30. So we ran down the winding path, past the spring through the primrose and anemone starred woods to the meadow, quarry, farm and road. I cannot think who the wild party were. They were like no one whom I ever saw before. They seemed as if they were the *genii loci* and always lived there. At all events I shall always connect them with Mouse Castle. And if I should ever visit the place again I shall certainly expect to find them there in full romp.

The air blew sweet from the mountains and tempered the heat of the sun. All round the brow of the hill the sloping woods budded into leaf, the birds sang in the thickets and the afternoon sun shone golden on the grassy knolls.

Wednesday, 20 April

Last night the stars glowed and glittered in the moonless sky with a strange peculiar beauty and the heaven seemed to be thicker sown with great stars than usual. I dreamed I was out coursing with two greyhounds each of which had only one eye. They started a hare apiece at the same moment, but each greyhound could only see the hare that the other was coursing. The consequence was that both hares escaped and both greyhounds knocked their heads against a stone wall.

Tuesday, 26 April

John Morgan was tottering about his garden with crutches, gathering stones off the beds and hoeing the earth between the potato rows. I took the hoe from the old soldier and hoed three rows for him, finishing the patch. Then we went indoors and sat down by the fire. It was quite warm working.

The whole country is now lighted up by the snowy pear blossoms among their delicate light-green leaves. The pear trees stand like lights about the gardens and orchards and in the fields. The magnificent great old pear tree opposite the Vicarage is in bloom.

Thursday, 28 April

Only Mr Venables was at dinner at Cae Mawr. The children had carefully put up my nosegay in water for me. Champagne at dinner and some splendid mutton and I was very hungry. Last night one of Cheese's clerks came to lodge here. I met him at the gate this evening and liked his looks, but when I came in after dinner I found the house poisoned with tobacco smoke.

Friday, 29 April

Last night the stars keenly glittered and sparkled with frost till the sky was all ablaze with them, and the night was strangely light, almost as bright as if there had been a moon. There seemed to be something that we did not know of giving light.

May Eve, Saturday

Mr Venables started in the Hay omnibus from Clyro Vicarage

for London for his two months' absence at 10.15.

This evening being May Eve I ought to have put some birch and wittan (mountain ash) over the door to keep out the 'old witch'. But I was too lazy to go out and get it. Let us hope the old witch will not come in during the night. The young witches are welcome.

May Day, Sunday

Two rainbows by 8 a.m. This looks like showery weather. After School I went to the Vicarage and found Mrs Welby in the drawing room and Mr Welby* came in from the dining room immediately afterwards. He is a pleasant looking, pleasant man-nered man with good features but with a light lackadaisical inconsequent unstable air. Mrs Welby is apparently older – also pleasant but a little prim, staid and stiff. Going out to Church we met the Crichtons at the door and they took Mrs Welby to sit in their seat. Mr Welby is rather given to light clerical slang and playfully alludes to his gown as his 'black' which he did not much approve of preaching in. He brought his own robes to Church in a bundle and wore a cassock in which I should think he must have been uncommonly cold sitting in the chancel. I read the prayers and those two splendid Balaam chapters. Mr W. preached on the character of Balaam – 'Let me die the death of the righteous etc.' – a short good striking sermon, but his voice has a peculiar faculty for stirring up every echo in the church to make it indistinct and defeat itself. I should think scarcely any one heard the Communion service, and I fear very few heard all the sermon.

Tuesday, 3 May

Started at noon to walk to Newchurch. Went by Whitty's mill. Stopped on the steep hill above the mill to enjoy the sight of the peaceful little hamlet, and the chink of the forge at Pentwyn sounded sweet, clear and busy across the dingle. I turned up by the old deserted kiln house, empty now, silent, desolate, with its

*Mr Venables's *locum tenens*.

high steep brown tiled roof and white dirty walls. This old field path is quite new to me. I have never travelled it before. Just above the kiln I saw and gathered the first red campion. Luxuriantly large cowslips grew on the bank and marsh buttercups in the ditch. It is a strange country between the kiln and Whitehall. The trees look wild and weird and a yew was stifling an oak. The meadow below Whitehall looked sad and strange and wild, grown with bramble bushes, thorns, fern and gorse. Poor White-hall, sad, silent and lonely, with its great black yew in the hedge of the tangled waste grass-grown garden and its cold chimney still ivy-clustered. I walked round and looked in at the broken unframed windows and pushed open a door which swung slowly and wearily together again. On another door at the house end were carved two figures of ploughs. A dry old mixen withered before and close to the front entrance. Here were held the Quar-terly Dances. What fun. What merry makings, the young people coming in couples and parties from the country round to dance in the long room. What laughing, flirting, joking and kissing behind the door or in the dark garden amongst the young folks, while the elders sat round the room with pipe and mug of beer or cider from the 'Black Ox' of Coldbrook hard by. Now how is all changed, song and dance still, mirth fled away. Only the weird sighing through the broken roof and crazy doors, the quick feet, busy hands, saucy eyes, strong limbs all mouldered into dust, the laughing voices silent. There was a deathlike stillness about the place, except that I fancied once I heard a small voice singing and a bee was humming among the ivy green, the only bit of life about the place. From the old long low brown cottage of Whitehall with its broken roof with a chimney at each gable end I went up the lane to Pant-y-ci speculating upon the prob-able site of the Coldbrook and the Black Ox which was the house of call on Clyro Hill for the drovers of the great herds of black cattle from Shire Carmarthen and Cardigan on their way down into England. I thought I saw the place where the house prob-ably stood. No one was at home at Pant-y-ci so I stuck a cowslip in the latch hole by way of leaving a card and went on to Crow-ther's Pool.

By Tyn-y-cwm Meadows to Newchurch village and in turning in at the old Vicarage garden door I heard the hum of the little school. The door under the latticed porch was open and as I went in a pretty dark girl was coming out of an inner door, but seeing me she retreated hastily and I heard an excited buzzing of voices within the schoolroom and eager whispers among the children: 'Here's Mr Kilvert – It's Mr Kilvert.' Not finding the good parson in his study I went into the schoolroom and fluttered the dove cot not a little. The curate and his eldest daughter were away and pretty Emmeline* in a russet brown stuff dress and her long fair curls was keeping school bravely with an austere look in her severe beautiful face, and hearing little Polly Greenway read. Janet* and Matilda* dressed just alike in black silk skirts, scarlet bodices and white pinafores, and with blue ribbons in their glossy bonny dark brown curls, were sitting on a form at a long desk with the other children working at sums. Janet was doing simple division and said she had done five sums, whereupon I kissed her and she was nothing loth. Moreover I offered to give her a kiss for every sum, at which she laughed. As I stood by the window making notes of things in general in my pocket book Janet kept on interrupting her work to glance round at me shyly but saucily with her mischievous beautiful grey eyes. Shall I confess that I travelled ten miles today over the hills for a kiss, to kiss that child's sweet face. Ten miles for a kiss.

The parson had been called away to receive strangers. After showing them the Church he had taken them up to the house to tea, and when 4 o'clock came and Emmeline gravely broke up the school I walked up to Gilfach y rheol with Janet and Arthur, while Emmeline and Matilda came after us presently. We went down the lane and across the swift flowing little brook, the Milw, by the old foot bridge, plank and handrail, and up the steep bank through the trees over a recognized shard. We were soon spied from the house and Sarah Vaughan stood in the door to welcome us with her pretty fair face, beautiful white brow, and luxuriant clustering dark brown curls. I do think the way the Vaughan girls wear their short curling hair is the most natural and prettiest in the world. Oh if fashionable young ladies

*Vaughan.

could but see and perceive and understand and know what utterly ludicrous guys they make of themselves, with the towers and spires and horns and clubs that they build and torture their hair up into! But slaves to fashion must its gods adore.

Wednesday, 4 May

Last night I heard a bull roaming and roaring about in the Bridge End grumbling and muttering deep low thunder. The crescent moon sparkled through a poplar and between the twin poplar spires hung the twin stars. I rose early, wrote, and loitered down the sunny lane before breakfast. A lovely morning and I heard the first turtle dove trilling. The voice of the turtle is heard in our land. I was standing on the bridge plank over the waste water looking at the black and white ducks and a fine drake preening themselves and splashing about in the mill pond when Price of the Swan came down the lane. 'So,' he said smiling, 'you are sunning yourself this morning.' Then he told me that Phillips of Penllan had ploughed up three fields of wheat on account of the drought. It is a very serious time for the farmers. Everything a month behindhand, stack and all. No grass, no wheat. We were standing talking where the waste water crosses the road and Price said, suddenly pointing, 'Look there'. There was a small animal running about the stones by the brook side in the sun – whirling round in circles and behaving very strangely. Price pronounced it to be a small kind of weasel catching flies. I said I thought it was a mouse, and it proved to be a shrew. Price called it 'a hardy straw'. It was whirling and whisking round swiftly among the stones in little circles, sometimes almost on its side, showing its white belly, tumbling about, darting to and fro rapidly, and conducting itself in the most earnest but ludicrous manner. It was so absorbed in catching flies or whatever it was about that it did not see us or care about us though we threw stones at it, and allowed us to come quite near and turn it over with a stick and push it into the water. It squeaked but did not run away and I took it up. It clung on to Price's stick, dropped on to the ground, and then vanished into a hole in the bank. . . .

I lent Hannah a book and brought away a fern green from off the great flat porch stone over the door of the Oaks. They are good for making ointment. The brook and Painscastle mill pond glancing like silver. A beautiful sunny afternoon and the cuckoo calling everywhere. Perhaps the cuckoo is the angel of the spring to remind us of the Resurrection. Met Mrs Cooper in the churchyard and she told me Cooper is very ill with stoppage.

Friday, 6 May

I had to set off for Newchurch again, my second visit there this week.

When I got out on to the open of the Little Mountain the lapwings were wheeling about the hill by scores, hurtling and rustling with their wings, squirling and wailing, tumbling and lurching on every side, very much disturbed, anxious and jealous about their nests. As I entered the fold of Gilfach y rheol, Janet issued from the house door and rushed across the yard and turning the corner of the wainhouse I found the two younger ladies assisting at the castration of the lambs, catching and holding the poor little beasts and standing by whilst the operation was performed, seeming to enjoy the spectacle. It was the first time I had seen clergyman's daughters helping to castrate lambs or witnessing that operation and it rather gave me a turn of disgust at first. But I made allowance for them and considered in how rough a way the poor children have been brought up, so that they thought no harm of it, and I forgave them. I am glad however that Emmeline was not present, and Sarah was of course out of the way. Matilda was struggling in a pen with a large stout white lamb, and when she had mastered him and got him well between her legs and knees I ventured to ask where her father* was. She signified by a nod and a word that he was advancing behind me, and turning I saw him crossing the yard with his usual outstretched hand and cordial welcome. I don't think the elder members of the family quite expected that the young ladies would be caught by a morning caller castrating lambs, and probably they would have selected some other occu-

*The Rev. David Vaughan.

pation for them had they foreseen the coming of a guest. However they carried it off uncommonly well.

Monday, 9 May

Now the various tints of green mount one over another up the hanging woods of Penllan above the dingle. Over the level line of brilliant larch green rises the warmer golden green brown of the oaks. But the most brilliant green of all is the young green of the beeches. The brilliance of the beeches is almost beyond belief. The turtles were trilling softly and deeply in the dingles as I went up the steep orchard. The grass was jewelled with cowslips and orchises. The dingle was lighted here and there with wild cherry, bird cherry, the Welsh name of which being interpreted is 'the tree on which the devil hung his mother'. The mountains burned blue in the hot afternoon and the air felt quite sultry as I climbed the hill.

Coming back up the fallow from the Oaks to Wern Vawr I saw Richard Jones, the eldest son, sitting on the hedge bank with his boot off and a man standing by him, while the horses and polished plough gleaming like silver in the sunshine stood waiting at the beginning of another furrow. At first I thought he had had an accident and hurt his foot. But the bystanding man was a shoemaker and the young farmer was trying on a pair of new boots – a very good accident. The shoemaker had a benevolent face and as we walked on to Wern Vawr together he asked me if I knew him and when I said no, he said he went every Sunday morning to read the Bible to Mrs Williams, but he had been told that if I ever caught him there I should be very cross with him. I begged him not to believe any such nonsense and said that so far from my being cross with him he had my warmest thanks. He was a Painscastle man and I should think a good man. These are the misconceptions that are spread abroad about the clergy.

Tuesday, 10 May

I went to luncheon at Clyro Court and there were present the

Welbys, the Crichtons, Mr Allen and Miss Marie Guise staying in the house. Afterwards we had croquet and archery and I played bowls with Baskerville, an old set that we rummaged out of an outhouse for the occasion, not having been used for years. His father used to play with them in Wiltshire and at Clyro Court and they are a fine old set. In the midst of the sports I was obliged to hurry away before post time to finish my letter to go to my Mother on her birthday, May 12th, with a birthday present of Miss Molesworth's *Stray Leaves from the Tree of Life*, the Pilgrimage which I have written on purpose to give her on her birthday, and a card of the verses 'Honest Work'.*

Wednesday, 11 May

A blessed, blessed rain. It began soft and gentle and silent about 3 a.m. and when I awoke everything was dripping, and already growing greener. How long it is since we have seen a dark cloudy dripping sky.

Thursday, 12 May

On going to Sackville Thomas' yesterday, I found little Mary Thomas at home because the ground was wet and her boots full of holes. When she heard her grandmother telling me how it was that she could not go to school, she went away by herself crying quietly and bitterly. Poor child it was touching to see her trying to write on the floor with a bit of chalk, and working as well as she could by herself with an old broken piece of slate and torn leaf of a book trying to think she was at school.

Saturday, 14 May

Over the great old fashioned house door of Court Evan Gwynne hung the sprigs of birch and wittan, the only remnants of the old custom I have noticed this May. The sprays had been hanging since May Eve and were rather withered.

*A poem by Kilvert.

Sunday, 15 May

Spoke to Wall about the desirability of trying to get James Allen to dislodge his immoral tenants at Cwmpelved Green.

Monday, 16 May

Morrell drove down and picked me and my luggage up at 7.30 and drove me to the station.

[*He goes to Langley and to the Bath flower show, returning to Clyro on 28 May.*]

Saturday, 28 May

From Langley to Clyro by early express. Galloped through Hereford in a fly with a white horse and just caught the Hay train at Moorfields. A pleasant journey – the weather fine and the country lovely. Charles Lacy met me with the elephant* and dog cart at Hay, and drove me over. . . .

Charles while driving me over told me of the charge brought against Brewer by Janet, late kitchenmaid at Clyro Vicarage, accusing him of being the father of her child. Janet wrote to him at Clyro, making the charge, as soon as the child was born, and poor Mrs Brewer opened the letter, read it, and sent it on to her husband. I am told she is nearly heartbroken. Poor child. Charles fears the charge is too well founded. I was thunderstruck. I always thought so well of Brewer and believed him to be such a very different man.

Mrs Chaloner† has put down a new carpet in my sitting room – a green and gold one bought at Capt. Lowrie's sale at Glasbury House. Not before it was wanted, for the old Turkey carpet was very filthy – full of oil and unwholesome.

Monday, 30 May

Mrs Smith of New Barn paid me an interminable visitation and hindered me a long while to no purpose, wanting me to write to

*Nickname for a horse. †Kilvert's landlady.

Mr Weere and ask him to let them have Pen-y-wyrlod, if her brother Stephen Davies has to leave. Mr Weere paid his tenant and farm an unexpected visit and finding him living in open concubinage with Myra Rees gave him notice. I told Mrs Smith that Mr Weere is a perfect stranger to me and that I could not interfere with what is not my business.

June Day, Wednesday

Going out to the School at 10 found Mary Brooks, the Vicarage housemaid, at the door just going to ring. She had run down breathless with an open letter just received in her hand to announce that Mrs Venables was confined of a nice little girl at 1.5 a.m. yesterday. Three cheers. The news flew through the village like wild fire. Charlie Powell, Richard Brooks and John Harris rushed to the Church and the bells were soon in full peal . . .

Hannah Whitney standing at her door knitting heard the bells ringing and asked 'What has God sent her?' The bells ringing at intervals all day. Mrs Price of the Swan sent the ringers a gallon of beer. I sent them another gallon, and went to the belfry to see them ringing. . . .

I went to bed early and saw a broad strong light striking through my NW. bedroom window on the wall opposite. I found afterwards it was a tar barrel bonfire which Cooper and Evans the schoolmaster were making upon the Bron in honour of Miss Venables.

Thursday, 2 June

Woke at 3 a.m. and looked out Eastwards. The sky clear as crystal and cloudless. The sun had not yet risen, yet the birds were singing loud and clear and 'the cuckoos were at their work again', as Richard Williams says. Clyro bells ringing again at intervals today. The great white clematis now in full bloom so sweet in the morning fresh air. The clematis seems to be strangling the mountain ash and has climbed almost to its top. The ash blossom has turned brown.

I am told that Mrs Preece's bees all swarmed the day she died.

Went to the Savings Bank. Sat an hour from 1 to 2 reading *The Times*, but not a soul came near the place. Miss Venables' birth announced in the first column.

To Llanthomas* at 4.30. Crichton and W. Thomas just going out trout fishing. They brought home a nice basket of fish. The ladies with Henry Thomas had gone up the bank sketching.

Heard that Kingcraft won the Derby yesterday instead of the favourite Macgregor who was thought safe to win.

The Llanthomas carriage took the Crichtons home and I went with them as far as Wye Cliff gate, Henry Thomas lending me a capital bearskin sort of coat to drive in. As we drove home the night was still and warm, the landrails were craking in the grass and the crescent moon was setting bright and clear. As I walked down the Long Mills hill the brickkiln glowed bright and red through the dusk.

Friday, 3 June

Went to see John Morgan and found the old soldier sitting out in his garden, so I brought a chair out of the house and sat with him reading and talking to him. The beans were deliciously sweet-scented and a white flower something like Whitsuntide stock. . . .

At the Lower House the orchard boughs were so thick and close that the sun could not penetrate them, and the sunlight only got into the orchard at a gap in the west side through which it came streaming in low in a long bright streak along the brilliant green rich velvety-looking grass like sunshine through a painted Cathedral window.

Sitting room windows open till very late. A group of people talking and laughing loud in the Swan porch and on the steps in the dusk. I was delighted to hear Teddy Evans proposing to some other children to play the old game of 'Fox a Dandley'. Then they chose 'dens' and began running about catching each other and I thought I heard the 'Cats of Kinlay' mewing. Perhaps that is part of the game, I had no idea the old game was

* Home of the Thomas family.

still played by the present generation of children. Teddy Evans
was singing

> *My Mother said that I never should*
> *Play with the gipsies in the wood, etc.*

Whitsun Day, 5 June

Woke in the night and saw the crescent moon setting red over
the dingle trees. Very hot in morning Church, and an enormous
bumble bee crawled over the white cloth and everything else
during the Holy Communion. A number of white dresses and
light colours in Church in honour of Whitsuntide. After afternoon Church walked across the fields to Hay. Went to the Castle
and found them all at tea. Went with them to Church and
preached for Bevan. Rather disconcerted at seeing Mrs Crichton
in Mr Allen's seat just below, for she had heard the same sermon
at Clyro in the morning.

A letter from Mr Venables confirming the Brewer scandal. I
had been hoping almost against hope that it might not be true.
It is a sad scandal for the Vicarage. He says he has never had
such a scandal in his house before. Mrs Venables does not know
of it yet. They were obliged to keep it secret from her lest it might
do her harm and shock her so as to hasten matters.

Whitsun Monday, 6 June

Called at Clyro Court. Mrs Baskerville said she had heard that a
lady had been carried out of Hay Church fainting under the
influence of a sermon from Mr Welby. The story is probably
untrue.

Whitsun Tuesday, 7 June

Up early and writing in my bedroom before breakfast. The
swallows kept on dashing in at the open window and rustling
round the room. The road sides are now deep in the dry withered
wych blossom blowing and rustling about lightly and falling
from the Churchyard wyches. Thunder muttering again this

morning, but still a cloudless sky, a wind from the E. and hot sun, everything parching and burning up. When are we to have rain? At the school Gipsy Lizzie looking arch and mischievous with her dark large beautiful eyes, and a dazzling smile showed her little white teeth, as she tossed her dark curls back.

Thursday, 9 June

In the night there came a cooler wind and fair showers out of the west. The falling white blossoms of the clematis drift in at the open window on the fresh morning breeze. In the garden there are red roses, and blue hills beyond. Last night the moon was shining in at my west window through the lacing boughs of the mountain ash – the moonbeams fell across the bed and I saw 'the gusty shadow sway' on the white bed curtain. Called at Cae Mawr at 3.30 and found Mr and Mrs Morrell playing croquet with his sister and Miss Morrell of Moulsford who are staying in the house, having returned with him on Tuesday. Joined them and we had two merry games. The two eldest Miss Baskervilles came in by the wicket gate while we were playing and we had tea on the lawn. I staid to dinner. After dinner we had archery.

Thursday, 16 June

The old soldier showed my brother his Peninsula medal with the Vittoria, Pyrenees and Toulouse clasps, and after some talk about the army and the Peninsula we left. It was fearfully sultry as we walked home and at 9 p.m. a thunderstorm came. It seemed as if three or four thunderstorms were rolling and working round far off. The lightning was exceedingly fine. Broad flares and flames of rose colour, violet, and brilliant yellow. Heavy rain came on and lasted for an hour. The air was much cooled and everything refreshed.

Friday, 17 June

Perch* went groping about in the brook and brought in a small
*Kilvert's brother Edward who was staying with him.

crayfish which crawled about the table, horns, tail and claws like a fresh water clean brown lobster. I did not know there were any crayfish in the brook.

We went to a croquet party at Clyro Court, calling at Cae Mawr by the way. The party divided between croquet and archery.

Tuesday, 21 June

Today we went for a picnic to Snodhill Castle in the Golden Valley. A great brake very roomy and comfortable came round with a pair of brown horses and we all got in. Mrs Oswald, Captain and Mrs Bridge, Perch, Jim Brown, Arthur Oswald and myself. The sun glared fiercely as we started, but driving made life tolerable and some heavy clouds came rolling up which made us fear a thunderstorm. The Haigh Allens drove up, then the Henry Dews, and the party was complete. So the company and provisions were packed into the four carriages and the procession set out through the narrow lanes. The girls ran out into the porches of the quaint picturesque old fashioned farm houses of the Golden Valley to see the string of horses and carriages, and the gay dresses of the ladies, an unwonted sight to the dwellers in the Golden Valley. At the foot of the Castle Hill we got out and every one carried something up the steep slippery brown bare grass slopes.

The first thing of course was to scale the Castle mound and climb up the ruins of the Keep as far as might be. It was fearfully slippery and the ladies gallantly sprawled and struggled up and slithered down again. Then a fire was to be lighted to boil potatoes which had been brought with us. Rival attempts were made to light fires, Bridge choosing a hole in the ruins and Powell preferring a hollow in the ground. Powell, however, wisely possessed himself of the pot and potatoes so that though the other fire was lighted first it was of no use and the divided party reunited and concentrated their minds and energies upon the fire in the hollow. Three sticks were propped together, meeting in a point, gipsy fashion, and from them was hung the pot, full of new young potatoes just covered with water. Wood was

Snodhill Castle, Golden Valley

Abbey Dore, Golden Valley

picked up off the ground and torn out of a dry hedge and a fierce fire was soon roaring under the pot making the trees and banks opposite quiver and swim in the intense heat. The flames soon burnt through one of the supports and when the fire was at the fiercest down came the three sticks and the pot upside down hissing into the midst of the flames. The pot lid flew off, out rushed the water and potatoes and a cloud of steam arose from the fire. Arthur Oswald gallantly rescued the pot with a pot hook in spite of the intense heat which was very difficult to endure. There were loud cries and everyone was giving unheeded advice at once. At length the pot was settled upright on the embers, more water having been poured in, and another armfull of dry wood heaped upon it, so that the pot was in the midst of a glowing fire. Twenty minutes passed, during which the gentlemen stood round the fire staring at the pot, while the ladies got flowery wreaths and green and wild roses to adorn the dishes and table cloth spread under an oak tree and covered with provisions. Then the pot hook was adjusted, the pot heaved and swung off the fire, a fork plunged into the potatoes and they were triumphantly pronounced to be done to a turn. Then there was a dispute how they should be treated. 'Pour away the water', said one. 'Let the water stay in the pot', said another. 'Steam the potatoes', 'Pour them out on the ground', 'Hand them round in the pot', 'Put them on a plate', 'Fish them out with a fork'. They were however, poured out on the ground and then the pot fell upon them, crushing some and blackening others. Eventually the potatoes were handed round the table cloth, every one being most assiduous and urgent in recommending and passing them to his neighbour. There was plenty of meat and drink, the usual things, cold chicken, ham and tongue, pies of different sorts, salads, jam and gooseberry tarts, bread and cheese. Splendid strawberries from Clifford Priory brought by the Haigh Allens. Cup of various kinds went round, claret and hock, champagne, cider and sherry, and people sprawled about in all attitudes and made a great noise – Henry Dew was the life of the party and kept the table in a roar. After luncheon the gentlemen entrenched themselves upon a fragment of the Castle wall to smoke and talk local news and politics and the ladies wandered away by themselves. At last we all met upon the mound where Mary Bevan and someone else had been trying to sketch the Keep, and sat in a great circle whilst the remains of the cup, wine, and soda water were handed round. Then we broke up, the roll of the carriages was heard coming through the lanes below and everyone seized upon something to carry down the steep slippery grass slopes.

At the Rectory we strolled about the garden. Dinner was announced, quite unnecessarily as far as I was concerned, for I wanted nothing. The room too was steaming hot. After dinner the carpet was taken up in the drawing-room and there was a dance on the slippery dark oak floor which was sadly scratched and scored by the nailed boots of the gentlemen and some of the ladies. Tom Powell slipped and fell. Tom Brown, dancing a waltz with his nephew Arthur Oswald, came down with a crash that shook the house and was immediately seized head and heels by Henry Dew and Mr Allen and carried about the room. We danced the Lancers, and finished with Jim Rufen but it was almost too hot. Then the carriages were ordered and we came away.

The drive home in the cool of the evening was almost the pleasantest part of the day. The light was so strong that we could hardly believe it was ten o'clock. The longest day, and the strong light glow in the North showed that the Midsummer sun was only just travelling along below the horizon, ready to show again in five hours. Passing by Hawkswood and the ghost-haunted pond we told ghost stories until Mrs Oswald was almost frightened out of the carriage.

Wednesday, 22 June

It was settled some time ago that my father* and Perch should go a-fishing to Llangorse Lake and stay a night there. Today was fixed on for the expedition. At dinner time my Father kindly asked me to be one of the party. My Father went down to the Lake while J. and I proceeded to Stephen Pritchard's house to see if we could get beds and a boat. Pritchard was out fishing on

*His parents were staying at the vicarage.

Boating

the Lake but his housekeeper told us we could have supper and
three beds, and the boatman Evans went down with us to the
landing stage. Stephen Pritchard's house stands upon the common very near the Lake, almost hidden in a bosoming bower of
trees. On the square hedge-guarded lawn in front of the cottage
a picnic party from Brecon, a number of girls in light dresses
and young men, were seated on green benches round a green
table covered with a white cloth in a shady corner having tea or
dinner.

Evans the Monmouthshire boatman rowed us past the island
to the edge of a field of perch weed, but the weather was too dry
and hot for fishing, the fish were sulky or sick, and all we caught
was five little perch. To me, however, the fishing was of very
little consequence. I had not expected to catch anything and
was not disappointed. The beauty of the evening and the Lake
was extraordinary, and in the west the Fan stood grand and
blue and peaked like a volcano. The feathery perch weeds waved
like forests under water, the cuckoo was calling about the hills
and around the lake, though he has done singing at Clyro and
is gone, or at least is silent. From the lake shores came musical
cattle calls, faint shouts, the barking of dogs and the melodious
sounds of evening. The boatman told us that within the last ten
years the American weed had crept into the dyke and was spreading fast all over it and doing much mischief. There used to be a
great quantity of grebe, he said, but they had been slaughtered
without mercy. Tern came here in numbers and last Christmas
a bittern was shot on the common near Pritchard's house.

Wednesday, 29 June

Going to the school I met two strange looking people, a young
man and a girl. He was dressed entirely in white flannel edged
with black and wore a straw hat. He looked like a sailor. They
hesitated a moment at the Churchyard gate, then turned in and
walked across the Churchyard and I saw them no more.

Saturday, 2 July

My father left us for Langley. At the station sitting in the waiting shed was a man dressed in a slop* with his head entirely covered with a black shawl except a patch of white handkerchief over the face. The shawl was arranged like an animal's snout. Not a feature was visible. He looked strange, horrible, unearthly, half like a masked burglar and half like a snouted beast. The station people knew nothing of him except that he came down the road from Clifford. I suppose he had met with some fearful accident which had disfigured his face.

There seemed to be a good deal of disputing and quarreling through the village about yesterday's sale and the things bought. A quarrel arose at the New Inn and Henry Warnell the gipsy came cursing, shouting and blaspheming down the road into the village mad with rage because someone had accused him of something and threatened 'to send him back to Hereford where he was before', the sting of the remark lying in this fact that the gipsy had just come out of Hereford jail where he has been undergoing sentence for assaulting and kicking William Price the innkeeper. The whole village was in uproar, some taking one part and some another, and it was long before the storm died away and the gipsy's wrath was appeased and his sense of honour satisfied.

I went to see old Sackville Thomas. He was evidently very ill and seemed as if he would never be better. He was lying in bed in a corner of the dark hovel hole which serves as a bedroom almost underground. A crimson coverlet was on the bed and he had a red cloth or handkerchief wrapped about his head. There were two beds in the room and on the other bed lay a rosy fair haired little girl of 4 years old flushed and just awakening from sleep, a strange and sharp contrast to the dying man of 82 on the opposite bed.

Monday, 4 July

Since the inspection† the classes and standards at the school have been rearranged and Gipsy Lizzie has been put into my reading class. How is the indescribable beauty of that most lovely face to be described – the dark soft curls parting back from

* A sort of smock.   †This took place on 1 July.

the pure white transparent brow, the exquisite little mouth and pearly tiny teeth, the pure straight delicate features, the long dark fringes and white eyelids that droop over and curtain her eyes, when they are cast down or bent upon her book, and seem to rest upon the soft clear cheek, and when the eyes are raised, that clear unfathomable blue depth of wide wonder and enquiry and unsullied and unsuspecting innocence. Oh, child, child, if you did but know your own power. Oh, Gipsy, if you only grow up as good as you are fair. Oh, that you might grow up good. May all God's angels guard you, sweet. The Lord bless thee and keep thee. The Lord make His Face to shine upon thee and be gracious unto thee. The Lord lift up His countenance upon thee peace, both now and *evermore*. Amen.

Mr Venables offered us the dog cart this afternoon, and we drove with the new bay horse from Tattersalls' to call at Wye Cliff. . . .

It seems the young gentleman in flannels and the young lady whom I saw walking through Clyro village last Wednesday are young Lyne and his sister. They are staying at the Swan at Hay with their Father and Mother. Their brother Ignatius* is soon expected down to look after his monastery in the Black Mountain. They seem to be very odd people. The two young people came to Clyro Church on Sunday afternoon and when my Mother went up to the Church door she had to run the gauntlet between them as they sat on tombstones opposite each other kicking their heels. They were at a croquet party at Hay Castle last week and young Lyne made himself very ridiculous taking off his hat when women spoke to him, and he persecuted poor little Fanny Thomas almost to the verge of distraction, taking off his hat to her whenever she made a stroke. After they came out of Clyro Church on Sunday afternoon young Lyne grinned in a boy's face and said, alluding to Mr Venables, who had performed the Service, 'What a very nice clergyman you have here'.

Wednesday, 6 July

At 3 o'clock went to Wye Cliff by the meadows. The targets

*See footnote on p. 45.

were pitched in the long green narrow meadow which runs down to the river and the summer houses, one of the prettiest archery grounds I ever saw, the high woods above and the river below. It was a pretty sight to see the group of ladies with their fresh light dresses moving up and down the long green meadow between the targets, and the arrows flitting and glancing white to and fro against the bank of dark green trees. At 6 tea, coffee, cider cup, etc. was laid out in the summer house and when 3 dozen arrows had been shot we left off shooting and went to tea and I made up the score. All through the hot burning afternoon how pleasant sounded the cool rush and roar of the Wye over its rapids & rocks at the end of the meadow.

Thursday, 7 July

At 5.30 started to walk to Clifford Priory to dinner, going to Hay across the fields. I arrived before any of the other guests and in the dark cool drawing room I found Mr Allen, his brother Major Allen, and Major Allen's two bewitching pretty little girls, Geraldine and Edith. Fair Helen* of Troy prettier than ever followed with her sister from Hardwick Vicarage, Henry Dew and Emily, Pope and Mr Allen, Llanthomas, Mary and Grace. I took Lucy Allen in to dinner but was forcibly separated from her and sat opposite by Louisa Wyatt who talked Switzerland and saved me much trouble in finding conversation. It was a very nice pleasant dinner. No constraint, plenty of ice. Good champagne and the first salmon I have tasted this year, a nice curry, and the Riflemen strawberries quite magnificent. Everyone in good spirits and tempers and full of talk. A sheep dog was spied devastating the flower beds on the lawn and it was proposed to shoot him with a bow. Clifford Priory is certainly one of the nicest most comfortable houses in this part of the country. The furnished hall is very charming. The evening was exquisite and the party wandered out into the garden promiscuously after dinner under the bright moon which shone alone in the unclouded sky. The flower beds in the lawn were beautiful, but most brilliant and dazzling were the riband

*Miss Webb, daughter of the vicar of Hardwick.

borders by the gate. When the party re-assembled in the drawing room there was music, and meanwhile I had a long talk in the recessed window and moonlight with Helen of Troy. She and her sister were dressed prettily in blue, the most elegant and tasteful dresses I have seen this year. Old times were revived and particularly one moonlight night at Hardwick Vicarage in the observatory, the same night I saw the light of the Great Meteor. Mrs Allen asked me to a croquet party here next Tuesday, and Mr Allen asked me to luncheon at Oakfield on Monday when the Foresters are coming to his house. He brought me as far as Hay in the rumble of his most antiquated most comfortable old yellow chariot on C springs, very large broad and heavy and able to carry 7 people. We had 6 on board, Mrs Allen, Thomas and Pope inside, I preferred the night air and the tramping of the fast mare. Going up the hills we had before us the antiquated figure of the old coachman against the sky and amongst the stars. So we steadily rumbled into Hay and there was a great light in the North shewing where the sun was travelling along below the horizon, and only just below.

Saturday, 9 July

It is a pretty lane this Bird's Nest Lane, very shady and quiet, narrow and over/bowered here and there with arching wyches and hazels. Sometimes my darling child Gipsy comes down to school this way, but more often she comes down Sunny Bank when the days are fine, and then over the stile by little Wern y Pentre. Yet often and often must those tiny feet have trodden this stony narrow green-arched lane, and those sweet blue eyes have looked down this vista to the blue mountains and those little hands gathered flowers along these banks. O my child if you did but know. If you only knew that this lane and this dingle and these fields are sweet to me and holy ground for your sweet sake. But you can never know, and if you should ever guess or read the secret, it will be but a dim misty suspicion of the truth. Ah Gipsy.

Savine, the Clyro Court coachman, who is going to be confirmed, rather amused me by saying that he had been preparing himself for confirmation by reading Revelations. 'I've read down Timothy too,' said he. How the Bishop would enjoy that.

Monday, 11 July

The view from my bedroom window looking up the dingle always reminds me of Norway, perhaps because of the spiry dark fir tops which rise above the lighter green trees. Often when I rise I look up to the white farm house of Penllan and think of the sweet grey eyes that have long been open and looking upon the pearly morning sky and the mists of the valley and the morning spread upon the mountains, and think of the young busy hands that have long been at work, milking or churning, with the sleeves rolled up round arms as white and creamy as the milk itself, and the bright sweet morning face that the sunrise and the fresh air have kissed into bloom and the sunny tresses ruffled by the mountain wind, and hope that the fatherless girl may ever be good, brave, pure and true. So help her God. The sun looks through her window which the great pear tree frames and lattices in green leaves and fruit, and the leaves move and flicker and throw a chequering shadow upon the white bedroom wall, and on the white curtains of the bed. And before the sun has touched the sleeping village in the shade below or has even struck the weathercock into a golden gleam, or has crept down the steep green slope of the lower or upper Bron, he has stolen into her bedroom and crept along the wall from chair to chair till he has reached the bed, and has kissed the fair hand and arm that lies upon the coverlet and the white bosom that heaves half uncovered after the restlessness of the sultry night, and has kissed her mouth whose scarlet lips, just parting in a smile and pouting like rosebuds to be kissed, show the pearly gleam of the white teeth, and has kissed the sweet face and the blue veined silky lashed eyelids and the white brow and the soft bright tangled hair, till she has unclosed the sweetest eyes that ever opened to the dawn, and risen and unfastened the casement and stood awhile breathing the fresh fragrant mountain air as it blows cool upon her flushed cheek and her half veiled bosom, and lifts and ruffles her bright hair which still keeps the kiss of the sun. Then when she has dressed and prayed towards the east, she goes out to draw water from the holy spring St Mary's Well. After which she goes about her honest holy work, all day long, with a light heart and a pure conscience.

Tuesday, 12 July

Walked to Clifford Priory across the fields with Crichton and Barton. Bevan and Morrell walked on before faster and got there before us. I had some pleasant talk with Barton, who is a clever well-read man, about Tennyson, Wordsworth, Mr Monkhouse, the Holy Grail, and at last we got to Clifford Priory, very hot, a few people out in the sun on the lawn, and Lucy Allen came to meet us. A crowd in the drawing room drinking claret cup iced and eating enormous strawberries. Gradually people turned out on the lawn. Pretty Geraldine and bewitching Edith Allen, I am sorry to say, were gone. Colonel Balmayne and his niece Miss Baldwin were there from Middlewood where he has lately come to live. The rest were the usual set that one meets and knows so well. Dews, Thomases, Webbs, Wyatts, Bridges, Oswalds, Trumpers, etc. No Baskervilles, no Bevans, Mary and Alice being away at Four Ashes. Everyone about here is so pleasant and friendly that we meet almost like brothers and sisters. Great fun on the lawn, 6 cross games of croquet and balls flying in all directions. High tea at 7.30 and croquet given up. A young gentleman caused some amusement by appearing on the lawn in full evening dress, tail coat, white tie and all. It proved to be the Miss Wyatts' brother come with the Webbs. I took Miss Barton in to tea and saw she had plenty to eat and drink. More than 40 people sat down. Plenty of iced claret cup, and unlimited fruit, very fine, especially the strawberries.

After tea we all strolled out into the garden and stood on the high terrace to see the eclipse. It had just begun. The shadow was slowly steadily stretching over the large bright moon and had eaten away a small piece at the lower left side. It was very strange and solemn to see the shadow stealing gradually on till half the moon was obscured. As the eclipse went on the bright fragment of the moon seemed to change colour to darken and redden. We were well placed for seeing the eclipse and the night was beautiful, and most favourable, not a cloud in the way. We watched the eclipse till all that was left of the moon was a point of brightness like a large three-cornered star. Then it vanished altogether. Some people said they could discern the features of the moon's face through the black shadow.

Wednesday, 13 July

Miss Lyne is a very nice sensible unaffected girl, rather pretty, with dark curls, grey eyes and a rich colour, and pretty little white hands. She is rather short. Her brother Clavering goes in for being comic and ends in being a bit of a buffoon. He has four dogs at the Swan now. His usual complement is thirteen. Miss Lyne told me a good deal about Father Ignatius and his monastery which she called 'his place' at Capel y Ffin. He has to keep on preaching to support the monastery and the building operations as everything depends on him. His average collection after each sermon is £20. Father Philip, one of the monks in residence at Capel y Ffin now, was a baker by trade. The other, Brother Cyrene, was a gardener and a very drunken man. He came to Father Ignatius and asked him to take him and reclaim him. He has been with Father Ignatius a year now and is an altered man.

Friday, St Swithin's Day

Familiar as this place is to me I am always noticing some fresh beauty or combination of beauties, light or shade, or a view from some particular point, where I have never been before at some particular hour and under some particular circumstances.

To Hay Church at 6.30. Afterwards I went to the Castle and found Mrs Bevan sitting in the drawing room in full chat with Miss Wybrow. We had tea and then I went down to the Swan with Fanny and Nelly to fetch Miss Lyne and her brother to play croquet. They were out and we went into the saloon to wait for them. Presently Miss Lyne passed the window with her quick decided step and we went out into the hall to meet her.

She came forward and held out her hand so pleasantly, the beautiful little hand just what a lady's hand ought to be, 'small, soft, white, warm and dry'. Then we all tramped up into the town together and walked about with her while she went round to the shops paying their bills as they leave the Swan and Hay tomorrow for Hereford. And I am very sorry they are going, at least that she is going. It is so provoking that just as I have become acquainted with her and like her so much, and just as her shyness and reserve were beginning to wear off, and she had become so friendly and cordial, she goes away and perhaps I shall never see her again.

Clavering Lyne told me some of the extraordinary visions which had appeared to his brother Father Ignatius, particularly about the ghosts which come crowding round him and which will never answer though he often speaks to them.

Also about the fire in the monastery chapel at Norwich, that strange unearthly fire which Father Ignatius put out by throwing himself into it and making the sign of the cross. When the Lynes went away I walked with them till our roads parted and I asked her if I might venture to call upon Father Ignatius when he comes to the Monastery at Capel y Ffin. She said, 'by all means', and added that her brother is always glad to see people and especially the clergy. Clavering Lyne rode over to Capel y Ffin yesterday and reports the monastery building going on very badly, his brother having paid the workmen in advance. One more cordial clasp from the pretty white hand, 'Good night and Good bye'.

Shall I confess how I longed to kiss that beautiful white little hand, even at the imminent risk that it would instantly administer a stinging slap on the face of its admirer.

Saturday, 16 July

To-day we heard rumours of war and war itself. Henry Dew brought the news stated in the *Globe* that war had been declared by France against Prussia, the wickedest, most unjust most unreasonable war that ever was entered into to gratify the ambition of one man. I side with the Prussians and devoutly hope the

French may never push France to the Rhine. Perhaps the war was a dire necessity to the Emperor to save himself and his dynasty. At all events the war is universally fearfully popular in France, and the French are in the wildest fever to go to the Rhine.

[*He goes to stay with friends in Cornwall, then to Langley, thence back to Clyro.*]

Monday, 15 August

This being the Napoleon Fête Day it has been supposed that the Emperor would hazard a battle for the sake of French sentiment. Went to see the old soldier and talk to him about the War. I asked him as an old enemy of the French which side he took, French or Prussian. He said he knew nothing of the Germans, the French were more natural to him and he wished them well. They were very kind to him, he said, when he was quartered in the Allied Army at a small village near Arras. He helped them to dig their fields, garden, cut wood or do anything that was wanted. In return they rewarded him by giving him their nice white bread, while the dark hard ration went to the pigs. Morgan said there was often a good and friendly feeling between English and French soldiers when they were in the field. He had often been on picquet duty less than 50 yards from the French sentries. He would call out, 'Bon soir'. The Frenchmen would sing out in return 'Will you boire?' Then they would lay down their arms, meet in the middle space and drink together. Morgan liked drinking with the French sentries because they mostly had something hot. He believes and believed then that if they had been caught fraternizing he would have been shot or hung.

Friday, 19 August

Ben Lloyd of the Cwm Bryngwyn reeling up the steep field above Jacob's Ladder carrying a horse collar and butter tub. Just as I came up the drunken man fell sprawling on his back. He got up looking foolish and astonished, and I gave him some good advice which he took in good part at first. I asked if he were married. Oh, yes, and had great-grandchildren. A nice example to set them, I thought. When I said how his wife would be vexed and grieved to see him come rolling home, I found I had touched a tender point. He became savage at once, cursed and swore and threatened violence. Then he began to roar after me, but he could only stagger very slowly so I left him behind reeling and roaring, cursing parsons and shouting what he would do if he were younger, and that if a man did not get drunk he wasn't a man and of no good to himself or the public houses, an argument so exquisite that I left it to answer itself.

On the Little Mountain the gorse that glowed and flamed fiery gold down the edge of the hill contrasted sharp and splendid with the blue world of mountain and valley which it touched.

Friday, 2 September

At 10.45 started across the fields to walk to Capel y Ffin. I came in sight of the little Capel y Ffin squatting like a stout grey owl among its seven great black yews. I hastened on, and in front of the Capel House farm there was the sunny haired girl washing at a tub as usual by the brook side, the girl with the blue eyes, not the blue of the sky, but the blue of the sea. 'Is Father Ignatius here?' I asked. 'Yes, at least he was here this morning.' I asked a mason at work upon the building if Father Ignatius was there. 'There he is with his brother,' said the mason. A black robed and cowled monk was walking fast along the bottom of the field towards a barn with Clavering Lyne. Clavering came up to me, but the monk walked quickly on without looking round. Clavering took me to his father and mother, who were sitting on a garden seat under a tree in a pretty little dingle. They had just arrived unexpectedly from Pontrilas having driven up the valley as I came down. It was curious, our meeting thus as it were by chance.

Mr and Mrs Lyne came up out of their dingle and Mrs Lyne brought up Father Ignatius and introduced us. He struck me as being a man of gentle simple kind manners, excitable, and entirely possessed by the one idea. He always spoke to his father

Father Ignatius

and mother as 'Papa' and Mamma' and called me 'Father'. I could not persuade him that my name was not Venables. His head and brow are very fine, the forehead beautifully rounded and highly imaginative. The face is a very saintly one and the eyes extremely beautiful, earnest and expressive, a dark soft brown. When excited they seem absolutely to flame.

He wears the Greek or early British tonsure all round the temples, leaving hair of the crown untouched. His manner gives you the impression of great earnestness and single-mindedness. The voice and manner are very like Clavering's and it was with difficulty that I could tell which of the two was speaking if I did not see them.

Father Ignatius wore the black Benedictine habit with the two loose wings or pieces falling in front and behind, two violet tassels behind, the knotted scourge girdle, a silver cross on the breast, and a brazen or golden cross hanging from the rosary of black beads under the left arm.

We walked round the place and then climbed the steep bank above and looked down upon the building. Mrs Lyne gathered some whinberries and gave them to us to eat. They were very nice. They grew along the ground on tiny bushes among a very small delicately twisted pink heath. We saw the monks and novices below issuing from a barn where they had engaged for an hour or so in an 'examination of conscience'. One of the monks was gazing at us. He had conceived an irrepressible desire to see Mrs Lyne again. He did not wish to intrude upon her approach or address her. He simply wanted to see her at a respectful distance and admire her afar off.

Mr Lyne said the monk was a man of few and simple wants, content with a little and thankful for small mercies. Because the monk had said that if he could see Mrs Lyne he would be perfectly happy.

Mrs Lyne not having much faith in the larder or resources of the monastery, especially on a Friday, had wisely taken the precaution of bringing with her an honest leg of mutton and two bottles of wine. The monasterial garden provided potatoes and French beans, very good, and we had luncheon under the tree in the dingle, waited on by the novices also cowled and robed in black like the monks. They addressed Father Ignatius as 'dear Father' whenever they spoke to him and bent the knee whenever they approached or passed him.

Whilst we were at luncheon we heard voices close to us proceeding from the bottom of a deep watercourse or lane, on the other side of the hedge. Then a man looked over the hedge and asked his way to Capel y Ffin. Father Ignatius had been sitting talking freely and at ease with his head uncovered, and his cowl lying back on his shoulders. But directly he heard the strange voices and saw the strange face peering over the hedge he dashed the cowl over his head and face and bolted up the bank among the shrubs like a rabbit. I never saw a man so quick on his legs or so sudden in movement. He was gone like a flash of lightning. He has been much intruded on and persecuted and dreads seeing strangers about the place. Last night some men came up from Llanthony Abbey and rung the monastery bells violently and were very rude and insolent. However he treated them kindly and they apologized for their conduct and went away conquered.

After luncheon we went up to the monastery again and Mr and Mrs Lyne, Clavering and I each laid a stone in the wall. We had to go up a ladder on to the scaffolding and hoarding. Each of us 'walled' our stone for the benefit of the masons. I laid a stone at the particular request of Father Ignatius. The building that the masons are at work on now is the west cloister which is to be fitted up temporarily for the accommodation of the monks. This work was begun in March and ought to have been finished long ago. But there was no one to look after the workmen and they did as much or as little as they pleased. Father Ignatius thinks every one is as good as himself and is perfectly unworldly, innocent and unsuspicious. He gave the contractor £500 at first, took no receipt from him. And so on. The consequence is that he has been imposed upon, cheated and robbed right and left. Father Ignatius took us into the Oratory, a tiny square room in the Cloister, fitted with a lace and silk-covered altar upon which stands a super altar or Tabernacle in which he informed us in a low awestruck voice was 'the Blessed Sacrament'. There was a couch in the room on which he sleeps. The altar lace came from France, and was very expensive. There was a crucifix above the altar. It came from Spain and had been broken, but it was a beautiful figure. Father Ignatius said that once when he was praying Gerald Moultrie who was present saw the crucifix roll its eyes, then turn its head and look at Father Ignatius. Father Ignatius confessed that neither he nor any of the monks had ever seen the crucifix move. He did not know what to think about it, but he could not help believing that Moultrie saw what he declared he saw. He says that Moultrie is not at all an excitable imaginative man. As he was talking about this in a low eager whisper, he looked strange and wild and his eyes were starting and blazing. He apologized for Mr Lyne's not kneeling at the altar by saying that his father did not believe in the Real Presence. He knelt for a moment at the side of the altar.

Mr Lyne was anxious to be going as they had ten miles to drive down a bad road to Pontrilas. So they got their dogcart. Clavering drove and we parted in the lane. They drove off and I remained in the lane talking to Father Ignatius. I had a good deal of conversation with him then and at luncheon time. He told me that Lord Bute came up to see him and the monastery a few days ago, and to make enquiries. He greatly hopes Lord Bute may help him and send him money. The Order of St Benedict, Father Ignatius says, is now worth about £60. The monks are supported entirely by his preaching. He makes £1000 a year. He gets on much better with the Low Church than with the High Church people he says, best of all with the Dissenters who consider and call him a second Wesley. He allows that a man must be of a very rare and peculiar temperament to become and remain a monk. A monk he says must either be a philosopher or a 'holy fool'. He also allows that monkery has a strong tendency to drive people mad. Out of 50 novices he could only reckon on making 3 monks. The rest would probably be failures. One in seven was a large percentage.

I stood in the lane near the Honddu bridge for some time talking with Father Ignatius. I asked him if he would not find an ordinary dress more convenient and practical and less open to insult and objection. But he scouted the idea of abandoning his distinctive monastic dress. He said he had once given it up for a few days, but he felt like a deserter and traitor till he took to the habit again. Then he again became happy. The Bishop of Gloucester and Bristol he said, had suggested the same thing, but he turned the tables on the Bishop by asking him why he did not discard his own foolish and meaningless dress, far more irrational than the Benedictine habit, every part of which has its meaning. The Bishop laughed and said there was a good deal in what Father Ignatius said. He thinks the Bishops are coming round to his side. We shook hands and departed. 'Goodbye, Father,' he said with an earnest kindly look, 'and thank you for your good wish. You must come and see us again when we have our guest house ready.' When we had parted a little way and our roads had diverged he called out through the half screen of a hazel hedge, 'Father! Will you remember us the next time you celebrate the Holy Communion?' 'Yes', I replied, 'I will.'

Saturday, 3 September

The news was brought from Hereford this afternoon that Mac-Mahon's army had been surrounded and had capitulated and that the Emperor had surrendered himself in person and given up his sword to the King of Prussia. What a tremendous collapse. We waited and waited dinner and at last it appeared that we were waiting for the Llanthomases. Presently they came in, a little before 8. They had walked from Llanigon, their waggon-ette having broken down directly they started. I sat next to Mrs Bridge at dinner and we had a very merry time. Coming home at midnight there was a pitiful thing. At Wye Cliff gate I over-took a little girl taking her tipsy father home. It was dark but I thought I recognized Sarah Lewis' plaintive voice.

Tuesday, 6 September

Gipsy Lizzie was at school again this morning, lovely as ever. Rode the elephant* to Llowes after school to ask Williams† to drive me to the Three Cocks on my way to Llysdinam‡ on Friday evening. Poor elephant, his best days are over, and his knees show the Cornish Coat of Arms from a recent fall, but he is a noble gallant old fellow.

We went into the green orchard where beautiful waxen-looking August apples lay in the grass, under the heavily loaded trees. Williams gave me a pocket full of apples. The postman came in with the latest news, the *Evening Standard*. Williams tore the paper open and we saw the reports of Saturday confirmed and that a Republic had been proclaimed in Paris under General Trochu. Crichton sent me $1\frac{1}{2}$ brace of partridges. Really people are very kind in sending me game.

Saturday, 10 September

A wild tempestuous night, with lashing storms of rain and high

*Nickname for a horse.   †Vicar of Llowes.
‡The Venables' own home, where Kilvert was going to stay on the following Friday.

wind. A new walk has been made at Llysdinam since I was last here. It is a great improvement to the place. We all left New-bridge for Clyro at 12.20. At Llechrhyd I saw Mary Bevan on the platform waiting to get into our train. She looked very pretty in her white feathered hat and red and black check cloak. An old gentleman had given her a *Graphic*, with some good pictures of the War. Mary of course got into our carriage. At Three Cocks she took Mr Venables aside and told him that a dreadful calamity had happened. On Wednesday morning the turret ship *Captain* went down at sea with 500 men. Capt. Cowper Coles who constructed her was on board and went down with the rest. Mary Bevan thought Capt. Coles was Mr Venables' brother in law and very sensibly refrained from saying anything of what she had heard or seen in the *Western Post* of this morning until she could speak to Mr Venables alone. He waited till they got home to break the news to Mrs V. It is a terrible blow to her and all the family. Poor Mrs Coles and her 9 children. And no one left to tell the tale, or why the ship went down. *The Times* of today confirms the sad news.

Thursday, 13 September

Mrs Venables gave me a letter of Captain Chandos Stanhope to read and letters from Lily and Edmund Thomas with others from Southsea, all about the loss of the *Captain*. We have the gunner's account now. He says the ship turned suddenly bottom upwards in a squall and then went down so. He and some other men scrambled upon her hull and for a minute or two actually stood upon her bottom. What a sight. What a moment. And what a terrible [   ] for the 500 men entangled and surprised below deck. She was top heavy, had too much 'top hamper' and too low a free board, so that when she heeled over in the squall she had no high broadside to oppose to and press against the water, and so she turned upside down at once.

Wednesday, 14 September

I dined at the Vicarage. Poor Mrs Venables terribly distressed

Clyro Church and the Baskerville Arms in Kilvert's time

by Capt. Cole's death in the disaster of the *Captain*. She utterly broke down at dinner time and cried quietly and bitterly. I never saw her cry before.

Thursday, 15 September

Hay Fair. Roads lively with men, horses and sheep. We were busy all day dressing the Church or preparing decorations. . . .

Mrs Price and Miss Elcox had got a quantity of wild hops from their fields and were arranging bright red apples for ornament. Also they had boughs loaded with rosy apples and quantities of bright yellow Siberian crabs. At the school the children were busy leasing out corn from a loose heap on the floor, sitting among the straw and tying up wheat, barley and oats in small sheaves and bundles. Gipsy Lizzie was amongst them, up to her beautiful eyes in corn and straw. The schoolmaster, the boys and I gathering stringed ivy from the trees in the Castle Clump. The Miss Baskervilles dressing the hoops for the seven window sills with flowers and fruit. After dinner while writing to Fanny I was told that Mrs Morrell wanted the keys of the Church. We got them and found her sitting on a tombstone near the Church door with Miss Sandell. She undertook to dress the reading desk, pulpit, and clerk's desk and did them beautifully. Then Cooper came down with his men carrying magnificent ferns and plants and began to work in the chancel. One fine silver fern was put in the font. Gibbins* undertook the font and dressed it very tastefully with moss and white asters under the sweeping fronds of the silver fern. Round the stem were twined the delicate light green sprays of white convolvulus. The pillars were wreathed and twined with wild hop vine falling in graceful careless festoons and curling tendrils from wreath and capital. St Andrew crossed sheaves of all sorts of corn were placed against the walls between the windows, wheat, barley and oats with a spray of hop vine drooping in a festoon across the sheaf butts and a spray of red barberries between the sheaf heads. Bright flowers in pots clustered round the spring of the arches upon the capitals of the pillars, the flower pots veiled by a twist of hop vine. Mrs

*Mrs Venables' maid.

Partridge returned from Worcestershire this afternoon and brought and sent us two magnificent branches of real hops from the Worcestershire hop yards. These we hung drooping full length on either side of a text Mrs V. had made, white letters on scarlet flannel, 'I am the Vine. Ye are the branches. Without Me ye can do nothing.' And from the corners of this text Cooper hung two bunches of purple grapes. Two texts in corn on green baize. 'Praise ye the Lord' in wheat ears, and 'Thanks be to God' in oats were placed over the doors, inside. Outside the great door branches of apples and pears hung over the door. The gates were dressed with ferns, fruit and flowers. Following the outer arch, within a border of Spanish chestnuts oak and acorn, elderberries, barberries and apples, was Mr Evan's text in scarlet letters on a bright blue ground. 'Enter into His Gates with Thanksgiving.' An avenue of tall ferns and coleus led up the chancel. A row of the same plants stood along the altar steps, and dahlias were laid on brae fern along the altar rail bars. On either side of the entrance to the altar hung a splendid cluster of purple grapes, and along the rails were tied at intervals small sheaves of wheat and tall heads of Pampas grass. On the altar stood two sheaves of all corn with a paten between them worked in scarlet flannel bordered with corn and IHS worked in wheat ears. Above this hung a cross covered with scarlet flannel and adorned with corn barberries. On the window sill above stood a larger sheaf of all corn in a moss field and upon the moss lay all fruit, plums, apples, pears.

Saturday, 17 September

Lady Joscelyn Percy says that in this neighbourhood she never hears people speaking unkindly of each other.

Monday, 19 September

The lights twinkled in the Hay and shone bright across the valley and there was a glare in the sky above the town. I went into the harmonious carpenter's Bengough. He was looking out some flute music for a young farmer whose cart and two horses stood meanwhile alone at the gate and so awkwardly that I could not get in at first. Bengough played for my edification 'Jenny Janes' upon a flageolet which drew piteous howls from a large black dog in the room. Bengough also played the flute and harmonium, but the dog did not disapprove of those. The crickets were chirping in the forge and near the forge I met a girl dressed entirely in white walking quickly towards the Lower House singing.

Tuesday, 20 September

Went up the orchard bank in preference to Jacob's Ladder, but found the spiked gate at the top locked and had to climb over it. Just below on the orchard bank grew an apple tree whose bright red boughs and shoots stood up in beautiful contrast against the light blue mountains and grey town and the blue valley. And the grey tower of Clyro Church peeped through the bright red branches. A sack half filled with apples stood under a tree but no one was about. A woodpecker was tapping loud some way down Jacob's Ladder. Partridge shooting on all round.

From the stile on the top of the hill above the plantation watched the sun set in a crimson ball behind the hills or rather into a dense ball of dark blue vapour. It was like seeing a sunset over the sea. He went down very fast. All the country round was full of evening sounds, children's voices, dogs barking, the clangour of geese. Meanwhile the sheep fed quietly round me. Then came the afterglow round the S. and E. Scarlet feathers floated in the sky, and the gorse deepened into a richer redder gold in the sunset light.

Wednesday, 21 September

Another dense white fog which cleared off to cloudless blue and brilliant sunshine at 11. As I sat with my windows open at noon writing, the rustle of the glossy bright poplar leaves filled the room as the leaves twinkled and shimmered up the green poplar spire into the blue.

Went to the Bronith. People at work in the orchard gathering up the windfall apples for early cider. The smell of the apples very strong. Beyond the orchards the lone aspen was rustling loud and mournfully a lament for the departure of summer. Called on the old soldier. He was with his wife in the garden digging and gathering red potatoes which turned up very large and sound, no disease, and no second growth, an unusual thing this year. The great round red potatoes lay thick, fresh and clean on the dark newly turned mould. I sat down on the stones by the spring and the old soldier came and sat down on the stones by me while his wife went on picking up the red potatoes. We talked about the war and the loss of the *Captain*. Mary Morgan brought me some apples, Sam's Crabs and Quinin's. The spring trickled and tinkled behind us and a boy from the keeper's cottage came to draw water in a blue and white jug.

It was very quiet and peaceful in the old soldier's garden as we sat by the spring while the sun grew low and gilded the apples in the trees which he had planted, and the keeper's wife moved about in the garden below, and we heard the distant shots at partridges.

I dug up the half row of potatoes for him which he had left unfinished.

Monday, 26 September

Magistrates' meeting at noon. Two Clyro cases. An unsuccessful attempt by Samuel Evans' daughter and wife of the Bird's Nest to father the daughter's base child upon Edward Morgan* of Cwmpelved Green. It came out that Mrs Evans had been shameless enough to let the young man sit up at night with Emily after she and her husband had gone to bed. Mrs V. most properly reprimanded her publicly and turned her out of the Club. Such conduct ought to be strongly marked and disapproved.

Wednesday, 28 September, Michaelmas Eve

I went out for a walk with Mr G. Venables over the Doldowlod suspension bridge across the Wye and up the Llandrindod road. We fell into conversation about Wordsworth and the

*See page 158.

following are some of Mr George Venables' recollections of him.

'I was staying at Ambleside with some people who knew Wordsworth and was introduced to him there. Then I went over to tea at his house, Rydal Mount. Wordsworth's sister Dorothy was in the room, an old woman at that time. She was depressed and took no part in the conversation and no notice of what was passing. Her brother told me he attributed the failure of her health and intellect to the long walks she used to take with him, e.g. from Llyswen to Llanthony.

'He said he met "Peter Bell" on the road between Builth and Rhayader.

'One evening riding near Rydal I saw Wordsworth sauntering towards me wearing a shade over his eyes, which were weak, and crooning out aloud some lines of a poem which he was composing. I stopped to avoid splashing him and apologized for having intruded upon him. He said, "I am glad I met you for I want to consult you about some lines I am composing in which I want to make the shadow of Etna fall across Syracuse, the mountain being 40 miles from the city. Would this be possible?" I replied that there was nothing in the distance to prevent the shadow of the mountain falling across the city. The only difficulty was that Etna is exactly North of Syracuse. "Surely", said Wordsworth, "it is a little N.E. or N.W." And as he was evidently determined to make the shadow fall the way he wanted it I did not contradict him. Wordsworth was a very remarkable looking man. He looked like an old shepherd, with rough rugged weather beaten face, but his features were fine and high cut. He was a grand man. He had a perfectly independent mind and cared for no one else's opinion. I called upon him afterwards at the Stow, Whitney. He was very kind to me there. He used to say that the Wye above Hay was the finest piece of scenery in South Britain, i.e. everything south of himself.'

Monday, 3 October

How odd, all the news and letters we get from Paris now coming by balloons and carrier pigeons. When Lord Lyons, the English Ambassador at Paris, went to Tours the other day he sat on his box in the street for some hours before he could get a lodging. . . .

The old Stonebreaker (James Jones) was exulting by the way-side on his heap of stones, about an ear trumpet Miss Bynon had given him. He said it was as long as his stone hammer and that now he should come to Church. Called on Mrs Corfield. Below her cottage at the mouth of the short narrow green lane I met a wild sharp-looking Welsh lad, with a bright face, laughing eyes and windy hair. He was driving a lean white pig, for whom he apologized saying she had been suckling young ones and was poor. While we were talking this pig cleverly opened a gate went through and shut the gate behind her, or else the gate shut itself.

Tuesday, 4 October

Today I sent my first post cards, to my Mother, Thersie, Emmie and Perch. They are capital things, simple, useful and handy. A happy invention.

A man crouching over the fire in his hovel said to me with touching earnestness and humbleness, '*I do pray Him to forgive me if Him please.*' This was Edward Evans in Clyro village.

Dinner at Clifford Priory. A fair haired pretty German girl dressed in blue staying in the house showed us some beautiful drawings and illuminated texts, and at her request I became a subscriber for a six shilling set, of which she has ordered 1000 copies to be printed.

The subject of Germany was started and we were talking about Baden, Strasburg, Heidelberg. 'Ah,' said Miss Schlienz to me, 'it is easy to see which way *your* sympathies lie.' She had (I learnt afterwards) been made painfully aware that other people's sympathies did not all lie the same way, for one after-noon when driving through Hay with Mrs Allen, she met Cap-tain Thomas and Captain Bridge, both strong French partizans. The two Captains naturally turned the talk upon the War and not knowing Miss Schlienz's nationality they both expressed their opinions freely. 'And now,' said Captain T., 'there is one of those beastly German Dukes shot.' 'I don't know if you are aware,' said Katie Allen leaning grimly down from the box, 'I don't know if you are aware that there is a German lady in the carriage.' The Captains routed horse and foot, bowed, and fled, one up, the other down street.

Wednesday, 5 October

A dark foggy afternoon. At the Bronith near the Cottage a yellow poplar spire stood out bright against the dark woods above. At the Bronith spring a woman crippled with rheumatism and crying with the pain, had filled her tin pail and was trying to crawl home with it. So I carried the pail to her house.

Friday, 7 October

. . . promised to administer the Sacrament to Edward Evans. Poor Edward is very ill. What a scene it was, the one small room up in the roof of the hovel, almost dark, in which I could not stand upright, the shattered window, almost empty of glass, the squalid bed, the close horrid smell, the continual crying and wailing of the children below, the pattering of the rain on the tiles close overhead, the ceaseless moaning of the sick man with his face bound about with a napkin. 'Lord have mercy. Lord have mercy upon me,' he moaned.

I was almost exhausted crouching down at the little dirty window to catch the light of the gloomy rainy afternoon.

Called on Esther Rogers, and found her at home after three times finding the garden gate padlocked. I gave her a copy of Uncle Francis' Bathwick Sermons. She told me that her brother was a heavy dragoon and was killed at Waterloo. His horse had been killed under him or disabled. Going to fetch a fresh horse, as he was walking in a lane with two other English soldiers, they came upon a troop of French cavalry, probably lancers. The three English soldiers lay down and pretended to be dead, but her brother was thrust through as he lay on his face on the ground (probably by a lancer). She just remembered her brother as a fine tall man, and has a vivid recollection of a picture of him in a scarlet uniform mounted on a black horse with white hoofs.

It was curious to hear the old Waterloo story told more

than half a century after by a quiet fireside in Wales.

Saturday, 8 October

Heavy rain in the night and in the morning the mists had all wept themselves away. In the night the wind had gone round from the cursed East into the blessed West. All evil things have always come from the East, the plague, cholera, and man.

Monday, 10 October

All the evening a crowd of excited people swarming about the Swan door and steps, laughing, talking loud, swearing and quarrelling in the quiet moonlight.

Here come a fresh drove of men from the fair, half tipsy, at the quarrelsome stage judging by the noise they make, all talking at once loud fast and angry, humming and buzzing like a swarm of angry bees. Their blood is on fire. It is like a gunpowder magazine. There will be an explosion in a minute. It only wants one word, a spark. Here it is. Some one had said something. A sudden blaze of passion, a retort, a word and a blow, a rush, a scuffle, a Babel of voices, a tumult, the furious voices of the combatants rising high and furious above the din. Now the bystanders have come between them, are holding them back, soothing them, explaining that no insult was intended at first, and persuading them not to fight. Then a quick tramp of horse-hoofs and a farmer dashes past on his way home from the fair. Twenty voices shout to him to stop. He pulls up with difficulty and joins the throng. Meanwhile the swarm and bustle and hum goes on, some singing, some shouting, some quarrelling and wrangling, the World and the Flesh reeling about arm in arm and Apollyon straddling the whole breadth of the way. Tonight I think many are sore, angry and desperate about their misfortunes and prospects. Nothing has sold today but fat cattle. No one would look at poor ones, because no one has keep for them during the winter. Every one wants to sell poor cattle to pay their rent and to get so many mouths off their hay. No one wants to buy them. Where are the rents to come from?

Tuesday, 11 October

Visited Edward Evans in the dark hole in the hovel roof which does duty for a bedroom, and a gaunt black and white ghostly cat was stalking about looking as if she were only waiting for the sick man to die, that she might begin upon him.

Dined at Pont Vaen and played chess with Bridge. Going down towards Chain Alley I saw a pair of dark beautiful eyes looking softly and lovingly through the dusk, earnest and eager to be recognized, and the slight delicate girlish figure of the Flower of the Border stood within her grandmother's door, her round olive cheeks shaded by her rich clusters of dark curls. A happy smile broke over her beautiful face, as she looked up shyly and spoke. When I came back a little before midnight the house was dark, but as I passed under the windows I heard the child's voice speaking in the bedroom. Chain Alley is a dangerous terrible neighbourhood for a beautiful girl to be reared in. God keep thee my child.

Friday, 14 October

Visited Edward Evans and the stench of the hovel bedroom almost insupportable. The room below was occupied by 12 bushels of potatoes just brought home from Cabalva Cwm where they were set. The gaunt ghastly half starved black and white cat was still sitting on a box at the bed head waiting for the sick man to die.

The children are many of them still busy picking acorns which they can sell to the farmers at 2/- and 2/4 a bushel. Acorns are so valuable this year that the farmers are jealous of them and exclude everyone from their fields. So the poor people are obliged to confine themselves to the road under the oaks. I went to Allt-y-Fedwas to learn the real story of the death of the little boy who was killed by the horse last week. Price wishing to describe the child's size said that 'he stretched out a good deal of a long boy after he was dead'. A little chubby-cheeked girl sitting on the settle proclaimed aloud in a triumphant voice as if she were repeating a well learnt lesson, 'Charlie's dead and in the grave', and then fetched a deep long sigh. The low grey woman with the grotesque face sat by the window sewing. A comely girl in russet brown swept up the hearth with a goose's wing and set on the kettle, and a large black and white sheep dog pushed open the door and wandered into the room, and was sent out again.

At Wern Vawr a girl with green eyes was washing bright red potatoes in a bowl in the yard. A sound of several voices from within the old hospitable house, and good Mrs Jones was bustling about.

Hannah was crouching over a glowing wood fire on the hearth in the outer kitchen knitting a stocking, and Mrs Morgan of Cold Blow was waiting to have her gallon tin filled with milk. It is an old custom in these parts for the poor people to go about round the farm-houses to beg and gather milk between and about the two Michaelmasses, that they may be able to make some puddings and pancakes against Bryngwyn and Clyro Feasts, which are on the same day, next Sunday, the Sunday after old Michaelmas Day or Hay Fair, October 10th. The old custom is still kept up in Bryngwyn and at some hill farms in Clyro, but it is honoured at comparatively few houses now, and scarcely anywhere in Clyro Vale. Wern Vawr is one of the best houses to go to, a hospitable old-fashioned house where they keep up the old customs. Besides being given a gallon of milk to be carried away, the poor people are fed and refreshed to help them on their journey to the next farm, for they wander many miles for milk and it is a weary tramp before they reach home. The women go round again to gather milk in May when the calves are weaned.

Wern Vawr has the character of giving 'Not very bad milk neither', which phrase, though so carefully qualified in the mouths of these hill people, is no slight praise.

I turned in to old Hannah's and sat with her an hour talking over old times, and listening to her reminiscences and tales of the dear old times, the simple kindly primitive times 'in the Bryngwyn' nearly ninety years ago.

She remembers how, when she was a very little girl, she lived with her grandfather and grandmother, old Walter Whitney (who was about ninety) and his wife. In the winter evenings, some of their old neighbours, friends of her grandfather, used to come in for a chat, especially old Prothero, William Price and William Greenway, contemporaries of her grandfather, and all men born about the beginning of the 18th or the end of the 17th century. Greenway's old wife was ill and helpless, and Hannah Whitney's grandmother used to go and look to her and take care of her. These old people would sit round the fire talking on the long winter evenings, and Hannah then a child of 8 or 10 would sit on a little stool by her grandfather's chair in the chimney corner listening while they told their old world stories and tales of faries ('the fairies') in whom they fully believed.

Then there was the 'Wild Duck Pool' above Newbuilding, where they used to run on first to frighten the wild ducks up when they were going out leasing*. To this pool the people used to come on Easter morning to see the sun dance and play in the water and the angels who were at the Resurrection playing backwards and forwards before the sun. There was also the 'sheep cot pool' below Wernwg, where Hob with his lantern was to be seen, only Hannah never saw him. But when people were going to market on Thursday mornings they would exhort one another to come back in good time lest they should be led astray by the Goblin Lantern, and boys would wear their hats the wrong way lest they should be enticed into the fairy rings and made to dance. Then the story of the girl of Llan Pica who was led astray by the fairies and at last killed by them, and the story of the old man who slept in the mill trough at the Rhos Goch Mill and used to hear the fairies come in at night and dance to sweet fiddles on the mill floor. Hannah living in 'the Bryngwyn' wore a tall Welsh hat till she was grown up. She remembers an old Welsh woman who always came to the Rhos Goch Chapel in a tall hat, 60 years ago.

Saturday, Clyro Feast Eve, 15 October

I found the old soldier sitting by his black fireplace and the door open, but soon a spark of fire showed and the flame leapt up,

*Leasing = gleaning.

and soon we had a glowing fire. We talked about the War and he amused me by telling me his remembrances of the wolves in Spain, how they were very large and fierce, much larger than any dog he had seen. 'We frightened them,' he said, 'by making a flash of powder in the pan of our muskets. When the wolves saw it they went away. They did not like to see that.' It is nothing to write, but the old man said it so quaintly as if the wolves disapproved of the proceeding and did not wish to countenance it, so they walked away.

Tuesday, 18 October

Old James Jones was breaking stones below Pentwyn. He told me how he had once cured his deafness for a time by pouring hot eel oil into his ear, and again by sticking into his ear an 'ellern' (elder) twig, and wearing it there night and day. The effect of the eel oil at first was, he said, to make his head and brains feel full of crawling creatures. The clouds were hanging low, dark and woolly and I asked him if he thought it was going to rain. He said there would not be much rain before night and until the 'sun got round to the butt of the wind'. And he was right.

A wild rainy night. They are holding Clyro Feast Ball at the Swan opposite. As I write I hear the scraping and squealing of the fiddle and the ceaseless heavy tramp of the dancers as they stamp the floor in a country dance. An occasional blast of wind or rush of rain shakes my window. Toby sits before the fire on the hearthrug and now and then jumps up on my knee to be stroked. The mice scurry rattling round the wainscot and Toby darts off in great excitement to listen and watch for them.

Wednesday, 19 October

When I looked out the last thing the night was pitchy dark and pouring with rain. The ball passed off very quietly. The rain choked off the usual number of loafers who lounge and row outside, and beyond the squealing of the fiddle and the tramp

of the dancers faintly heard across the road there was no sound.
. . . Mrs Chaloner told me this morning that when the Harrises,
now living at the Wine Vaults at Hay, kept the Baskerville
Arms, at one of the Clyro Feast Balls the Whitcombs of the
Bronith got in. A fight followed, the house was in an uproar,
the company were fighting all night instead of dancing, and in
the morning all the respectable people had black eyes.

At that time the inn was very badly conducted, people sat up
drinking all night and fought it out in the morning in the road
before the inn. Frequently they were to be seen at 11 o'clock in
the morning stripped and fighting up and down the road, often
having drunk and vomited and wallowed in the inn all night. . . .

Went in to see Richard Meredith the Land Surveyor and sat
talking to him for some time. He said the old folks used to rise
very early, never later than five even in winter, and then the
women would get to their spinning or knitting. His grandmother
was always at her spinning, knitting or woolcarding by 6 o'clock
in the morning.

It was fashionable to breakfast just before daylight in winter
and 9 o'clock at night was a very late hour for going to bed.
When people rose very early it was a saying that they were
'beating for day', because it was supposed that they went out
and knocked on the earth for day to come.

Thursday, 20 October

Next to visit old Laver (W. Price). He was all in confusion and
excitement, not able to splutter out his words fast enough, all up
on end, dancing first on one leg and then on the other. It was
his washing day (the first I should think which had occurred to
afflict him for a very long time). His hovel had just been washed
out and goodness knows not before that operation was needed,
so I promised to call another day, and Price much relieved, yet
fearing to be rude and inhospitable, assented in great excitement, hopping on alternate legs, and swarming with lice.

It was so dark in Edward Evans' cabin that I could not see
his face or him all the time I was in the low and crazy loft in the
roof, and only heard a feeble voice proceeding out of the dark-

Hannah Whitney's cottage, Clyro

ness, 'Bless God, Bless God'. A small and filthy child knelt or
crouched in the ashes of the hearth before a black grate and
cold cinders. No one else was in the house and the rain plashed
in the court and on the roof and the wind whistled through the
tiles. Almost all the glass was smashed out of the bedroom or
rather bed loft window, and there was only a dirty cloth hanging before the ruin of the window to keep the wind away.
Imperial Caesar dead and turning to clay would have done
better, and could not have done worse. It was a real wind-door.

Turned in to old Hannah Whitney's. The old woman cloaked
and with her rusty black bonnet fiercely cocked and pointed,
crown uppermost, on the top of her head was standing in the
doorway taking an observation of the weather, the world and
the stream of water flowing fast down the gutter before the door.
This gutter is of great importance to her and she takes a deep
interest in it, for if it gets choked with leaves etc., in a violent
rain storm, the water all rushes immediately into her house. The

old woman was preparing to shut the door for the night for she felt chilly and said that let the wind be uphill or down it always came in at her door. I went in and sat chatting with her an hour, listening reverently to the words of wisdom which dropped from her. Hannah is a very wise woman, wise with mother wit matured and broadened by the wisdom of age. I asked if the water had come into her house in the late storm. 'No, God be thanked for it, the water hanna been in *yet*.' We talked about the old days. She said that people 'adored old Christmas Day', even after they began to keep the new. 'And now,' she burst out indignantly, 'no one minds the old Christmas Day, they all keep the new.' Then she calmed down and went on to say philosophically, 'I do believe the Old Day is the right day, but them as have studied the matter say that we had gained too much time and that the new day is the right day. It may be, I don't know, not I, God only knows which day it is. If we keep one day and keep it in sincerity and truth that is the main.' Formerly, she said, there were more holidays than there are now. On Good Friday they were used not to 'gear, but to Garden'. I observe that Hannah rightly always talks of Whitsun Sunday, Whitsun Monday, Whitsun Tuesday. 'There was one cruel flash of lightning yesterday,' she said. 'Clyro Feast,' she said, 'went down the road, for I saw nothing of it.' But turning her withered grey face and white hair, the fine delicate features whose ancient beauty is still perceptible, she looked earnestly at me, and her eyes shone as she took up her parable and spoke of the blessing of being cheerful and contented and of being able to sit by her own fireside and eat her crust of bread in peace and quietness.

Saturday, 22 October

I went up the common to White Ash, the air blowing fresh and fragrant on the open hill side green. Read to Sarah Probert, the story of the Raising of Lazarus. Hannah came in and sat by the fire listening with grunts of assent between the whiffs of her short pipe. She said she had been 'tugging and tearing firewood up the old dingle'. A squirrel's skin hung over the hearth. The cat killed the squirrel and several others a month ago. 'I couldna think,' said Hannah, 'what she was a-tushing down the fold.' Hannah had preserved for me some Columbine seeds and some seed of the blue flower Scabious called 'Kiss at the garden gate'.

Monday, 24 October

8 p.m. Mrs Chaloner has just called me out into the passage to look through the great window at a strange light in the sky. It was evidently an Aurora though it did not appear in the North. Overhead the sky was covered with a deep burning rosy flush which spread down into the East and showed in patches in the South and West, everywhere but in the North. The glow at first looked like the reflection in the sky from a great fire. There was no flashing, shooting or streaming. The light was quite steady. The effect of the bright stars shining through the rosy flush was very beautiful. The sky was wild, broken and stormy, especially in the North with black clouds, and there was a fresh cold wind. The night was very light though there was no moon, and for hours after the flush of rose had faded a white strong flare shone in the N.

Tuesday, 25 October

At Maesllwch Castle last week four guns killed seven hundred rabbits in one afternoon.

Wednesday, 26 October

Carrie Gore let me in to the Mill kitchen through the meal room and loft over the machinery, and there was Mrs Gore making up the bread into loaves and putting them into the oven. Good-natured nice Carrie, with her brown hair arranged in a bush round her jolly broad open frank face, and her fine lusty arms bare, entertained me by playing on the jingling old harpsichord sitting very stiff and straight and upright to the work with her chair drawn in as near as possible to the key-board so that she was obliged to lean a little back quite stiff. She played some hymn tunes correctly, but what I admired most was her good nature, good breeding and perfect manners in sitting down to play directly she was asked without any false shame or false modesty, without shilly-shallying or holding back that she might be asked again, but just sitting straight down, doing what she was asked and doing her best at once without any nonsense, in a good-tempered cheerful way that many young ladies might copy with advantage. She is as nice and good a girl as you will meet in a day's march.

A pretty little girl sat in an armchair by the fire reading. Mrs Gore had made her some apple hop-abouts, but forgot to put them in the oven till I reminded her of them. Mrs Gore showed me with great and lawful pride a very nicely drawn and coloured map of England and Wales, which Carrie had done at Clyro School and which her sister Mary had had framed and glazed.

Mrs Gore wanted me to have some gin and when I declined offered me tea as an alternative. I accepted the tea. While they were getting it ready Mary came back from a long round among the hills on horseback, collecting bills and money for her father. The Gores of Whitty's Mill are very well-off, make at least £200 a year*, the schoolmistress says, and have a matter of £300 in the bank. Carrie had gone upstairs, and I heard Mrs Gore calling in a loud voice, 'Carrie dear, there's Mary come back, go to the door and take the mare off her'. I rose and looked through the window into the yard below. Carrie was leading a bay mare to the stable and a pretty girl who had just dismounted, the Miller's daughter, was coming towards the house with her riding whip in her hand, dressed in a dark riding habit which she was holding up as she walked, and a black jaunty pretty hat with a black feather sat upon her flowing fair hair. It was a pretty picture. She came into the kitchen straight, with the manners, bearing and address of a lady, shook hands and welcomed me cordially. 'Well, Miss Mary, you've had a cold stormy ride.' Her little hand was cold with riding. She began to tell me where she had been, then went upstairs, took off her riding habit, and came down in a pretty maize print dress, and sitting in an armchair by the fireside went on with the account of her

*Kilvert earned about £150.

ride. The dog and cat fawned on her and jumped into her lap. Everybody and everything seemed glad when 'Mary' came home. She appeared to be the strong gentle ruling spirit of the house. Oh the dear old Mill kitchen, the low, large room so snug, so irregular and full of odd holes and corners, so cosy and comfy with its low ceiling, horse-hair couch, easy chair by the fire, flowers in the window recess, the door opening into the best room or parlour. Oh these kindly hospitable houses about these hospitable hills. I believe I might wander about these hills all my life and never want a kindly welcome, a meal, or a seat by the fireside. And the kindness and earnest gratitude one meets with when one calls at the houses is quite touching. Mary brought me a small round table to my side of the fire. Mrs Gore herself brought me tea and bread and butter and preserves. So we sat round the hearth and talked about the War. And when I rose to go, 'Goodbye, Sir,' said the Miller's daughter, with a warm hearty clasp of the hand. 'I'm *very* glad to see you here.' Blessings on the dear old Mill, and the brook that turns the wheel, and on the hospitable kitchen and the rooftree of the Gores, and blessings on that fair brave honest girl, the Miller's daughter of Whitty's Mill.

Saturday, 29 October

Reading *Puck*. Last night we heard that Metz has fallen and that four Marshals of France and 150,000 men have surrendered as prisoners of war.

Today I found in a book a red silk handkerchief worked with the words 'Forget me not', and I am sorry to say that I have entirely forgotten who gave it to me. One of my many lovers no doubt. But which? Ah this is 'Manner true' indeed.

Friday, 18 November

Next to the Pant, where Mrs Powell was entertaining a sister-in-law from Huntington at tea. We were talking about parishes and boundaries. 'I'm sitting in Brilley (England and Hereford-shire) now,' said I, feeling for the boundary notch in the chimney. 'It's further this way,' she said. 'I suppose,' she said, 'there have been some curious disputes about the boundary running through this house.' 'Very odd indeed,' I said, remembering the extraordinary story which old Betty Williams of Crowther used to tell me about the birth of a child in this house (the Pant) and the care taken that the child should be born in England in the English corner of the cottage. 'Stand here, Betsey, in this corner,' said the midwife. And the girl was delivered of the child *standing*. Last summer the Manor folk walked and beat the bounds and pushed a stick through the window of the Pant as usual first removing a pane of glass. At Cae Noyadd in its black yews and hedges covered white with drying linen Mrs Harley was washing, the floor was littered with dry fern, and a big girl had of course 'cracked a commandment', run away from her place ('started' as they call it) and come home in this fashion, i.e. in the family way. The usual old story.

Sunday, 20 November 1870

I went back with Mrs Venables to the Vicarage to tea and we had a long confidential talk between the lights and far into the dark, sitting by the drawing room fire, talking about the prevailing scepticism of the day. I said if I had children I should teach them to believe all the dear old Bible stories. She said she hoped to see me some day with a number of children about me, my own children. Never, I said adding I did not believe that I should ever marry. Then came out by degrees my attachment to C. She was very much surprised when she guessed the right name after trying Mary Bevan, Fanny Higginson, Flora Ross, Lily Thomas. 'She'll never marry,' she said gravely. 'I know it,' I said.

Wednesday, 23 November

I dined at the Vicarage with Lord and Lady Hereford who came today and stay till Saturday for the shooting at Clyro Court.

Thursday, 24 November

A wild rainy night and the rain poured all day so that the Clyro Court party could not shoot and played battledore and shuttle-cock in the hall, gentlemen and ladies.

Monday, 28 November

A plaintive mew outside the door. I open the door and tabby Toby comes trotting in with his funny little note of affection.

When visiting John Morgan of the New Inn I asked him if he trusted that he was forgiven by God. 'I cannot answer you fully,' he said. 'I make my appeals to Him,' said the sick man solemnly.

Baskerville sent me a brace of pheasants. I put up a notice of the next Penny Reading in the Post Office window and called at Annie Powell's and found her better. Walked up the Cwm and found old James Jones stonebreaking. He told me how he was once travelling from Hereford to Hay by coach when the coach was wrecked in a flood by Bredwardine Bridge because the coachman would not take the bearing reins of the horses off. The bearing reins kept the horses' noses down under water, they plunged and reared and got the coach off the road and swim-ming like a boat, and an old lady inside screaming horribly, 'Don't keep such a noise, Ma'am,' said Jones, throwing himself off the roof into a hedge-row against which the coach was swept by the fierce current. 'We won't leave you before we get you out somehow.' He was followed by most of the passengers on the roof, though one very tall man fell into the water on his face all along like a log, and waded through the flood out on to the Bredwardine side. One outside passenger was a miller of the neighbourhood who had a boat on the river. This was sent for and the old lady pacified and pulled into it through the coach window. The coachman was prayed and entreated to loose the bearing reins, but refused to do it. Two horses were drowned, one wheeler went down under the pole. The other, a leader, broke loose and plunged and pawed and reared at the bridge out of the flood till he was exhausted, and then fell over backwards into the stream and was rolled away by the current.

Tuesday, 29 November

A letter from my mother enclosing one from Perch. She tells me that Maria Kilvert of Worcester died last week after a few days' illness. Mr Hooper, her Worcester lawyer, wrote to ask my Father to come immediately. He and my Mother went to Worcester yesterday. My Father said on reading Mr Hooper's letter that he thought she had probably left all the bulk of her property to the Cathedral.

Wednesday, December Eve

A letter from my Mother from College Green, Worcester – Maria Kilvert's house, where they are staying. When my Father and Mother arrived, the servants were crusty and evidently did not intend them to stay there, saying there was no spare bed and nothing to eat in the house. Mr Hooper, the acting executor, was out of town, so not liking to take any step without his sanction they went to the Star for the night, until they could see him. Next morning he told them, 'Certainly, they had a perfect right to go to the house, and stay there'. So armed with his authority they went to College Green and took up their quarters there. My Mother sent a rough sketch of the will which Mr Hooper read over hastily to them. £15,000 left to charities, Clergy widows and orphans, Home Missions and S.P.G., by a right but by no moral right and a most unprincipled unnatural act and piece of ostentation and a most erroneous injustice. Still more monstrous, £600 had been left by the will to Lord Lyttelton and his son. Happily this had been revoked by codicil. Her beautiful prints she left to the Bishop of Worcester and the magnificent volumes of engravings were left to the executors. To my Father she left her *rose trees* and to my Mother her furs and lace, which my Mother thinks may be worth a few shillings. There are many legacies to old servants etc., some of them heavy ones. After the sale of the house everything in it, including the fine old plate with the family arms engraved upon it, is to be sold, and after all legacies, debts and expenses have been paid what remains of the property, which will probably be a mere trifle, is to be equally divided between my Father, Aunt Marianne and the Motherwells. A most iniquitous will, not a shilling was left to any of the Francis Kilverts, the old grudge and malice against Uncle Francis* for writing Bishop Hurd's life ruling strong in death.

My Mother has been very busy making inventories and lists for Mr Hooper as a check on the servants, as everything was left to their mercy. The funeral is to be on Friday after Cathedral morning service. The funeral service is to be choral. The six pall bearers to be the Canons. My Father and Mother the only mourners. I decided to go over tomorrow and stay over the night and see the funeral and Worcester, and wrote to offer to attend the funeral.

Thursday, December Day

Walked to Hay and took the 11.30 train to Hereford, passing throngs of market folk on the road.

[*The diarist arrives at Worcester and a girl of whom he has asked his way offers to guide him.*]

We passed along an irregular quadrangle formed by the N. side of the Cathedral on one hand and houses on the other sides. A carriage drive swept round an iron-railed grass enclosure within which were some ancient elms with almost all their limbs lopped or broken off. This was the Cathedral Close or College Green. Most of the houses were red brick, some stuccoed white, all irregular and unlike each other. 'There,' said the girl with the baby, 'that is Miss Kilvert's house, the last house, red brick with white blinds down.' It was a curious looking house in an inner recess of the Close, red brick, white window frames, a conical roof with tiles, and a small front. In the middle of this inner recess was a smaller open grass plot. The Close may be pretty in summer but it looked bare and dreary in December. The Cathedral Tower close by, just restored by Lord Dudley, is a grand rich object. The first impression the Cathedral exterior gave me was one of plainness, bareness, newness, produced by the new

*See page 19.

grey sandstone with which it has been cased, not yet weather-fretted or lichen-grown.

The maid-servant announced me at the library door where my Father and Mother were sitting, as 'a visitor for Mrs Kilvert'. My Mother, who was writing at a table between the two windows, rose and took off her spectacles, expecting to see a stranger, as I had written that I was coming by a later train. Dinner had just gone out but a charwoman brought me in a tray of luncheon. The three servants are too grand to wait upon us so they employ a charwoman. Then my mother related all their adventures. I had a particular wish to see Miss Kilvert though I usually loathe and abhor the sight of a corpse, so Charlotte Haynes, the ladies' maid, was summoned and she gladly conducted us upstairs into the bedroom and drew up the blinds. It was a small room very plainly furnished, but some exquisite engravings hung on the walls. The bed stood in the middle of the room and the room was full of chloride of lime. It was a four post curtained bed, covered with a white sheet. Charlotte drew back the sheet. The dead woman 80 years old lay in her coffin, a lead coffin fitted into an outer one of dark oak and lined with white satin. The coffin lid with its brass breastplate leaned upright in a corner of the room. The face that lay still, frozen down into silence, in the coffin was a very remarkable one. It was a distinguished face with aristocratic features. A firm mouth, fine highly formed nose delicately and sharply cut. There was a slight frown and a contraction of the brows. It was the face of a person of considerable ability, stern, severe, and perhaps a little contemptuous, an expression which with the contraction of the brows was so habitual that death had smoothed neither away. It did not look like the face of a woman of fourscore. The 'likeness to some one of the race' had 'come out'. There was a strong family resemblance to my Father, and there was a look which brought back a vague fleeting dim recollection which I could not catch or define. It was the least repulsive dead face I have seen. My Father went downstairs to bring my Mother up, as she had at first declined accompanying us to the bedroom. I think we were all glad that we had visited the room and seen the noble face of the dead uncovered. She must have been very handsome in her youth. My Father says she was more than this, 'she was bewitching'. She seems to have been a singularly clever accomplished person of refined and elegant tastes. She played and sang exquisitely and one of the canons compared her to Jenny Lind. The drawing room upstairs was hung round with beautiful proof prints, some of the most exquisite engravings I ever saw, so soft and clear. There also lay on a side table the noble volumes of engravings of the ancient Mansions of England. These were brought down by a servant for us to look at.

I went out into the town for a walk with my Father. As we were returning we were met by the charwoman saying she could get no fowls for the funeral breakfast tomorrow. 'Should she get a small turkey?' – 'Yes, she should get a small turkey.'

Friday, December morrow

I had a comfortable dry warm bed and nice bedroom at the Star. I walked up to College Green and my Father and Mother drove up to 8.30 breakfast. At 10.30 the canons and prebendaries who were to be pall-bearers began to assemble with the other people who attended the funeral. Cathedral morning prayer at 10.15 and as it was Litany Day they were not over till 1.30. Meanwhile breakfast, scarves and hatbands. Mr Hooper the lawyer and Mr Wheeler the Cathedral Precentor were there. The former reminds me much of Haman of Boatside. There was an old Mr Gresley who knew my great uncle and said he remembered often being blessed by Bishop Hurd. It was not on the whole a distinguished looking company. They met in the dining room where over the mantelpiece hung a nice portrait of old Doctor Green, Chancellor of the Diocese, in his scarlet D.D. robes, old Mrs Kilvert's father, or brother. Opposite hung a Paul Potter, and on the side wall a quaint view of Rome in a very long narrow picture. There was a piano in the dining room and another upstairs, and there was a little funny old-world picture of two children playing together, one of them being old Mrs Kilvert. The coffin had been brought downstairs and was waiting in the hall covered with the black velvet sweeping soft pall, white bordered. Boom went the great bell of the Cathedral.

Church was over, and someone said they ought to have used the tenor bell, but they were using the great bell and no mistake. Boom went the bell again. The coffin went out immediately and the pall bearers filed out in pairs after it, taking their places and holding each his pall tassel on either side. My Father and I followed as Chief mourners in crape scarves and hatbands. All the rest in silk. The bearers had been selected not at all with reference to their fitness for the task, but with reference to the friendship entertained for them by the servants of the house. One of the bearers on the right side was very short, so short that he could not properly support the coffin level. The coffin seemed very heavy. As the procession moved across College Green to the Cloister arch, the men staggered under the weight and the coffin lurched and tilted to one side over the short bearer. One very fat man had constituted himself chiefest mourner of all and walked next the coffin before my Father and myself. The bearers, blinded by the sweeping pall, could not see where they were going and nearly missed the Cloister arch, but at length we got safe into the narrow dark passage and into the Cloisters. The great bell boomed high overhead and the deep thrilling vibration hung trembling in the air long after the stroke of the bell.

So the clergy and choir came to meet us at the door, then turned and moved up the Cathedral nave chanting in solemn procession, 'I am the Resurrection and the Life saith the Lord'. But meanwhile there was a dreadful struggle at the steps leading up from the Cloisters to the door. The bearers were quite unequal to the task and the coffin seemed crushingly heavy. There was a stamping and a scuffling, a mass of struggling men swaying to and fro, pushing and writhing and wrestling while the coffin sank and rose and sank again. Once or twice I thought the whole mass of men must have been down together with the coffin atop of them and some one killed or maimed at least. But now came the time of the fat chief mourner. Seizing his opportunity he rushed into the strife by an opening large and the rescued coffin rose. At last by a wild effort and tremendous heave the ponderous coffin was borne up the steps and through the door into the Cathedral where the choristers, quite unconscious of the scene and the fearful struggle going on behind, were singing

up the nave like a company of angels. In the Choir there was
another dreadful struggle to let the coffin down. The bearers
were completely overweighted, they bowed and bent and nearly
fell and threw the coffin down on the floor. When it was safely
deposited we all retired to seats right and left and a verger or
beadle, in a black gown and holding a mace, took up his position at the head of the coffin, standing. The Psalm was sung
nicely to a very beautiful chant. The Dean had the gout and
could not appear, so Canon Wood read the lesson well and
impressively in a sonorous voice. The Grave Service was intoned
by the Sacristan Mr Raisin and sung by the choir, standing on
the planking round the vault whilst a crowd of people looked in
through the cloister windows. After the service we went for a
moment into the Chapter Room where we found Canon Wood
and the Sacristan. I reminded the Canon of our having met at
luncheon at the High Sheriff's (Baskerville's) lodgings at
Presteign Summer Assizes, in August 1868.

It must have been an expensive funeral. Everyone had hatbands down to the Choristers who wore them round their college caps. And there was a heavy fee to the Choir for the Choral
service. Canon Wood floated down College Green from the
cloisters to his own house next to Miss Kilvert's, and we went
home with the two executors, Mr Wheeler and Mr Hooper, to
read the will. Mr H. gave Mr W. and myself each a copy of the
will and read it aloud. The estate proved to be £36,000, and
about £7000 will come to my Father. When he left Langley he
did not even know if he should have enough left him to pay his
expenses. The cook was entirely ignored, except £5 for mourning like the others. The other two servants had £100 apiece.
Charlotte, the ladies' maid, asked Mr Hooper to announce this
fact to the cook himself. She was summoned and he broke the
news to her. She retired in dudgeon and I expect the other
servants had a breezy time of it as the cook was said to be a
bad-tempered woman. Luncheon off the turkey and other
funeral baked meats and Mr Wheeler went away to another
funeral, exhorting me first to see his son's church. We went
down into the rose garden to choose the roses that are to go to
Langley. The library looks out on this strip of garden, then on

to the low flat mud banks of the dreary cold black Severn. In the distance beyond the river there is a pretty view of the Malverns. You descend into the garden by flights of steps from a broad stone terrace that runs along the face of the house. The gardener was there to take orders.

Then we went into the town to see Hobbs the auctioneer near Foregate St Station, to tell him to come and value the furs, laces, etc., for the legacy duty and probate. Back to Evensong at the Cathedral. The Anthem, with a beautiful accompaniment like the rippling of water, was chosen probably with reference to the funeral in the morning, the words being, 'Though the body can die, the soul endureth for evermore'. Mr Hooper passed through the Cathedral and came to the house with some calculations about the estate. We passed a very cosy evening and about 7 o'clock Mr Hobbs made his appearance with an assistant laden with a box containing a pair of scales, which we had ordered him to bring to weigh the plate. When he arrived we discovered the plate ought not to be weighed now. But the scales were solemnly produced to weigh a silver seal which Hobbs pronounced worth 2/6 and which I immediately stole from the estate in consideration of my having come from Clyro to lend my support and countenance on the occasion. I should like to have stolen a great many things, books, plate, etc., but I did not dare. The deep soft muffled tones were still echoing the grand pealing of the bells from the lighted Tower and the dark night was all in a tremble from the sweet vibration. 'That is for Miss Kilvert,' whispered the officious ladies' maid to me in the porch.

Saturday, 3 December

I am 30 years old today. Well, well. . . .

We went back to the Star to pick up our luggage and there we parted, my Father and Mother going to the Shrub Hill and I to the Foregate St. Station. But first I went to the Office in High Street and got a *Worcester Journal* hoping to find an account of Miss Kilvert's funeral in it, but there was none. Then I had my hair cut and I told the man to cut my beard square. 'Now,' he said, 'this is very inconsistent. Your features are round and you want your beard cut square.' 'Still,' I said, 'I prefer it.' My Mother had given me some money, five shillings, to buy a book as a birthday present. Part of it, 2/-, I spent on buying a copy of *Faust*, an English translation, one of Tischendorf's series, at the Foregate St. Station, as a remembrance of Worcester.

[*The diarist returns to Clyro.*]

Thursday, 8 December

I went to Pope's and walked with him across the fields to David Price in Broad Meadow who is ill and whom Mr Webb had left in our charge. We found him in bed in a little hovel by the roadside opposite Broad Meadow Farm, a noble-looking handsome white-bearded patriarch of 77, a shoemaker by trade. He gave me much interesting information about the Black Mountain on the Northern side of which his forefathers have lived for 300 years. He lived at Moyadd Newydd. He had talked much with his grandfather who was born in 1726. He told me of the three chieftains' graves near Twyn y beddau (the mound of graves) between Ashford and Achalofty, the sole remaining monuments of the great battle fought on the mountain in the reign of Edward III. Near the same place stood the church of St Cellon built by Cellon, son of Caractacus and brother of Ifon. St Paul converted Caractacus and Cellon at Rome. Cellon returned to Britain and built this Christian Church and when St Paul visited Britain he crossed the Black Mountain and preached in this Church. In modern times it was called the 'Church of the Three Yews'. The only remains of the Church or Churchyard left are some rude stones and the stump of one of the yews which David Price remembers standing a perfect tree. He promised to show me the stump of the old yew if he ever got well and strong again. . . .

Capel y Ffin is a third part of Llanigon parish. The Chapel was built partly for the convenience of the people on the Southern side of the Mountain. Owing to the snow and terrible storms these poor people were sometimes in the winter obliged to keep

Capel y Ffin

their putrifying dead in their cottages for weeks before they could carry them to Llanigon for burial.

David Price, who understands Welsh, thinks that Bwlch y Fingel means, not the Gospel Pass, but a narrow notch between two hills.

I asked him what the feeling was when he was a boy between the English and Welsh. Very bad, he said. The Welsh distrusted the English and disliked their coming into the Welsh country. But in the last century they were beginning to 'interlink' and intermarry with the English. 'I don't believe,' said the old man, 'that I have a drop of English blood in my veins. I am a pure Welshman.' 'I suppose,' I said, 'that you like your own people best.' 'No,' said he, 'I like them both the same. I like always to see any of the Lord's Ministers and anyone who names the Name of Jesus.'

Monday, 19 December

The sick woman at Cross Foot, Mary Price, cowering before a roaring fire. She said, 'Six weeks ago I was in bed at night and suddenly a young one came on my left arm, like a little angel. It was not one of my own. It was dressed in white clothes long and it had a cap like the dear little children when they are put into their coffins'. She told the story in such a strange weird way that I felt uncomfortable. It was not a dream, she said, she was broad awake.

Wednesday, 21 December

East wind and struggling snow flakes. Bitter miserable cold. The wind flew round to the E. in the night.

Coming in to the Vicarage from the school I found Sir Gilbert Lewis pacing round the gravel walk round the lawn in gloves and stick and great coat trying to get warm before starting on his cold journey to Harpton. He told me a good deal about Maria Kilvert of Worcester whom he knew, as he is a Canon of Worcester. He said she was tall and thin. She used to come rapidly into Church (into the Cathedral) to receive the sacrament two or three times a month, but for the last three years she had not attended the other services. She used to come in a respirator. She shut herself up almost entirely ever since he had been Canon of Worcester, 15 years. Lady Lewis used to call and was sometimes admitted. Sir Gilbert had not called for three years. The house looked most melancholy and dreary, like a house of the dead, no movement, the blinds never drawn up, no carriage ever stopping at the gate, scarcely any one ever going out or in at the door. Sir Gilbert does not believe she had the slightest acquaintance with Lord Lyttelton, or that she even knew him by sight. He said mad people are apt to come to Cathedrals. There was a mad woman who came to Worcester Cathedral and gave him a great deal of trouble by screeching out. There was a Mr Quarrell who used to make antics at the time of the Communion. At a certain point in the service this man would bow down till he got his head on the pavement and his movements were so extraordinary that all they could do was to look at him and watch him. The authorities did not know what to do with him. They could not say, 'You shall not be a Communicant', but they let him know indirectly that they thought his proceedings very ridiculous. 'Ah,' said Sir Gilbert, 'you don't know all the little games that go on in Cathedrals.'

Saturday, Christmas Eve

An intense frost in the night. Lowest point 14 degrees. When I went in to my bath I sat down amongst a shoal of fragments of broken ice as sharp as glass. Everything was frozen stiff and stark, sponge, brushes and all. After I had used the sponge and put it into the basin it was frozen to the basin again in less than 5 minutes.

Up to Cae Mawr again and the people began to pour in for their beef, pudding and beer with their baskets and bottles. I took the opportunity of finding out who wanted bedding most. When I went down to the Church again the clerk and the schoolmaster were dressing the outer porch arch. The inner arch was wreathed with one beautiful ivy spray.

Sunday, Christmas Day

As I lay awake praying in the early morning I thought I heard a sound of distant bells. It was an intense frost. I sat down in my bath upon a sheet of thick ice which broke in the middle into large pieces whilst sharp points and jagged edges stuck all round the sides of the tub like chevaux de frise, not particularly comforting to the naked thighs and loins, for the keen ice cut like broken glass. The ice water stung and scorched like fire. I had to collect the floating pieces of ice and pile them on a chair before I could use the sponge and then I had to thaw the sponge in my hands for it was a mass of ice. The morning was most brilliant. Walked to the Sunday School with Gibbins and the road sparkled with millions of rainbows, the seven colours gleaming in every glittering point of hoar frost. The Church was very cold in spite of two roaring stove fires. Mr V. preached and went to Bettws.

Monday, 26 December

Much warmer and almost a thaw. Left Clyro at 11 a.m.

[*He goes to Langley until January 31.*]

1871

Wednesday, February Day, Candlemas Eve, Sproutkele 1

Sarah Whitney came to my rooms this evening for an old pair of trousers I had promised her. She told me that Mrs Jones, the jockey's wife at the corner, had a fortnight ago left some linen drying out on the churchyard hedge all night having forgotten to take it in. By morning Mrs Jones declared two pairs of drawers and a 'shimmy' had been stolen, and her suspicions fell on some of the neighbours. She and her husband consulted the ordeal of the key and Bible (turning the key in the Bible). The key said, 'Bella Whitney'. Then Jones the jockey went to the brickyard and got some clay which he made into a ball. Inside the ball he put a live toad. The clay ball was either boiled or put into the fire and during the process of boiling or baking the toad was expected to scratch the name of the thief upon a piece of paper put into the clay ball along with him. Some other horrible charm was used to discover the thief, the figure of a person being pricked out on a piece of clay. It is almost incredible.

Friday, 3 February

This evening we had our 4th Penny Reading. The room was fuller than ever, crammed, people almost standing on each other's heads, some sitting up on the high windowseats. Many persons came from Hay, Bryngwyn and Painscastle. Numbers could not get into the room and hung and clustered round the windows outside trying to get in at the windows. The heat was fearful and the foul air gave me a crushing headache and almost stupefied me. I recited Jean Ingelow's 'Reflections' and my own 'Fairy Ride'.

Saturday, 4 February

I hear that last night there were some 60 people standing outside the school during the whole time of the Readings. They were clinging and clustering round the windows, like bees, standing on chairs, looking through the windows, and listening, their faces tier upon tier. Some of them tried to get through the windows when the windows were opened for more air.

Monday, 6 February

I looked out at dawn. The moon was entangled among light clouds in the North and made a golden maze and network across which the slender poplars swayed and bowed themselves with a solemn and measured movement in the west wind. The morning flushed red and shone upon the pools and sheets of water in Bridge End, and the day grew lovely. Old Hannah sat knitting coarse grey stockings within her door. I asked her how she liked the tea and sugar my mother sent her. 'Ah,' she said, 'it is beautiful. I keep the sugar to honour the Sabbath morning and evening and God bless the sender.'

The afternoon was so beautiful that I walked over to Broad Meadow to see old David Price again. David Price's young good-humoured-looking slatternly wife opened the door to me. The old man was in bed and weaker than when I saw him last. . . . Price said, 'One day a lady was walking on a hill in Flintshire when she met Prince Caradoc who wanted to be rude with her but she spurned him. Whereupon he drew his sword and cut off her head. And a monk coming by at the moment clapped her head on again and she lived 15 years afterwards'.

Friday, 24 February

Wrote to my Father for his birthday and sent him an *Illustrated London Almanac* as usual.

Villaging about to Mrs Jones at the Infant School, Jo Phillips and Margaret Griffith, who told me that in the old-fashioned farm houses a steen of butter and something particularly good was always kept till March and not touched because March was reckoned a very severe trying month and people were thought to want some special support then. Old-fashioned folks called March 'heir-loun' or some such name.

Saturday, 25 February

Sophy told me of the murder of 'Sammy', son of Rees Pritchard, the Great Vicar of Llandovery. He was murdered by the two half-brothers of the heiress of Maes y Felin whom Sammy was courting. They did not wish the property to go with her away from them and out of the family, so they waylaid their sister's lover, murdered him, put him in a sack, and threw him into the Towy. Ever after that 'the will of God' was upon Maes y Felin and nothing grew, trees nor grass.

A servant girl living at Pant y weil near Llandovery 150 years ago was told by her mistress overnight to get up very early in the morning and go to the town to fetch something. She got up at midnight and thinking the full moonlight was dawn started for Llandovery without looking at the clock. When she came to the bridge over the Towy she met four men carrying a dead man whom they threw into the river. The girl went home and died of the fright in two days. 'They murdered him,' said Sophy in her broken English, 'according to money.'

Monday, 27 February

Tossing about with face ache till 3 o'clock this morning. Clyro Petty Sessions. Fifteen people summoned for neglecting to have their children vaccinated, but they got off by paying costs. A full bench of magistrates, 5, and the Chief Constable was present. An old magistrate, Mr Bold, came in late and in long riding leggings, very dirty, for he had ridden from Boughrood. He amused himself during a dull part of the proceedings by combing his grey hair with a pocket comb. Then he lay back in his chair with his hands clasped behind his head.

Wednesday, March Day, Lenet Monat, 1

After dinner last night Mr V. kindly anxious to cure my face ache made me drink four large glasses of port. The consequence was that all night and all today I have been groaning with a bursting splitting sick headache.

Thursday, March Morrow

I went up the lane to see the old soldier and read him from *The Times* a notice of Lord Palmerston's tours in France in 1814 and 1818, mentioning the occupation of Paris by the Allies, and giving some anecdotes of the Duke and his opinion of the British soldiers, especially of the Peninsular regiments. The Duke's kind words pleased the old Peninsular Veteran. He remembered the time so well. He had seen them all in their pride. Emperors, King, Duke.

Then I read to him by the fast fading light Matthew ix and after some talk he asked to receive the Sacrament shortly. As I came home alone in the dusk the banks above and the meadows below the road were filled with the sweet last singing of innumerable birds.

Monday, 6 March

I like wandering about these lonely, waste and ruined places. There dwells among them a spirit of quiet and gentle melancholy more congenial and akin to my own spirit than full life and gaiety and noise.

Sunday 12 March

After evening service I went in to see Joe Phillips and read some of the Evening Prayers for him. He told me that on the night when Anne Phillips, Jane Phillips' daughter, ran down from

Clyro Court, threw herself into the river and was drowned, some of the Sheep House lads across the river who were out in the meadows late looking after the sheep and cattle, heard loud and repeated screams from the river. It was getting dark, and they could see nothing. The poor girl's father was in prison and some of her fellow servants had been twitting her with this and saying, 'When your father comes out of prison there will be a place for you'. She jumped up, ran straight down to the river and plunged in. Her grandmother hung herself at the Burnt House, behind the door.

Tuesday, 14 March

The afternoon had been stormy but it cleared towards sunset.

Gradually the heavy rain clouds rolled across the valley to the foot of the opposite mountains and began climbing up their sides wreathing in rolling masses of vapour. One solitary cloud still hung over the brilliant sunlit town, and that whole cloud was a rainbow. Gradually it lost its bright prismatic hues and moved away up the Cusop Dingle in the shape of a pillar and of the colour of golden dark smoke. The Black Mountains were invisible, being wrapped in clouds, and I saw one very white brilliant dazzling cloud where the mountains ought to have been. This cloud grew more white and dazzling every moment, till a clearer burst of sunlight scattered the mists and revealed the truth. This brilliant white cloud that I had been looking and wondering at was the mountain in snow. The last cloud and mist rolled away over the mountain tops and the mountains stood up in the clear blue heaven, a long rampart line of dazzling glittering snow so as no fuller on earth can white them. I stood rooted to the ground, struck with amazement and overwhelmed at the extraordinary splendour of this marvellous spectacle. I never saw anything to equal it I think, even among the high Alps. One's first involuntary thought in the presence of these magnificent sights is to lift up the heart to God and humbly thank Him for having made the earth so beautiful. An intense glare of primrose light streamed from the west deepening into rose and crimson. There was not a flake of snow anywhere but

In the Black Mountains

on the mountains and they stood up, the great white range rising high into the blue sky, while all the rest of the world at their feet lay ruddy rosy brown. The sudden contrast was tremendous, electrifying. I could have cried with the excitement of the overwhelming spectacle. I wanted someone to admire the sight with me. A man came whistling along the road riding upon a cart horse. I would have stopped him and drawn his attention to the mountains but I thought he would probably consider me mad. He did not seem to be the least struck by or to be taking the smallest notice of the great sight. But it seemed to me as if one might never see such a sight again. The great white range which had at first gleamed with an intense brilliant yellow light gradually deepened with the sky to the indescribable red tinge that snow-fields assume in sunset light, and then the grey cold tint crept up the great slopes quenching the rosy warmth which lingered still a few minutes on the summits. Soon all was cold and grey and all that was left of the brilliant gleaming range was the dim ghostly phantom of the mountain rampart scarce distinguishable from the greying sky.

Saturday, *18 March*

A heavenly day, reminding one of Wordsworth's 'March Noon', larks mounting, bees humming in the hot afternoon, lambs playing. Children in the lanes gathering violets and primroses, and the mountain streaked and striped and ribbed with snow.

Midlent, *Mothering Sunday, 19 March*

And all the country in an upturn going out visiting. Girls and boys going home to see their mothers and taking them cakes, brothers and sisters of middle age going to see each other. It is a grand visiting day. And what a magnificent day. As I walked to Bettws it was so sultry that I thought it would thunder. The sun was almost overpowering. Heavy black clouds drove up and rolled round the sky without veiling the hot sunshine, black clouds with white edges they were, looking suspiciously like thunder clouds. Against these black clouds the sunshine showed the faint delicate green and pink of the trees thickening with bursting buds.

Monday, *Brothering Monday, 20 March*

Miserable news from Paris. Another Revolution, barricades, the troops of the line fraternizing with the insurgent National Guards, two Generals shot, two more in the hands and tender mercies of the beastly cowardly Paris mob. Those Parisians are the scum of the earth, and Paris is the crater of the volcano, France, and a bottomless pit of revolution and anarchy. Reading Bishop Cotton's life.

Friday, *24 March*

After luncheon I spent a happy half hour in the lovely warm

afternoon wandering about Clyro churchyard among the graves.
. . . I sat awhile on the old Catholic tomb of the 'Relict of Thomas
Bridgwater' under the S. Church wall, near the chancel door.
This is my favourite tomb. I love it better than all the tombs in
the churchyard with its kindly 'Requiescat in pace', the prayer
so full of peace, with its solemn reminder 'Tendimus huc omnes'
and the simple Latin cross at the head of the inscription. There
is something much more congenial to my mind in these old
Catholic associations than in the bald ugly hideous accompani-
ments which too often mark the place of Protestant or rather
Puritan burial. The Puritans of the last century seem to have
tried to make the idea and place and associations of death and
burial as gloomy, hideous and repulsive as possible, and they
have most signally succeeded. What a difference between the
orthodox and horrible 'Affliction sore long time I bore, Physi-
cians were in vain', and the unorthodox but beautiful and soothing words of prayer, 'Requiescat in pace'.

A small and irreverent spider came running swiftly towards
me across the flat tombstone and scuttling over the sacred words
and memories with most indecent haste and levity. Here it was
very quiet and peaceful, nothing to disturb the stillness but the
subdued village voices and the cawing of the rooks nesting and
brooding in the tops of the high trees in the Castle clump. Some-
where near at hand I heard the innkeeper's voice behind the
church and across the brook giving orders to a workman about
planting some quick and privet. Near the old yew I found the
flat tombstone of 'Eustace Whitney 1669'.

Wednesday, 29 March

Went down the meadows to Mrs Tudor's. Handsome Tudor
was working in his garden. By the door lay a salmon rod on the
ground, so I knew the Squire was having luncheon in the cottage. I went round and there he was with old Harry Pritchard.
He brought out his telescope and we had a look at Crichton and
Mrs Nicholl both wading in the river and fishing under the red
cliff. I crossed the ditch climbed the bank and went along the
beautiful cliff walk on the edge of the cliff looking over the edge

at Mrs Nicholl standing on a rock fishing far below till I came
to a steep path leading down the rocks to where Crichton was
fishing. Crichton went on fishing and wading a little way out
into the stream, and I sat down on a ledge of rock in the warm
sunshine and watched him and Mrs Nicholl a little higher up
stream alternately. It was very still and pleasant in the sun out
of the reach of the cold E. wind. Three boys lay on the grass of
the Warren Meadow across the river looking on, and between
us the broad river flowed quietly among its reefs and rocks.
'Henry,' called Mrs Nicholls' voice faintly down the river. 'She
has got a good fish,' said Crichton, winding up his line after
looking at her a moment. We scrambled over the rocks to her,
but she had landed her fish before we reached her. She thought
it was a fine trout at first but it proved to be a chub. I was
amazed to see Mrs Nicholl coolly wading more than ankle deep
in the river with her ordinary lady's boots on. She walked about
in the river as if she were on dry land, jumped from rock to rock,
slipped off the rocks into the river, scrambled out again, splashed
about like a fish. Standing on a rock in the river she looked very
much like a heron fishing. Many men would not have cared to
go into the water now even with wading stockings on. March
water is cold. Mrs Nicholl must be an uncommonly plucky
woman. Crichton says she rides to hounds and nothing stops her.
She does not care what she does. He hooked a salmon the other
day and his boy was clumsy in landing the fish, so Mrs Nicholl
plunged into the water on the edge of a deep hole, embraced the
great fish round the body, and carried him out in her arms.

Friday, April Eve

A letter from Emily Dew asking me to go to Whitney Rectory
either tomorrow or next Tuesday to meet Miss Hutchinson, the
niece of William Wordsworth by marriage and the god-daughter
of his sister Dorothy, for whom I have a great admiration. I
shall certainly go. I remember seeing this Miss Hutchinson at
Whitney Rectory with her sister years ago, but then they were
very shy and hid behind a hedge.

Saturday, April Day, All Fools' Day, Oster Monat, 1

I went to Whitney by the 2.6 train. Stopped a minute to look at the grey church above the river and to think of the many generations that have worshipped and lain down to rest in its God's Acre. Miss Hutchinson was at home at the Rectory. She is the niece of Mary Hutchinson, the wife of William Wordsworth the poet. And she was the god-daughter of Dorothy Wordsworth, William's sister. We had some interesting talk about the Wordsworth family. She showed me first a large brooch she was wearing containing on one side a beautiful coloured photograph of the poet, and on the other side two locks of grey hair from the heads of the poet and his wife. This photograph is far the best and most pleasing likeness I have seen of the poet. It was taken from a picture painted by H——* almost entirely from memory. The poet had written to the painter telling him with pride that he had ascended Helvellyn when he was 70 years old, and sending him a sonnet on the occasion. The painter was extremely pleased with the letter and the sonnet and immediately drew Wordsworth in a meditative mood composing the sonnet.

Miss Hutchinson said that once, when she was staying at the Wordsworths', the poet was much affected by reading in the newspaper the death of Hogg the Ettrick Shepherd. Half an hour afterwards he came into the room where the ladies were sitting and asked Miss Hutchinson to write down some lines which he had just composed. She did so, and these lines were the beautiful poem called the Graves of the Poets. He was very desultory and disinclined to write. His ladies were always urging him to do so however. And he would have written little if it had not been for his wife and sister. He could not bear the act of writing and he wrote so impatiently and impetuously that his writing was rarely legible. He was very absent and has been known to walk unconsciously through a flock of sheep without perceiving them. He had many books read to him in his later years when his eyesight grew weak. He did not care much for society and preferred the society of women to that of men. With men he was often reserved.

*Presumably Haydon.

When William Howitt was at Rydal Mount looking about after Wordsworths' death he fell in with old James the gardener and asked him which was the poet's study. 'This,' said James pointing to the arbour and the grass mound from which Rydal Mount takes its name. William Wordsworth was a tall man. Dorothy was short and spare. She was a great walker in her youth and suffered physically and mentally as she grew old for having overtaxed her strength when she was young with excessively long walks. When she was middle aged and growing elderly she thought nothing of walking from Brinsop into Hereford, six miles and back, if she wanted a thimble. When she was staying at the Hutchinsons' farm in Radnorshire she would walk into Kington and back on the smallest excuse. During her imbecility she had frequent intervals when all her old brightness, liveliness and clearness of mind returned. Then she relapsed into her sad state. She and her brother used often to stay at Mrs Monkhouse's at the Stow farm, Whitney. Her diaries are now in the possession of her nephew. Dorothy had a lucid interval at her brother's death. She was deeply affected at his loss, left her room and came to his bedside when he was dying.

Friday, 14 April

In the cross lane below Tybella old deaf Tom Gore was mending a ruined dry stone wall. He said he had only one pair of boots in the world, they were cracked and full of holes and he had asked in vain of the relieving officer to beg the Board of Guardians to give him a new pair. He told me his wife was ill and he hoped he should not lose her. He remembered what it was after he lost his first wife, how he often came home wet through to the skin and no fire and no food cooked. Four little children of his lay side by side in Bryngwyn Churchyard. He had seen trouble. He didn't know but he thought it was a fate. I could scarcely make him understand a word. He went on building up his stone wall at half a crown a perch* and I went on to see his wife.

*A perch equals 5½ yards.

Saturday, 15 April

I went to read to Sackville Thomas. Being tub night Polly with great celerity and satisfaction stripped herself naked to her drawers before me and was very anxious to take off her drawers too for my benefit, but her grandmother would not allow her. As it happened the drawers in question were so inadequately constructed that it made uncommonly little difference whether they were off or on, and there was a most interesting view from the rear. Then her grandmother washed her head with soft soap and hot water in a tub, the little image kneeling down in her drawers on the cold stone floor with her head in the tub close to the open door into the road.

Wednesday, 19 April

Mr Venables heard this morning from Chelsea Hospital. The authorities have granted a pension of ninepence a day to our old Peninsular veteran John Morgan of the Bronith with arrears from February. Mr V. went to the old man's house to announce the good news.

Monday, May Day, 1, Trimilki

Up early, breakfast at 7 and the dog cart took Sharpe and me to the station for the 8 train. . . . As we drove to Hay Charles said, 'That was a lovely sermon you gave the Volunteers yesterday, Sir. They did all seem to give such an ear to it. Captain Williams did speak about it to them afterwards'. It was a lovely May morning, and the beauty of the river and green meadows, the woods, hills and blossoming orchards was indescribable. At Hereford two women were carrying a Jack in the Green about the High Town and we fell in with Llewellyn Lloyd of Llowes and his brother going to Cheltenham. In the next carriage a man was playing a harp and a girl a violin as the train travelled.

[*He goes to Langley until May 13.*]

Friday, 12 May

My Mother's birthday. I gave her a travelling brass inkstand. Please God that she may long be spared to us.

Saturday, 13 May

Started for Clyro by the usual 8.42 train. Mrs Dew got in at Whitney and out at Hay and went up to the Castle in the only public conveyance that Hay boasts now, a ramshackle filthy omnibus drawn by two cart horses and driven by a man in a white slop with another agricultural labourer sitting by him on the box to open the door. This equipage came up the town chiefly at a crawling walk and stopped with Mrs Dew at two public houses between the station and the Castle. It was very pleasant to see the Bevans at home again and all the familiar faces in the old house. . . .

It was bitterly cold and I overtook some Clyro village children who had been out to get some green. The children smiled as they looked up. I asked them what they had been gathering. 'Even', (wild parsley) they said, 'for the pig'. I went to Cae Mawr and had a long chat and tea with Mrs Morrell. The verandah and the green house brilliant with geraniums.

Monday, 15 May

At 10 Morrell called and we walked down to Cabalva where the river was to be netted for salmon. It was bitterly cold when we started, but the day soon began to mend, and the afternoon turned out brilliantly beautiful. Young Blisset and Trevellyn came from Letton and Clifford Place, Baskerville rode down with neuralgia and Hodgen came down, Crichton also appeared later in the day, Whitecombe brought the beating poles down, and old Harry Pritchard came down in the coburg with the nets. The first cast was made at the Dole 'pitch'. The net is carried round and dropped in a semi-circle like the seine, but is not allowed to be drawn. There is a double wall of netting, corked and leaded, the inner wall fine mesh and the outer wall larger mesh. Within the semicircle the water is beaten with poles to frighten the fish and drive them into the net. When a fish 'strikes', i.e. rushes into the net he bolts through the large mesh of the outer net carrying with him a bag or purse of the inner fine net which he cannot get through and there he hangs helpless. The party went up and down inside the net in two punts, beating the water with long poles and dashing their poles to the bottom of the river. Then they began to draw in the net. 'Fish', shouted Trevellyn and a salmon of 8½ lbs. was heaved struggling, splashing, and lashing his tail into the boat and knocked on the head. The Stone catch was drawn blank. Then we had luncheon under the great yew on the bank and Morrell produced from his basket an admirable pie, rissoles, bread, cheese and butter, beer and sherry.

A little higher up the river men were washing sheep on the Herefordshire bank.

After luncheon we all went up the long straight reach towards Hay in two boats and drew three pitches on the Moor water, all blank. No more salmon were caught but when the 'Stone' pitch was being drawn again, there was a yell and a great fish came floundering and lashing over the side into the boat with fierce struggles, and the noise as they were knocking it on the head was as if they were driving a pile or felling a tree. It was a pike of 16 lbs. When the pike was taken out of the boat and laid on the grassy bank by the salmon seemingly dead, Crichton put his foot into its mouth and the pike revived enough to grip the boot viciously. At one moment as the net was being drawn into the boat the attitude of the fishermen stooping over the boat's side remined me vividly of the cartoon of the miraculous Draught of Fishes.

The May fly was up, hovering over the river in the golden afternoon, and across the river from Herefordshire came the craking of the first landrail I have heard this year. I landed on the Radnorshire bank and walked down to the Dole, crossing the Gwynddwr by the little gate bridge. Two carpenters were at work sawing up young oaks into gate posts in the narrow meadow under the steep wooded bank.

It was very beautiful, the sunny river, the glassed shadows of the brilliant green and golden-brown trees, the gliding of the boats, the blue mountains rising over the reddish-brown poplars at the head of the long straight still river reach, the distant voices of the fishers and the rattling of the net leads over the gunwale, in that stillness, far down the river. At 6 o'clock the party separated, Blisset and Trevellyn going down the river towards Whitney in the boats with the nets, with shouts of Good night from both sides and the rest of us coming home across the meadows by the banks of the Gwynddwr.

Wednesday, 17 May

The great May Hiring Fair at Hay, and squadrons of horse came charging and battalions of foot tramping along the dusty roads to the town, more boys and fewer girls than usual. All day long the village has been very quiet, empty, most of the village folk being away at the fair. Now at 8 p.m. the roads are thronged with people pouring home again, one party of three men riding on one horse, (outvying the Templars). It was a horribly cold grey leaf-shivering morning, but it broke into a glorious sunny afternoon.

Holy Thursday, 18 May

The second day of the Hay Fair and plough boys etc. going to the town in droves to hire. Morning Prayer at 11. No sermon. Elizabeth Pugh came to ask me to write a note for her to take to Llanthomas as a recommendation. She has heard they want a housemaid and she is tired of living at Little Pen y Fforest and wishes to get into service in a gentleman's house. I wrote the note, and she went off with it highly pleased. Certainly they do want a housemaid at Llanthomas for the last young woman who occupied that responsible situation gave birth to a child in the house, and the child was found in the morning sprawling on the floor in the highest health and spirits.

Sunday, 21 May

Before school I went to see Sackville Thomas. Jimmy said he

took no food and added in a quaint despairing way, which almost made me laugh, 'How the creature do live I dinna know'. I went to see the old man again before afternoon church and took him some biscuits to be soaked in wine. He burst into tears and broke into a loud cry like a child who had been just left at school by his father for the first time. 'I want to go home', he cried, 'I want to go home.'

After Church visited some of the cottages. Elizabeth Pugh told me that when she was living at Little Pen-y-fforest she used to go to the Baptist and Independent Chapels at Painscastle. Stones were frequently thrown into the Chapels among the congregation during service, and once a dog was hurled in. There was a great laugh when the dog was seen flying in.

Monday, 22 May

[*The diarist walks to Glascwm.*]

First I went to the Vicarage. A pair of shears lay on the door step and a beautiful luxuriant sweet briar* climbed a trellis by the door and filled the whole porch with fragrance. . . . I met the old Vicar magistrate in the hall with his stout frame, ruddy face, white hair, stern long sweeping eyebrows and a merry odd twinkle in his eye. One of the last of the old-fashioned parsons. He gave me some splendid Herefordshire cider and some bread and butter and there came in with him a very small black and tan terrier named Ti (or Tiger I suppose), a waddling wheezing gasping mass, a ball of fat. The Vicar said his daughter Miss Marsden was gone out in the trap with his nephew Bevan of Talgarth, late of Newbridge, who had come in quite unexpectedly on Saturday evening, but most fortunately, for his uncle was in bed on Sunday with a violent cold, and sent him round to his three churches at Glascwm, Colva and Rhulen to do duty. I asked what happened supposing the Vicar were ill and no nephew dropped in opportunely on Saturday night. A merry twinkle stole into the old man's eye. 'I give them a holiday,' he said. He had scarcely ever been kept away from his duty by

*Some pressed leaves of the briar are inserted in the MS. at this point.

illness however, though he had occasionally got stuck in a snow drift and been unable to proceed.

'I am bishop here,' said the Vicar. Then fetching the church key he added, 'Come and see the Cathedral'.

The Cathedral lay a little distance down a pretty lane over-arched and avenued with sycamores and limes. A noble avenue of limes used to reach from the churchyard gate to the S.E. corner of the chancel, arching over the churchyard path, but a former Vandal of a Vicar cut them all down except the first pair by the gate. Some respectably dressed people came down the path from the church, an elderly woman dressed in black and looking like a farmer's widow and her two sons, come from Abergavenny to visit the land and the graves of their fathers. It was one of the very large Welsh Churchyards, two acres in extent and thinly peopled. The church long low and whitewashed, an unbroken line of roof without a tower or bell-turret of any kind. An immense chancel and an equally large belfry and a small nave. The belfry is the village school, fitted up with desks, forms and master's desk and a fireplace. The village clerk is village schoolmaster. Three large rich perpendicular windows in the chancel two on the S., one on the N. side. The Vicar had caused these windows to be scraped free from whitewash and had sent in the bill to the bishop who is the Rector. Under the S. chancel wall is the burying place of the Vicars of Glascwm, a colony of 8 or 10 flat tombs some with curious inscriptions. One Vicar is described as 'the Right Reverend the Rector'. In a huge deep Church chest were an old parish accounts book, an enormous flagon of pewter and a pewter paten and a fragment of one of the Church bells. There used to be three good bells in Glascwm Church brought by the enchanted bisons from Llandewi Brefi. Just before the present Vicar came there was a tremendous wedding of a farmer's daughter. There was great enthusiasm and excitement and the bells were required to ring very loud. One bell did not ring loud enough to satisfy the people so they took an axe up to the bell and beat the bell with the axe till they beat it all to pieces. The Vicar said that after preaching a sermon to gather money for the Sick and Wounded Fund or the distress in France, he got from the people 6/11, all in coppers. There is no real dissent in the parish, no chapel, only an endowed fortnightly Baptist sermon and meeting in a farm house. All the people come to Church. But there are no church rates. The old merry twinkle came into the Vicar's eye as he said that he had long foreseen the failure of Church rates, so he stripped the church* and made the parish put a new roof on. 'And now,' he said with a comical smile and shrewd turn of his merry eye, 'it will last my time.'

At the west end of the churchyard almost hidden in trees is the Yat, Squire Beavan's house, or as the Squire tries to have it called, Glascwm Court. Just outside the churchyard the Beavan family have a private burial ground, unconsecrated, where a number of them are buried.

I declined going into the Vicarage again so Mr Marsden walked with me up the long slope of the road leading eastward out of the cwm towards the Harbour. We stopped now and then to look back at the sunny sycamore-embosomed village and the blue hills and cwms beyond, westward, and Mr Marsden entertained me with some reminiscences of his own. 'A public house in the village, haven't we?' he said. 'We just have, and they keep a fearful noise there sometimes. Then I put my head out of my bedroom window and holla to them and they fly like the wind. When I was curate of Llangorse,' he said, 'the Vicar of Talgarth was ill and I had to procure an assistant curate. So I wrote to Llewellyn, now Dean of St David's – then Principal of Lampeter – to send me a man who wanted a title for orders and could speak Welsh and English. Llewellyn wrote that he had the very man for me, *doctus utriusque linguae*. The man came. The first thing he did was to read a funeral service in Welsh. I saw his Welsh was very shaky, but he went on till he came to the passage in the Burial Lesson "in the twinkling of an eye", instead of which he pronounced the Welsh words so that they meant "in the rattling of mice".

'Another time he was publishing Banns. He meant to say, "Why these two person's may not lawfully be joined together in Holy Matrimony". But what he did say was, "Why these two backsides may not lawfully be joined together in Holy

*To sell the lead?

Matrimony". Everyone in Church hid their faces. When we came out of Church I said, "Well, you *have* done it now". "What?" said he. I told him. "God forbid," said he. "It is true," I said.'

Mr Marsden told me that only 4 years ago died the last old woman who could speak her native Radnorshire Welsh, her northern tongue which she had learnt as a child from her mother and grandmother, never having lived out of her own parish. No one else in the parish could talk Welsh to her except Mr Marsden and her great delight was when he would read to her from a Welsh book.

Wednesday, 24 May

Dined at Cae Mawr and we had a capital stuffed and roasted pike. Baron Meyer Rothschild's Favonius has won the Derby today.

Thursday, 25 May

Today we read in the paper that the Assembly troops are in possession of Paris, but that Paris is on fire, the Communists having yesterday drenched with petroleum the Tuileries, the Louvre, Nôtre Dame, the Hôtel de Ville and La Sainte Chapelle and set them in flames. When the telegram left Paris at 6.30 last night the Tuileries were a heap of ashes, the Louvre not much better and no hope of saving anything, the petroleum flames were so furious.

Friday, 26 May

Today the Woolhope Naturalists' Field Club came to Hay and formally opened Twyn-y-beddau. Some bones and a broken skull were found, and a curious Saxon coin bearing a crowned head. The crown had high spikes and the face wore a beard. The coin was photographed. I had intended to be present, but I did not go as I hate going about in a herd and hated the idea of seeing the mountain desecrated by this particular herd. . . . Sackville Thomas died at 4 o'clock this morning.

Saturday, 27 May

At the top of Jacobs Ladder met Miss Sandell with the Morrell children carrying home from their ramble a beautiful rich nosegay of wild flowers. They had found the bog bean, the butterwort, milk-wort in four varieties, butterfly orchis, mouse ear, marsh valentine, marsh buttercup, hawkweed fumitory, yellow pimpernel, yellow potentilla. The children showed me what I never found out for myself or knew before, that the bog bean grows in the wern below Great Gwernfydden. And I have walked 14 miles for that flower, when it grew close by. Miss Sandell taught me more about these flowers in ten minutes than I have learnt from books in all my life. She knows a great deal about flowers. She did not know the comfrey or the yellow hill-violet, some of which I promised to bring her from the Warren Hill today.

Whitsun Monday, 29 May, Oakapple Day

A letter came yesterday from Mr Webb of Hardwick describing the opening of the tumulus Twyn y beddau on the Black Mountain last Friday and urging me to go and see it before it is filled up. He sent a little sectional sketch of the mound which I sent on to Mr Venables. So I made a pilgrimage to the place today starting at 3 p.m. Imagine my delight to find the place perfectly silent and solitary except for the sheep. . . . It is a fine thing to be out on the hills alone. A man can hardly be a beast or a fool alone on a great mountain. There is no company like the grand solemn beautiful hills. They fascinate and grow upon us and one had a feeling and a love for them which one has for nothing else. I don't wonder that our Saviour went out into a mountain to pray and continued all night in praying to God *there*.

Friday, June Morrow

I am told that the hoax about the coin at Twyn y beddau was perpetrated in this way. Penrose, the Master of the Workhouse, went to see the mound with Cyrus Morgan and Lewis Price.

They buried the manufactured false coin for him to find and suggested to him to dig in the mound. He dug accordingly and found the coin and being persuaded in his heart that it was a genuine antique, in the innocence and honesty of his heart sent it to the Woolhope Club, who were taken in, and to the British Museum, who were not. An antiquarian named Evans* pronounced the coin at once to be a fraud and showed how it had been made with punches. It seems to me a very unworthy practical joke.

Monday, 12 June

Last Friday evening Southgate, the druggist at Hay, was in Birmingham and saw snow fall for an hour. That was the 9th of June.

Hay June Fair and the roads thronged with sheep and cattle and folks ahorse and afoot.

[*He and his father start on an expedition to North Wales and stay at Dolgelly.*]

We drove to Miss Roberts' Hotel, the Golden Lion. 'Did you had your luggage?' asked the omnibus driver. I was very much struck and taken with the waitress at the Golden Lion. She said her name was Jane Williams and that her home was at Bettws y Coed. She was a beautiful girl with blue eyes, eyes singularly lovely, the sweetest saddest most weary and most patient eyes I ever saw. It seemed as if she had a great sorrow in her heart. Into the soup the cook had upset both the salt cellar and the pepper box. After dinner we went out and strolled round the town. . . . It seemed so strange to hear the little children chattering Welsh. I have always had a vision of coming into a Welsh town about sunset and seeing the children playing on the bridge and this evening the dream came true.

Tuesday, 13 June

Up at 5.30. Not a soul stirring in the house, the front door locked and the key gone. I got out by the garden door and through the

*Perhaps Sir John Evans, an emminent numismatist.

wicket into the Marian Mawr. . . . In the town I met the guide, old Pugh, coming to meet me. He took me to his house and furnished me with an alpenstock while his good wife gave me some tea and bread and butter for I could get nothing at the inn.

As we went towards the mountain my old guide told me how Mr Smith (Tom Colborne's clerk at Newport), was lost on Cader Idris some 6 years ago. He was on a tour in N. Wales, walking with his knapsack and had come to Machynlleth. He wanted the guide on the Machynlleth side to go over the mountain with him and offered him 2/6. The guide refused, saying his fee to go to the top of the mountain was 5/- and if he went on down the other side it was 10/-. Moreover the guide strongly advised Mr Smith not to attempt the ascent alone that evening, for night would soon fall and the weather was bad. However Mr Smith persisted in going on and the guide went a little way with him to put him in the right road. Two days after this guide was in Dolgelly and meeting my guide, old Pugh, he asked if he had seen anything of the gentleman who had crossed the Cader from Machynlleth to Dolgelly two days before. Pugh said he had neither seen nor heard anything of him although he had been up Cader Idris twice that day, one time being late in the evening. So they supposed Mr Smith had changed his mind and had gone down from the top of the mountain to Towyn. But 6 weeks passed. Nothing was heard of him and his wife grew uneasy. His brother came to Machynlleth, Towyn, and Dolgelly to make inquiries but could hear nothing, and the mountain was searched without result. Mr Smith disappeared in September, and in the following May a man was up on Cader Idris looking for a quarry. He heard his dog bark suddenly and looking over a precipice he saw a dead body. He hurried back to Dolgelly and fetched a doctor and policeman and the coroner, and Pugh came along with them. When the body was turned over Pugh was horrified. He said he never saw such a sight and he hoped he should never see such another. It was what had been Mr Smith. It was a skeleton in clothes. The foxes and ravens had eaten him. His eyes were gone. His teeth were dashed out by the fall and lay scattered about the mountain. His head was bent double under him and crushed into his chest so that his neck was broken. The only piece of flesh remaining on the bones was where the coat buttoned over the chest. One leg was gone and one boot. Pugh looked up and saw something white lying on a ledge above where the body lay. It was his knapsack. When it was brought down there were his things, his papers, his money. Then his stick was found. And some months afterwards Pugh found his hat. Pugh said he had probably tried to come down a short way to Dolgelly and must have fallen down a precipice in the mist and growing darkness. He showed me the place where the body was found. He found the marks the body had made in falling and knew exactly the point it had fallen from. He had carefully measured the distance and declared the body must have fallen 440 yards.

My old guide comes of a family of Welsh harpers. His brother is now harper to [   ] Sir Watkin's sister. Another brother who is dead won a silver harp at an Eisteddfod and was one of the best harpers in Wales. Pugh said there was a harper at Corwen and another at Llangollen and he knew an old bard at Corwen. He told me he had once been up Cader Idris 4 times in one day for a £10 wager against a reading party of 4 or 5 Cambridge men who declared he could not do it. On the last day of September a pouring wet day he did it and won the wager easily. He could have gone up the 5th time. A man on each side was posted on the top of the mountain and a man on each side at the bottom to see fair play and that Pugh did not ride up. It was stipulated that he should go up by the pony road and come down any way he liked. Coming down the first time he nearly came to trouble and was delayed 20 minutes in this way. He had noticed often when on the mountain that at a particular place his dog usually put up a fox and that the fox always disappeared down a cleft in the rocks. When walking for the wager he thought of this fox path and thought it would take him down quicker. Supposing that he could go where a fox went he slid down the narrow chasm and found that it led to the brink of a precipice. He could not go back and he was obliged to go on so taking off his boots and slinging them round his neck he clambered down. He did not try that way again.

By this time we had come to a place where was a lake by the roadside and in a boat on the lake were two men fishing. Leaving the road here we turned up a rough lane and crossing a little brook by a farm house were on the open mountain. As we sloped up the mountain side we had beautiful views of the Harlech mountains opposite, blue Cardigan Bay and dim Snowdon. The zig-zag path was steep in parts and a great wind blew over the mountain so that I had to sit down in a sheltered place and tie the band of my hat to my button-hole with the old guide's neckerchief, for, said the old man, 'Many hats have been lost on this ridge.' We aimed for a great stone on the top of the first ridge. After this the climbing was not so severe. The old man came up very slowly. Soon after we passed the great stone we passed through a gateway the posts of which were large basaltic pillars. Here we saw a mountain standing apparently close by waiting upon Cader Idris. It was Plynlimmon. Here we passed round over the back of the mountain and began ascending the summit from the S. We came to a little round pool or rather hole full of water. The old man pulled a little tumbler out of his pocket rinsed it and gave me a glass of the clear bright water. It was delicious. Then he drank himself. He said the pool was the head water or spring of the Dysyni River. He had never known it dry in the driest summers. We saw from the spring the winding gleam of the Dysyni wandering down a desolate valley to join the Dyfi, its sister stream.

About this time the wind changed and flew suddenly round into the S. The head of Idris, which had been cowled in cloud, had cleared for a while, but now an impenetrable dark cloud settled down upon it and the mist came creeping down the mountain. The sky looked black and threatened rain. Now there lay before us vast tracts and belts of large stones lying so close together that no turf could be seen and no grass could grow between them. It was broken basalt, and huge lengths of basalt, angled, and some hexagonal, lay about or jutted from the mountain side like enormous balks of timber and with an unknown length buried in the mountain. We passed quarries where some of the great columns had been dug out to be drawn down the mountain on sledges. Cader Idris is the stoniest, dreariest, most

desolate mountain I was ever on. We came now to the edge of a
vast gulf or chasm or bason almost entirely surrounded by black
precipices rising from the waters of a small black tarn which lay
in the bottom of the bason. Here the guide showed me the place
at the foot of an opposite precipice where Mr Smith's body had
been found. Then we stumbled and struggled on again over
rough tracts and wilderness of slate and basalt. The sun was
shining on the hills below, but the mist crawled down and wrapped us as if in a shroud blotting out everything. The mists and
clouds began to sweep by us in white thin ghostly sheets as if
some great dread Presences and Powers were going past and we
could only see the skirts of their white garments. The air grew
damp and chill, the cloud broke on the mountain top and it
began to rain. Now and then we could discern the black sharp
peak which forms the summit looming large and dark through
the cloud and rain and white wild driving mist, and it was hidden
again. It is an awful place in a storm. I thought of Moses on
Sinai.

The rain grew heavier. The old guide could not get on very
fast and told me to go on alone to the top and shelter in the hut
as I could not miss the path. So I went on up the last sharp peak
looming black through the dark mist and cloud, by a winding
path among the great rocks and wildernesses of loose stone. For
a few minutes I was alone on the top of the mountain. The
thought struck me, suppose the old man should be seized with
cramp in the stomach here, how in the world should I get him
down or get down myself in the blinding mist? The cloud and
mist and rain swept by and drove eddying round the peak. I
could hear the old man chinking his iron-shod staff among the
rocks and stones, as he came up the path, nearer and nearer, but
till he got close to me I could not discern his white figure through
the dense mist. 'This is the highest point of *Cader Idris*', he said,
laying his hand upon a peak of wet living rock, 'not *that*', looking
with contempt at the great conical pile of stones built upon the
peak by the sappers and miners during the Ordnance Survey.
He said, 'The Captain of the surveying company had his tent
pitched on the top of Cader Idris for 3 summer months and
never left the place. He had 18 men to wait upon him. And how

many clear views do you think he got in that time?' 'Twelve',
I hazarded. 'Nine', he said.

He took me down to a rude 2-roomed hut built of huge stones
by his father just under the shelter of the peak, and produced
for my benefit a hard-boiled egg and some slices of bread and
butter. Also he gave me a woollen comforter to wrap round my
neck. Then he vanished. The mist drove in white sheets and
shapes past the doorless doorway and past the windows from
which the window frames had been removed and the wind
whistled through the chinks in the rude walls of huge stones.
A large flat block of stone in the middle of the room on which I
sat formed the table. It is said that if any one spends a night
alone on the top of Cader Idris he will be found in the morning
either dead or a madman or a poet gifted with the highest degree
of inspiration. Hence Mrs Heman's fine song 'A night upon
Cader Idris'. The same thing is said of the top of Snowdon and
of a great stone at the foot of Snowdon. Old Pugh says the fairies
used to dance near the top of the mountain and he knows people
who have seen them.

Presently I heard the old man clinking his stick among the
rocks and coming round the hut. He came in and lighted his
pipe and we prepared to go down by the 'Foxes' Path'. And
indeed it was a path fit only for foxes. After leading me a few
steps he began to go over what seemed to me to be the edge of a
precipice, depth unknown and hidden in the mist. The side of
the mountain was frightfully steep here and required great care
in going down. Suddenly the old man stopped at a beautiful
little spring in the almost perpendicular bank, pulled out his
tumbler and gave me a draught of the clear sparkling water,
much colder than the water from the spring of Dysyni. About
the spring the grass grew brilliant green and there was a long
winding riband of bright green where the waters overflowing
from the spring trickled down through the grass stems to feed
the lake at which the foxes drink just below. Next we came to a
broad belt of loose rocks lying close together which the guide
cautioned me to beware of and not without reason saying they
were as slippery as glass and that a sprained ancle was an awk-
ward thing on the mountain. Down, down and out of the cloud

into the sunshine, all the hills below and the valleys were bathed in glorious sunshine – a wonderful and dazzling sight. Above and hanging overhead the vast black precipices towered and loomed through the clouds, and fast as we went down the mist followed faster and presently all the lovely sunny landscape was shrouded in a white winding sheet of rain. The path was all loose shale and stone and so steep that planting our alpenstocks from behind and leaning back upon them Alpine fashion we glissaded with a general landslip, rush and rattle of shale and shingle down to the shore of the Foxes' Lake. The parsley fern grew in sheets of brilliant green among the grey shale and in the descent we passed the largest basaltic columns of all protruding from the mountain side. In the clefts and angles of the huge grey tower columns grew beautiful tufts and bunches of parsley fern. We passed another lake and after some rough scrambling walking over broken ground at the mountain foot we came back into the turnpike road at the lake that we had passed in the morning. As we entered Dolgelly the old man said, 'You're a splendid walker, Sir', a compliment which procured him a glass of brandy and water.

[*The diarist and his father continue their tour and go to Llangollen.*]

Friday, 16 June

We walked up through the town to the Hand Hotel, stopping a moment on the fine quaint old grey stone bridge of Dee with its sharp angled recesses, to look down into the clear rocky swift winding river, so like the Wye. As we came near the Hand we heard the strains of a Welsh harp, the first I ever heard. The harper was playing in the hall the air 'Jenny Jones'. I would have come all the way to Llangollen on purpose to hear the Welsh harp. This is the only hotel in Wales where a Welsh harper can be heard. I stood by him entranced while he played Llwyn-on and the Roaring of the Valley, and several of the other guests in the house gathered round the harp in the corner of the hall. The harper was a cripple and his crutch rested by his side against a chair. He was a beautiful performer and he was playing on a handsome harp of sycamore and ash, which he had won as a prize at an Eisteddfod. I had a good deal of talk with him after he had done playing. He told me there were very few people now who could play the Welsh harp, and the instrument was fast going out of use. The young people learn the English harp which is much easier being double stringed instead of treble stringed. The Welsh harp has no silver string and it is played from the left shoulder while the English harp is played from the right shoulder. Sir Watkin keeps no harper. His sister does, and her harper is the brother of old Pugh of Dolgelly who took me up Cader Idris. The Llangollen harper said he knew him and thought him a good harper, but his brother whom he also knew and who is dead was much better, the first harper in Wales.

Presently the harper covered his harp and limped away to his own house in the town, saying he should come and play again at 9 o'clock. He plays in the hall at several stated hours every day. He gets nothing from the Hotel and subsists entirely on what visitors give him. At 9 o'clock he came again and played while we were at supper. It was a great and strange delight to listen to the music of this Welsh harp. The house was full of the melody of the beautiful Welsh airs. No wonder when the evil spirit was upon Saul and when David played upon the harp, that Saul was refreshed and was well and that the evil spirit departed from him.

[*The diarist returns to Clyro.*]

Monday, 19 June

Palmer, the new Cae Mawr gardener, and his wife have moved down from the Vineyards Cottage to the Old Mill. Mrs Palmer could not bear the Vineyards. She said it was so lonely. Miss Bynon, to whom the cottage belongs, took great exception to Mrs Palmer and the fault she found with the cottage. 'Lonely indeed! What does the lady on the hill want?' asked Miss Bynon. 'She can see my backdoor.'

Tuesday, 20 June

An angel satyr walks these hills.

Wednesday, 21 June

The longest day, and one of the darkest dreariest wettest coldest Junes that I ever remember. I went this afternoon to see old John Morgan at the Bronith and found the old soldier thinning his onions and giving the thinnings to the keeper who lives just below.

Saturday, 24 June

Midsummer Day. The coldest and most cheerless I ever remember.

Thursday, 29 June

Villaging. I went to the Old Mill to see the beautiful child. A group of girls on their way home from market loitered by the stile above the Old Mill, resting and chattering over the stile. The Old Mill was silent, deserted, locked. I left a leaf in the latch hole. The brook twinkled past the house. Two cows grazed in the orchard slope across the brook above the house, and the gate of the poor little garden leaned and tottered, a frail defence against a cow with proclivities for cabbage.

Annie Corfield is better but we fear that she and her sisters, the twins Phoebe and Lizzie, are very miserable and badly treated by their father since their dear mother's death. What would she say if she could see them now, ragged, dirty, thin and half-clad and hungry? How unkindly their father uses them. The neighbours hear the sound of the whip on their naked flesh and the poor girls crying and screaming sadly sometimes when their father comes home late at night. It seems that when he comes home late he makes the girls get out of bed and strip themselves naked and then he flogs them severely or else he pulls the bedclothes off them and whips them all three as they lie in bed together writhing and screaming under the castigation. It is said that sometimes Corfield strips the poor girls naked holds them face downwards across his knees on a bed or chair and whips their bare bottoms so cruelly that the blood runs down their legs. The neighbours fear there is little doubt that the girls are flogged on their naked bodies till the blood comes, and it has been proposed that Mrs Lewis or some woman should examine the children naked and see if there are marks of violence and cruelly severe whipping on the poor girls' backs and bottoms and thighs. We fear the soft tender flesh would be seen if the poor thin ragged frocks were lifted, sorely cut and wealed by the cruel stripes of the whip.

Tuesday, 4 July

This afternoon I went up the Cwm. Violent storms of rain came on and I had to shelter under the trees in the Cwm road on the edge of the broad deep dingle and the rain came sweeping down the dingle below me from the West in white sheets reminding me of the sweeping of the white sheets of mist and rain on Cader Idris. After a while the rain abated and I went on and dried myself by Hannah Jones' fire. She was smoking when I came in. Read to Sarah Probert and then went to John Williams. An old bowed man bent nearly double with a long white frock and white hair covering his forehead and falling over his eyes was wandering with his staff up the little stream. It was old John Lloyd of Cwmgwanon. He came into John Williams's while I was there and he told me his sister Mrs Watkins had gone mad and was living with them at Cwmgwanon, and they did not know what to do with her. Hannah Jones had told me about the madwoman of Cwmgwanon. They keep her locked up in a bedroom alone, for she will come down amongst them stark naked. She has broken the window and all the crockery in the room, amuses herself by dancing naked round the room and threatens to wring her daughter-in-law's neck. Then she will set to and roar till they can hear her down the dingle at John Williams's house, nearly half a mile.

Wednesday, 5 July

This morning Edward Morgan of Cwmpelved Green brought his concubine to Church and married her. She was a girl of 19, rather nice looking and seemed quiet and modest. She had a pretty bridesmaid and they were both nicely prettily dressed in lilac and white. After the ceremony I saw the stout dwarf Anne Beavan pinning on bright nosegays.

Friday, 7 July

I went up the Bird's Nest dingle calling at Bowen's and old Meredith's and Richard Jones' and then across the wern to Cross Foot where Mrs Watkins told me the scandal about the daughter of Shene of the Lane Farm and the child found dead in the water closet at the Three Cocks Station.

Monday, 10 July

A beautiful haymaking morning and the village was astir early and all in a bustle of people going out to turn the hay as soon as possible. It is the best and almost the only haymaking day we have had.

Wednesday, 12 July

The Government Inspector, Mr Shadrach Pryce, came to inspect our school today. He brought his wife with him and they came to my rooms for a glass of wine and a biscuit after the inspection, refusing anything more substantial. He seemed to me a pleasant kindly fair examiner and the children passed a good examination. We presented 35 for examination out of an average attendance of 51, while Hay school, which was examined yesterday, presented only 42 out of an average attendance of 105. Passed two hours at the school house in the afternoon, talking over the examination with the Evanses who were very much pleased and satisfied with the result.

There came begging through the village today three girls dressed in ragged black with naked legs and feet. The eldest was a tall street girl with a profusion of curling chestnut hair. The second girl was slighter. Her tattered black frock hardly covered her knees, her delicate beautiful slender limbs were bare and whiter by contrast with her black dress, and her pretty white feet small and shapely were bruised and worn with travel.

Thursday, 13 July

As I sat at breakfast I heard the drone of bagpipes. A man was playing at the New Inn. He came playing down the road and stopped in front of the forge droning on while the blacksmith's children danced before him. He could not complain that he had piped to the Clyro children and they had not danced. He was a wild swarthy Italian-looking man, young, with a steeple-crowned hat, and full of uncouth cries and strange outland words. He moved on from the forge to the inn still playing while the children still danced before him. I could see the group through the screen of chestnuts. They reminded me of the children in the Book of Job who 'rejoiced at the sound of the organ'. The innkeeper's wife came to the door. 'Ma'am', cried the wild swarthy creature in a strange uncouth voice, 'Ma'am'.

Friday, 14 July, St Swithin's Eve

I went to Hereford to see the dentist McAdam. He took out a temporary tooth stopping and put another temporary stopping in and I have to go to him again in a fortnight. He showed me the apparatus for giving people the new anaesthetic laughing gas which he thinks much safer than chloroform, indeed quite safe. In the street two or three French or Italian boys were singing the Marseillaise to a beautiful harp and violin accompaniment. I had my hair cut by a political barber who denounced the ballot* with great energy and lashed himself into needless excitement. The afternoon became lovely, very hot, and being early for the 3.15 return train I strolled across the meadows near the Moorfields Station. I got out at Whitney and went to the Rectory.

*The secret ballot was introduced by the Ballot Act of the following year.

Whitney Church

Emily and Jane were at home with their father, the rest of the children gone with their mother to Rhyl, except Helen and Armine who are at school at Kensington. I dined with the girls and their father. He told me of the sermons which old Mr Thomas the Vicar of Disserth used to preach as they were described to him by the Venables. He would get up in the pulpit without an idea about what he was going to say, and would begin thus. 'Ha, yes, here we are. And it is a fine day. I congratulate you on the fine day, and glad to see so many of you here. Yes indeed. Ha, yes, very well. Now then I shall take for my text so and so. Yes. Let me see. You are all sinners and so am I. Yes indeed.' Sometimes he would preach about 'Mr Noe'. 'Mr Noe, he did go on with the ark, thump, thump, thump. And the wicked fellows did come and say to him "Now Mr Noe, don't go on there, thump, thump, thump, come and have a pint of ale at the Red Lion. There is capital ale at the Red Lion, Mr Noe." For Mr Noe was situated just as we are here, there was the Red Lion close by the ark, just round the corner. Yes indeed. But Mr Noe he would not hearken to them, and he went on thump, thump, thump. Then another idle fellow would say, "Come Mr Noe – the hounds are running capital, yes indeed. Don't go on there thump, thump, thump." But Mr Noe he did never heed them, he just went on with his ark, thump, thump, thump.'

Miss E. Hutchinson had sent to Whitney for me to keep for my very own a relic very precious to me, a little poem of her aunt Dorothy Wordsworth in her own handwriting.

Tuesday, 18 July

A superb cloudless morning. The summer has come at last. The soft velvety shadow of the nearest poplar rested across a sister poplar in the early morning, and then as the sun moved southward the shadow slipped off the poplar, and fell lying up the dingle. A sudden distant clangour of geese, and the geese of Penllan in a white cloud came flying down the bright green hill and settled upon the steep slopes of the Lower Bron.

I went to Wern Vawr. The sun burnt fiercely as I climbed the hills but a little breeze crept about the hill tops. Some barbarian – a dissenter no doubt – probably a Baptist, has cut down the beautiful silver birches on the Little Mountain near Cefn y Fedwas.

Wednesday, 19 July

At the Brooms old Mrs Edward Thomas was sitting by the fire with a long clay pipe in her mouth which she was just about to light, but when she saw me at the door she snatched the pipe out of her mouth and crammed it into her pocket with the tobacco. 'Don't let me disturb you in the enjoyment of your pipe,' said I politely. 'I'll call another day.'

Saturday, 22 July

I went up to Cross Foot, turned down the farm lane to the huge

Gospel Oak which overshadows the farm, and across the meadow to the beautiful green lane which leads down to Cwmpelved and Cwmpelved Green. At Cwmpelved Green the low garden wall was flaming with nasturtiums which had clambered over it from the garden.

Within the cottage sat old Richard Clark and the pretty girl lately Edward Morgan's concubine, now happily his wife. I had thought Edward Morgan had a comfortless, miserable home. I was never more mistaken or surprised. The cottage was exquisitely clean and neat, with a bright blue cheerful paper and almost prettily furnished. A vase of bright fresh flowers stood upon each table and I could have eaten my dinner off every stone of the floor The girl said no one ever came near the house to see it, and she kept it as clean and neat and pretty as she could for her own satisfaction. The oven door was screened from view by a little curtain and everything was made the most and best of. I don't wonder Edward Morgan married the girl. It was not her fault that they were not married before. She begged and prayed her lover to marry her before he seduced her and afterwards. She was very staunch and faithful to him when she was his mistress and I believe she will make him a good wife. She was ironing when I came in and when I began to read to old Clark she took her work and sat down quietly to sew. When I had done reading she had me into the garden and shewed me her flowers with which she had taken some pains for she was very fond of them. No one ever came to see her garden or her flowers she said. The only people she ever saw passing were the people from the farm (the Upper Bettws where her husband works). They come on Market days along a footpath through the field before the house. The girl spoke quietly and rather mournfully and there was a shade of gentle melancholy in her voice and manner. I was deeply touched by all that I saw and heard. I went on up to Pentwyn Forge and had a long chat with Mrs Nott the blacksmith's wife. She told me her next door neighbour Mrs Williams was 'a wicked woman' and prostituted herself to her lodgers, while her husband as bad as herself took the money and asked no questions.

Sunday, 23 July

This morning Mr Bevan went up to the Volunteer Camp above Talgarth, on the high common under the Black Mountain. He is Chaplain to the Forces and attended to hold an open air service and preach a sermon to the Volunteers. He started at 8 o'clock and for the sake of greater comfort and expedition he took a large hired carriage and pair. Near Talgarth one of the horses fell and lay like a pig, stubbornly refusing to get up or move, till two farmers coming by opportunely dragged the beast up by main force. Then when the Chaplain arrived on the Common, the Builth Volunteers were already well drunk. They were dismissed from the ranks but they fought about the common during the whole service. The officers and the other corps were bitterly ashamed and scandalized.

Thursday, 27 July

Gipsy Lizzie never looked more beautiful than this morning. I wish I could get a likeness of the child. If her picture were in the Academy it would be thronged, unapproachable.

In the afternoon I took the old soldier the first instalment of his pension £8 0 4 for half a year. Mr Venables has got the pension for him at last after a long correspondence with the War Office. The old soldier told me some of his reminiscences. In the Battle of Vittoria as they were rushing into action his front rank man, a big burly fellow, was swearing that 'There wasn't a bloody Frenchman who had seen the bullet yet which should strike him'. A few minutes after he was shot dead. After the battle when old Morgan was shaking out his blanket to wrap himself up at night in the bivouac he shook three or four bullets out of it, and one ball had gone through his cap, so close as almost to graze his head.

Friday, 28 July

Gipsy Lizzie was at the School. Again I am under the influence of that child's extraordinary beauty. When she is reading and her eyes are bent down upon her book her loveliness is indescribable.

Saturday, 29 July

Torrents of lashing and streaming rain all the evening, a thunder-storm without thunder breaking into a beautiful sunny afternoon. I walked to Hay to pay some bills. On the crest of the hill above Hay I met a tall woman smoking a clay pipe and driving a black donkey. A raven sailed down croaking hoarsely from the hills to the Wye side meadows.

Sunday, 30 July

I lay awake sleepless almost all night and had a vision of myself as Vicar of Builth, to the accompaniment of the rushing and roaring of torrents of rain.

[On the next day the diarist leaves Clyro until 26 August.]

Wednesday, 30 August

Busy all the morning putting up swings for the school feast this afternoon, with the help of the schoolmaster. Baskerville was crossing the park and came up into the cherry orchard and helped us. . . .

The school feast began at 4 o'clock. There were 110 children and 120 people went to tea in the Vicarage dining room by relays of 40. The Crichtons and Baskervilles and Hodgsons were present and all made themselves useful and agreeable and played with the children. The schoolchildren were especially delighted with Rosie Hodgson and wanted to cheer her among the rest at the end. The beauties were Eleanor and Florence Hill and Gipsy Lizzie and Esther and Pussy of New Barn.

The sports were kept up by the visitors and elder children long after we left, till dark, and stout Mrs Williams of the Lower House was romping with the girls and playing Oranges and Lemons and Thirds by moonlight.

'Gipsy Lizzie'

Thursday, September Eve

I went up to Lower Cwmgwanon to see the old madwoman Mrs
Watkins. Her son was out in the harvest field carrying oats, and
I had to wait till he came in to go upstairs with me. While I
waited in the kitchen the low deep voice upstairs began calling,
'Murder! John Lloyd! John Lloyd! Murder!' They sent up into
the oatfield for her son, but I had waited nearly an hour before
the oatladen waggon came creaking and swaying and sweeping
the hedge along the edge of a brow high above the house and
then down a steep rough path into the rickyard. The women
folk of the house were unloading the oats, as their 'harvest man'
Griffiths of Tylyhilog had gone off on a drinking bout and had
left them in the lurch.

The madwoman's son, a burly tall good-humoured man with
a pleasant face, came to the garden gate and thought I could
not do any good by seeing his mother. So I went away. But when
I had got half way down the meadow Cwmside on my way to
the Burnt House he shouted to me to come back and asked me
go up and see her. He led the way up the broad oak staircase
into a fetid room darkened. The window was blocked up with
stools and chairs to prevent the poor mad creature from throwing herself out. She had broken all the window glass and all the
crockery. There was nothing in the room but her bed and a chair.
She lay with the blanket over her head. When her son turned
the blanket down I was almost frightened. It was a mad skeleton
with such a wild scared animal's face as I never saw before. Her
dark hair was tossed weird and unkempt, and she stared at me
like a wild beast. But she began directly to talk rationally though
her mind wandered at moments. I tried to bring some serious
thoughts back to her mind. 'Whom do you pray to when you
say your prayers?' 'Mr Venables.' It was the dim lingering idea
of someone in authority. I repeated the Lord's Prayer and the
old familiar words seemed to come back to her by degrees till
she could say it alone. When I went away she besought me
earnestly to come again. 'You'll promise to come again now.
You'll promise,' she said eagerly.

Sunday, 3 September

I went to Bettws in light rain and preached extempore on the Good Samaritan from the Gospel for the day. A red cow with a foolish white face came up to the window by the desk and stared in while I was preaching.

Tuesday, 5 September

The day was lovely and I went over to Newchurch. Near Tynessa I met a tall pale yellow-faced woman with two empty bottles in a basket. She said it was so hot she could scarcely go. She was moving westward. A solitary fern cutter was at work on the Vicar's Hill mowing the fern with a sharp harsh ripping sound. In the first Newchurch field the turkeys, black and grey and fawn-coloured, were mourning in the stubbles and a black pony was gazing pensively over the hedge. I passed through two fields of thin stunted wheat almost choked with sow thistle which covered me with its downy blossom. From the Little Mountain the view was superb and the air exquisitely clear. The Clee Hills seemed marvellously near. The land glittered, variegated with colours and gleams of wheat, stubble and blue hill. The yellow potentilla jewelled the turf with its tiny gems of gold and the frail harebell trembled blue among the fern tipped here and there with autumn yellow. The little lonely tree bowed on the mountain brow, and below lay the tiny village deep in the valley among the trees embosoming the little church with its blue spire and Emmeline's* grave.

Thursday, 7 September

Fanny and Dora† came by the 4.10 train in very good form except that Dora had a headache. Fanny promises to play the harmonium in Church for us next Sunday and we went to the church to practise before supper.

---

*Emmeline Vaughan, daughter of the vicar of Newchurch, who has died since Kilvert's description of 3 May 1870.   †His sisters.

Friday, 8 September

Perhaps this may be a memorable day in my life. . . .

At 2 o'clock I walked to Llan Thomas. A gentleman was carrying chairs out of the house on to the lawn, a stranger to me, deeply sunburnt, but I soon recognized him as Lechmere Thomas, the Ceylon coffee-planter, from his likeness to Henry and Charlie. A nice fellow I should think. It was some time before the party began to arrive. The 3 Crichtons, 2 Miss Baskervilles and Miss Howard, Col. Balmayne and his niece Miss Baldwin, Mr and Mrs Webb and 2 Miss Estcourts of Gloucestershire, Tom Williams and Pope.

Some played croquet. Some went to archery. There were two croquet games going. I played with Daisy and a Miss Estcourt against Miss Baldwin, Tom Williams and Mrs and Major Thomas alternately. Daisy was very kind and charming, just home from school for good, she said. 'Three cheers', I said. 'I quite agree with you', said she laughing. We lost our game partly through my fault, but she was so good-tempered about it. I sat next her at supper at the bottom of the side table in the window and we were very merry. Her father wanted me to sit elsewhere, but she overruled him, saved my place, and kept me by her. I was telling her about Alice Davies of Cwm Sir Hugh. She became interested and when she heard what a treat fruit was to the sick child she sent the footman for a dish of grapes. 'Here,' she said, taking two bunches and putting them on my plate, 'take her these.' 'I do like you for that,' I said earnestly, 'I do indeed.' She laughed. I think she was pleased. I demurred about taking them. So when the ladies rose she went coaxingly up to her father and to satisfy me asked if she might send the grapes to the sick child. 'Certainly,' he said. So she said she would put the grapes in a little basket and be sure to give them to me when I went away.

To-day I fell in love with Fanny* Thomas.

I danced the first quadrille with her and made innumerable mistakes, once or twice running quite wild through the figure like a runaway horse, but she was so good-humoured and long-suffering.

*Fanny was evidently Daisy Thomas's nickname.

Llanthomas

It was a very happy evening. How little I knew what was in store for me when I came to Llan Thomas this afternoon.

Sunday, 10 September

Mr Venables preached in the morning and went to Bettws. Fanny played the harmonium capitally at both services and everyone was very much pleased.

I have been in a fever all day about Daisy, restless and miserable with uncertainty.

Monday, 11 September

This morning I went to Mrs Venables and unburdened my mind to her and asked her advice. She was enchanted to hear of my attachment and wish to marry, though I did not tell her it was Daisy. She gave me a great deal of good kind advice and encouraged me very much. Still I was very restless and feverish all day.

Tuesday, 12 September

A wretched restless feverish night. This morning I went to Mrs Venables in the drawing room bow-window and told her that it was Daisy I was in love with. She liked the idea extremely. I asked her to guess who it was. 'The Grapes', she said at once. 'It is', I said. Then she went to discuss the matter with Mr Venables. I went away, but soon she came down to tell me that he was very glad, highly approved of it and would talk to me about the matter at ten o'clock tomorrow morning.

Wednesday, 13 September

An ever memorable day in my life. I went to the Vicarage at 10 o'clock and had a long talk with him on the lawn about my attachment to Daisy. Ways, means and prospects. Major Thomas told Mrs Venables last night that his father was going to Brecon this morning but would be at home in the afternoon. So I decided to drive to the Hay Station with Mrs Venables when she went to meet Miss Warde by the 2.6 train and ask the guard if Mr Thomas came from Brecon by this train. The guard said he had and got out at Glasbury. So I started off for Llan Thomas on foot rather nervous. As I crossed the bridge over the Digedi I wondered with what feelings I should cross the bridge an hour later. The whole family at home came into the drawing room to see me and I was wondering how I could get Mr Thomas away for a private talk, when he said suddenly, 'Come out into the garden.' Daisy came into the room. I thought she coloured and looked conscious. I delivered up to her the basket she had lent me to take the grapes in to Alice Davies and gave her Alice's message of thanks. Then we went out into the garden, her father and I. I said, 'You will be very much surprised but I hope not displeased at what I am going to say to you.' 'What is it?' he said eagerly, 'have you got the living of Glasbury?' 'No, something much nearer to you than that'. 'What is it?' I was silent a minute. I was frightfully nervous. 'I-am-attached-to-one-of-your-daughters,' I said. Just as I made this avowal we came suddenly round the corner upon a gardener cutting a hedge. I feared he had heard my confession, but I was much relieved by being assured that he was deaf. Mr Thomas said I had done quite right in coming to him, though he seemed a good deal taken aback.

He said also a great many complimentary things about my 'honourable high-minded conduct', asked what my prospects were and shook his head over them. He could not allow an engagement under the circumstances, he said, and I must not destroy his daughter's peace of mind by speaking to her or showing her in any way that I was attached to her. 'You have behaved so well that I don't know which of them it is, unless it is Mary.' 'No, it is your youngest daughter.' 'Poor little girl, she is so young.' 'She is nineteen.' 'Yes, but a mere child, and so guileless and innocent. She would be so fond of you. If I were a young man I should have done just what you have done and chosen her out of the rest. When you were here on Friday I saw she liked you. I said to my wife after you were gone, "That little Fanny likes Mr Kilvert." Long engagements are dreadful things. I cannot allow you to be engaged but I won't say "Don't think of it". Go on coming here as usual, if you can put constraint on your feelings and not show her that you like her more than the others. It is a cruel thing for you, I know, but it would be a still more cruel thing to tell her and destroy her peace of mind.'

Well, I thought to myself, whatever I suffer she shall not suffer if I can help it.

We had been walking along the path between the house and the garden and down the middle garden walk. The place is inextricably entwined in my remembrance with the conversation and the circumstances. I felt deeply humiliated, low in spirit and sick at heart. But it was a great deal to learn from her father that he had observed her liking for me. I believed she liked me before. Now I am sure of it. But it was hard to know this and yet not to be able to tell her or show her that I loved her. I was comforted by remembering that when my father proposed for my mother he was ordered out of the house, and yet it all came right. I wonder if this will ever come right. The course of true love never does run smooth. What has happened only makes me long for her more and cling more closely to her, and feel more determined to win her.

On this day when I proposed for the girl who will I trust one day be my wife I had only one sovereign in the world, and I owed that. . . .

I went back across the brook with a sorrowful heart. At Clyro Vicarage every one was out. I left a note for Mrs Venables. 'He was very kind but gave no encouragement.' At Cae Mawr I found my sisters and Tom Williams playing croquet and just driven into the verandah by the rain. The afternoon had been grey, dull and dismal with an E. dark wind. Everything seemed gloomy and cold and the evening was irksome. Thersie went to dine at the Vicarage and we called for her as we went home. I could not feel able to join in the Bezique at Cae Mawr.

Thursday, 14 September

I went to the Vicarage after breakfast and told them the result of my visit and proposal yesterday. They were much pleased and very hopeful and thought the answer was as favourable as I could have expected at first. Somehow things seem to look brighter and more cheerful this morning. Mr and Mrs Venables were very much amused at Mr Thomas' approval of my choice of the one sister out of five, whom he should have chosen himself. I wrote to my father to tell him of my attachment and ask what my prospects were as far as he knew.

In the evening I went out for a walk with Thersie half way to Llowes in the dusk, startling her with all the horrors of the lonely evil road. We met the gleaning children coming home at the edge of night with great bundles of leased wheat poised on their heads, drooping over and hiding their faces.

Thersie, Fanny and Dora walked up to Cwmgwanon to sketch this afternoon.

Friday, 15 September

Lying in bed this morning dozing, half awake and half asleep,

I composed my speech of thanks at my wedding breakfast, a very affecting speech, and had visions of myself with Daisy at Langley and other places.

Thersie and Dora in the churchyard sketching the Church from different points. Fanny in the Church practising on the harmonium.

Sunday, 17 September

I preached in the morning from Psalm xv, 1, 2, and went to Bettws with Dora who skipped about like a goat.

I had to-day very kind letters from my Father and Mother about my attachment to Daisy. They say if they had inherited their natural share of the Worcester money they might have retired from Langley in my favour, but now that is impossible. They cannot afford it. My mother is very curious to know the young lady's name. I believe she thinks it is Mary Bevan. I am told by my father that I shall have one day £2700.

Monday, 18 September

I went to the Vicarage with Mrs Venables and had a talk with Mr Venables about my prospects. He most kindly promised to write to the Bishop to ask him for a living for me. Then we went out into the Churchyard where Webb the carpenter was painting the tombstones of his father and mother and his wife.

At 2.30 we all drove to Llan Thomas with Mrs Hilton, meeting Major Thomas, Lechmere and Charlie at the Brecon turnpike coming into Hay on foot to pay calls. Mrs Thomas and Mary came into the drawing room first. I was very nervous when Mrs Thomas came in, but she received me very kindly and cordially just as usual. The croquet things were got out, two sets playing on the same ground across from either peg. The girls gradually came out on to the lawn. I began to fear Daisy was not coming. She was the last of all. I was horribly afraid she had been advised not to appear, because I was there. Presently I turned and there she was in a black velvet jacket and light dress, with a white feather in her hat and her bright golden hair

Hay Castle

tied up with blue riband. How bright and fresh and happy and pretty she looked. . . .

I love her more and more each time I see her. I think she loves me a little. I hope so. God grant it. I am sure she does not dislike me, and I believe, I do believe, she likes me and cares for me. I fancy I can see it in her clear loving deep grey eyes, so true and fearless and honest, those beautiful Welsh eyes that seem to like to meet mine. I think she likes to be with me and talk with me, or why did she come back to me again and again and stand by me and talk to no one else? I wish I could tell her how dearly I love her but I dare not. I must not, because of my promise. Perhaps I am deceiving myself and mistaken after all. Perhaps what I think is love is only her innocent childlike affectionate way with all, and she might be the same with anyone else. I cannot believe it. I will not believe it. How proud and glad I felt every time she came and stood by me. And I thought she seemed proud and fond too. How fond we should be of each other. I wonder what she thinks of my poor disfigured eyes, whether she loves me better or worse for that. She must know. She must see. Yet it does not seem to make any difference against me with her. Perhaps she is sorry for me. And they say pity is akin to love.

My own dear girl. My own precious love. May God give her to me in His own good time. What should I do if anyone else were to come and take her from me? I believe this is one of the matches that are made in Heaven. All is hers now. It is all for her, life, talents, prospects, all. All for her sake, valuable only that they may be laid at her feet, with fond pride. I look at everything now only in relation to her. If I am and have anything that is good I prize it and rejoice in it for her sake, that it may be hers.

Wednesday, 20 September

I went to the Vicarage to speak to Mrs Venables and settle the Psalms and Lessons with Mr Venables for the Harvest Festival next Tuesday. As I was coming down the steps he tapped his study window and came out on to the lawn to have a talk. He said he thought he ought to caution me not to think my prospects better than they were and not to do anything precipitate.

At 2.30 I walked across the fields to Hay Castle to a croquet party. Daisy was at the Castle already with Charlotte and Charlie. Part of the people went out into the archery field. She went with them, inseparable from her friend Fanny Bevan. I and some of the rest played a slow game of croquet. Presently Daisy came on to the lawn again. I thought her manner was altered, more quiet, guarded and reserved. Perhaps it was only that she was more shy in a strange place than at home. But it seemed to me as if she had received a hint not to be too forthcoming.

Saturday, 23 September

A letter came from Mr Thomas. Kindly expressed and cordial, but bidding me give up all thoughts and hopes of Daisy. It was a great and sudden blow and I felt very sad. The sun seemed to have gone out of the sky. I wrote a courteous reply saying that I must abide by his decision, but that an attachment would not be worthy of the name which could be blown out by the first breath of difficulty and discouragement and that I should be more unworthy of his daughter than I was if I could give her up so lightly and easily. I said that all that was left me was to hope and quietly wait for her, but I could not conceal from myself that the lapse of years and a long unbroken separation might alter feeling which at present appeared to me unalterable.

Monday, 25 September

Up early, ran down to the Lower House before breakfast to ask the farmer Williams for some corn for dressing the church. We had ten sheaves of wheat, barley and oats at the school and the children were busy between lessons leasing out the corn tidy and regular in little sheaves ready for me to make my crossed sheaves on the Church walls between the windows etc. The St Andrew crossed sheaves were looped across the butts with wild hop and tied across the bands at Mrs Venables' suggestion with red flannel bands. The work was divided as follows. Cooper brought down his ferns and arranged them in the Chancel. The Crichtons did the East window, the Hodgsons the desk and pulpit. Mrs Venables and Mrs Hilton the texts, white cardboard letters on red flannel stretched on wooden frames. Mrs Hilton two banners, green baize with white raised tapioca crosses, hanging on each side of the E. window. Mrs Hilton the two chancel windows. Mrs Morrell and Miss Prothen the windows in the nave. Mrs Partridge the Font, the Baskervilles the altar rails. Gibbins the altar sheaf. Fanny and Dora the pillars and capitals. The schoolmaster the porch.

The Cabalva ladies, Mrs Hodgson and her two sisters, came and put up their magnificent pulpit and desk hangings, violet flannel covered with beautifully worked designs in corn, a sickle and sheaf, I.H.S., Faith, Hope and Charity represented by an anchor, a cross, and a heart respectively. Bunches of purple grapes were mixed with the corn. A deep fringe of oats, flax and rye was looped up with bright rosy apples.

Tuesday, 26 September

The morning opened gloomy and threatening with a cold wind from the E. and a little misty rain. I was in the church by 7 o'clock dressing my sheaves with fresh wild hop which the clerk's boy brought me from Court Evan Gwynne. Then I cut down some branches of Spanish chestnut with clusters of the green prickly fruit for Dora's wreaths for the capitals of the pillars. The clerk and I put up the remaining wreaths and 9 o'clock came and he was obliged to go away to chime the bells, I to breakfast, returning to finish our work at 9.30. Crichton brought his pretty decoration for the E. window at 10 o'clock and went back to breakfast. Last touches were given. By 10.30 all was ready and the morning had brightened and opened into a lovely day. Mr Webb of Hardwick Vicarage walked over to the service and Mary and Cousie Bevan came with their father. We had a hymn before the service. Mr Venables read prayers and I the lessons from the clerk's lectern.

The collection was £10.16.1., the best we have ever had in

this church. The service and singing were admirable, short, lively and hearty. Never has the Church been dressed so beautifully, and on the whole it has been the most successful Festival we have had.

Saturday, October Eve

A glorious morning after the dark hopeless rain of yesterday. The land was rejoicing in the sunshine, the jewelled green of the meadows, the brilliant blue of the Beacons.

The river swollen by yesterday's rain was tumbling and rushing brown and tumultuous under Hay Bridge and sweeping round the curves below where the yellowing trees leaned over the brown water hurrying along the winding shore.

Poor little Katie Whitney no better, tossing about naked in bed in great pain. Her grandmother old Hannah Whitney, 90 years old, sat by the bedside of the child of 9 knitting, with her old black bonnet cocked quaintly on the top of her head.

Then to see John Williams the gardener and old Sarah Probert. As I sat by their fireside old Hannah Jones lighted her pipe, began to smoke, and told me the tragic story of Mary Meredith's suicide. She lived at New Barn and a son of Juggy (Joan) Price, Bill Price, lived close by at Sunny Bank. They went together and he got her with child. She had a little money of her own in the bank but she could not draw it out without her brother John's consent for their money was mixed up together. Mary thought that if she could get her money her lover would marry her for the sake of the money. But her brother would not yield to let Mary draw her money. Moreover he and his father were very angry with Mary for being with child and disgracing them. Whereupon poor Mary seeing no hope of marriage became melancholy mad. 'Often,' she said to Hannah Jones my informant, 'often I have gone out on moonlight nights and sat down by the spring and cried for hours, thinking that I would drown myself in the river.' What a picture. The solitary figure of the weeping girl sitting by the well in the moonlight. The many bitter tears shed on many a cold night by the moonlit well.

Then her father died and she grew worse and worse. At last

there came an outbreak. One day she suddenly declared she
would do no more for her brother, left the bacon half salted and
the meat was spoilt. Not long after she was seen walking and
'prancing' about down by the river on Boatside. But she left the
river and in the evening she was seen 'prancing' about in the
Bron. John her brother went down and brought her up home to
New Barn. He suspected she was up to something, for she asked
him to let her little boy who always slept with her sleep with
him that night, and when they went to bed he locked the front
door and put the key in his pocket forgetting that the backdoor
had no fastening but a bolt on the inside. In the night Mary got
up and left the house and was seen by people who were abroad
very early in the morning dodging and ducking behind the
hedges and going down the Cwm. The carter boys at Boatside
were at Plough that morning when they saw a woman coming
up from the river with her head buried in her breast. She was a
long way from them and they thought it was Mary Pugh who
lived then at Tump House. They called out, 'Mary, you are out
early this morning'. They thought she had been down gathering
wood by the river. The woman lifted her head, looked at the
teams, turned and ran down the river as hard as she could go
and plunged headlong in. It was a fortnight before she was
found, and then a flood cast her body up near Whitney Court.
It was surmised that she would be buried as a suicide without
any service on the 'backside of the Church', but she was buried
by Mr Venables with the usual ceremony.

Sunday, October Day. Wine Monat I

I preached extempore on Love and Duty and St John from 1
John iii. 18. Somehow I cannot confine my 'extempore' sermons
within less than half an hour. Half an hour seems like five minutes when you are talking or preaching.

On Cabalva bridge I met a man and a woman in the heavy
rain driving home the Upper Cabalva turkeys. The woman
studiously hid her face under her umbrella.

When I reached the village it was dark. I went up to see little
Katie Whitney. Her mother was in great distress and said she

was talking 'wittily'. A bad sign. The great change was stealing over her. Death was stamped on her face. I saw the child was dying then and I knew she would not live to see the morning light of this world. I said to her, 'Jesus loves little children. He said, Suffer the little children to come unto me and forbid them not, for of such is the Kingdom of Heaven'. I repeated the verse, 'Gentle Jesus, meek and mild'. She said the Lord's Prayer after me. She knew me perfectly but her words came with difficulty and her blue eyes were glazing then. She had seen a beautiful bright place, a garden, and numbers of beautiful little children and was much vexed because her sister Bella could not see them too.

Monday, October morrow

In the afternoon I went to see John Morgan, the old soldier, at the Bronith. He amused me very much by repeating his wife's criticisms on our Harvest Thanksgiving Service. She said there were two maids who had 'alarmingly strong voices' and who 'sang alarmingly strong'. And she considered that Mr Bevan 'finished up his sermon very genteel'.

Wednesday, 4 October

I went down to Saffron Hill to visit the poor people in their affliction at the death of the child who was drowned in one of the peat pits on the Rhos Goch last Saturday week, September 23rd. Watkins took me into the house where his wife was washing and sat down to tell me about the accident in a quiet resigned sorrowful way that was very touching, while his deaf wife sat by crying.

[*Here follows a long account of the accident.*]

Then the poor woman took up the tale and the lament. Exactly a fortnight before his death the child had what she now thought must surely have been his death warning. She had sent him with some bacon to Tynycwm and Mrs Owens had given him a piece of bread and cheese for bringing the bacon. As he

Hay from Clyro

came back it was dark and when he came home to Saffron Hill he was frightened, and brought his bread and cheese in his hand half-eaten for he was too terrified to finish eating it. 'Mother', he said, 'I've seen a ghost.' She tried to laugh him out of the idea, but he said that as he came back he saw a ghost on the bridge over the Milw on the Castle brook that divides the two parishes of Clyro and Newchurch. 'What was it like?' 'Like a tall person dressed in white and it looked down upon me. When I had got past I looked back and I saw it looking after me.'

Mrs Watkins thought it must be the apparition of his mother who died when the child was four days old and prayed with her dying breath that the child might never be reared, but that it might be spared the miseries of this world.

Friday, 6 October

Miss Watkins took me into her telegraph office at the Post Office and showed the new instrument and easy method which she despises after having gone through the drudgery of learning the old method. It is a beautifully simple instrument. In the telegraph room a beautiful fair-haired girl with a delicate pink complexion, a dazzling beauty, was writing at a table and working the telegraph and receiving messages by turns.

Tilly, the Hay innkeeper, killed a pike on the Moor water the other day opposite the Dolau catch on Morrell's water and weighing 38 lbs.

Saturday, 7 October

The *Hereford Times* has misprinted our report of the Clyro Harvest Festival as follows, 'The *widows* were decorated with Latin and St Andrew's crosses and other beautiful devices in moss with dazzling flowers.' This was irresistible and the schoolmaster roared with delight.

The afternoon was superb, and the country full of golden and gilding trees. 'The gold hand gildeth the falling leaf.' The Cabalva orchards with their traces of crimson and yellow apples glowed brilliant in the quiet afternoon sun and one tree was so loaded with fruit that it had to be propped all round.

There was a murderous affray with poachers at the Moor last night. Two keepers beaten fearfully about the head with bludgeons and one poacher, Cartwright, a Hay sawyer, stabbed and his life despaired of.

Wednesday, 11 October

I wanted to send a note to the school this morning to say that I should not be there to day. While we were at breakfast a troop of schoolchildren came down the road, and when I went out to the gate under the lilacs and laburnums Gipsy Lizzie was passing. With an arch shy smile and a toss of her brown curls and a merry glance from her blue eyes the lovely child took the note and promised to give it to the schoolmaster.

I went to Hay to meet my Father coming back from Llangorse by the 6.40 train. As I went across the fields the white monks' house shone ghostly down in its lonely hollow in the dusk. The station lights glanced and trembled in the river and the train came down the Wye side sweeping round the curves and blazing with white and green lamps.

My father brought back 4 nice jack from Llangorse, one 6 lbs, some 18 or 20 pounds of fish altogether, and the best day's fishing he has ever had.

Friday, 13 October

After school about 12.20 I started to walk over the hills. The fern cutters were hard at work on the Vicar's Hill mowing the fern with a sharp ripping sound. Two fair fern gatherers with their pitchforks, comely rosy girls, the Gores from Whitty's Mill, had just come down off the Vicar's Hill and were going home to dinner, passing in the road with a courtesy and a sunny bright smile and 'Good Evening, Sir'. A hearty salutation came also from the fern cutters at work on the hill among the ruddy russet golden fern. It was half past one o'clock. The mountain and the great valley were blue with mist and the sun shone brilliantly upon the hill and the golden fern.

No longer.

O'er lone Tynessa's cabin roof.
The wind-blown larch was bending.

The old stunted larch has been cut down that used to bow itself amost at right angles over the humble roof like a guardian angel bending over its charge.

At Tymawr James Pitt with his wooden leg was working on the road. He began talking about the fern gatherers and the fern cutting. Now Mr Baskerville has bought the glebe and the Vicar's Hill he said the tenants will not be allowed to cut and sell the fern as they had been doing under Mr Venables. A great deal of the fern will have to grow for cover to the birds. It is very hard to shoot a bird or get near a bird on the Vicar's Hill now. The tenants will only be allowed to cut patches of fern. The continual cutting of the fern especially in August weakens the fern very much. Formerly the fern on the Vicar's Hill used to grow up to a man's middle. It is only of late years that they have taken to cutting the fern for bedding. A few years ago not a frond of fern was cut from the hill and then there was grass all through the winter, sheltered and nourished up by the fern. James was lamenting over the probability of Mr Venables leaving Clyro and saying how sorely he would be missed. There is a universal suspicion and growing belief that he is soon going to give up the living and move to Llysdinam.

I had put a flask of ginger wine in my pocket and a sandwich of bread and bacon which I ate by the Milw Bridge at the meeting of the three parishes and wished I had another for I was as hungry as a hunter.

Up the long Green Lane

And when we came to Fuallt Banks
We set the grouse a-crowing.

But the heather bloom was long over and the heather was dark, speckled with the little round white bells. I looked for Abiasula along the green ride narrowing between the fern and heather, and looked for her again at the Fforest, but the great dark heather slopes were lonely, nothing was moving, the cottage was silent and deserted, the dark beautiful face, the wild black hair and beautiful wild eyes of the mountain child were nowhere to be seen.

Round the great dark heather-clothed shoulder of the mountain swept the green ride descending steeply to the Fuallt farm and fold and the valley opened still more wide and fair. In the green fold of the Fuallt a dog lay before the door barking viciously, and in the fold hedge near the old ruinous house stood a tall mountain ash loaded with bunches of scarlet berries drooping and blending with the leaves now thinning and turning russet brown. The beautiful Glasnant came leaping and rushing down its lovely dingle, a flood of molten silver and crystal fringed by groups of silver birches and alders, and here and there a solitary tree rising from the bright green sward along the banks of the brook and drooping over the stream which seemed to come out of a fairy land of blue valley depths and distances and tufted woods of green and gold and crimson and russet brown.

As I stood upon the plank foot bridge where the Glasnant crosses the road, and leaned upon the hand rail, a squirrel darted across the lane and through the hedge and then galloping across the intervening corners of the meadow with long leaps, it rushed through the brook partly running, partly swimming, partly flying, in a shower of spray.

Up the lane past the Harbour and the Duvawr, and there

> *The Clogan on her greensward mount*
> *Sat like a queen for ever*
> *With tresses crowned of waving woods*
> *Green throned beside the river.*

But to get at it. That was the question. Between the house and me rushed the swift Arrow. No wonder that the mount was fortified and strong. I could see no way to attack it. And the Arrow streams appeared to me to have something less than a hundred arms. I tried one place of the river bank after another, and finally I had to cross the Arrow twice and break through two stiff hedges. At last I found my way up a rich green orchard tenanted by a flock of geese and through a gate into the fold sheltered by some noble sycamores. The farm house, long, low and yellow-washed, looked towards the N.E. and under the porch extended a rude ancient wooden bench. Nothing seemed to be stirring and the place seemed deserted when suddenly three fierce dogs rushed out of the open front door barking furiously. A girl came to the door and said Mrs Jones was at home, and bade me sit down in an easy leather-covered arm chair by the fire in the comfortable kitchen. On a shelf beneath the round three-legged table lay purring an enormous fat black cat, and the dogs came fawning upon me to make friends. Toss a black and white collie with a long sweeping feathery white-tagged tail, Lady a beautiful brown and white dog like a water spaniel, and Gip a rough wiry blue Scotch terrier. Mrs Jones came in and I introduced myself and thanked her for the nice cream cheese she sent me. She brought me a jug of nice porter and some sweet delicious farm house bread and butter. She wanted me too to have some cold mutton which she said was very good, but I declined. She said they killed a sheep every week. They are substantial well-to-do people, kindly excellent folks and hospitable with the true old mountain hospitality. Lady was sleeping in the chimney corner. Mrs Jones said it was a favourite amusement of the dog when the ducks were swimming in the Arrow to dive, come up gently under the ducks and pull them down under water by their toes.

She took me out and showed me round the place. It must have been a great house once and a very strong place, so easily defensible. The old walls which now surround the garden stretch a long way back to the brow of the steep green mounds. The house is said to be the oldest inhabited building in these parts. It stands high above the Arrow on its green mount, embosomed and almost hidden by its sycamores and other trees. The steep sides of the mount fall suddenly away from the house and garden at the back of the house, down to the two streams of the Arrow brawling far below under the dark shadow of the thick woods that fringe the river. In a dark secluded recess of the wood near the river bank an ice-cold never-failing spring boils up out of the rock. Mrs Jones said it makes her arms ache to the shoulder to put her hand into the water from this spring in the hottest day of summer. In the hot summer days Louie and the other girls take the butter down the steep bank, across the Arrow and make up the butter in the wood by the icy spring. Then they bring the butter up and it remains as if it had been iced.

There are beautiful trout in the river and large eels. While I was looking about Mrs Jones said she would go in and hurry tea for she would make me have some. She made me eat a quantity more bread and butter and two eggs, bringing me some butter to butter them with for she thought they were hard-boiled. Meanwhile she talked much of the wicked old Squire, Beavan of the Yat Glascwm and of Mrs Irvine and his two other poor daughters [   ] into idiots.

When I went away Mrs Jones came out without her bonnet and accompanied me across two sunny meadows belonging to the Clogan till we got to the bridge over the Arrow. Then she kindly bade me Farewell and come again.

At the Green Lane I went into the cottage to ask for Mrs Jones, the old soldier Morgan's daughter, who was tossed by a heifer a short time ago. A laughing glance from a pair of beautiful wild dark eyes, and there stood Abiasula just where I saw her first. Rarely have I seen such eyes, so large and magnificent with such long sweeping lashes. Her sister Mary had come over the hill from the Fforest with her to meet their mother who had been taking their sister Elwina to service. Both the girls were very merry and Abiasula laughed so much that her sister reproved her saying, 'Aby, be tidy with Mr Kilvert'. Then Aby suddenly became shy. I reminded her of the first day I ever saw her with the black shawl hooded over her head like a little gipsy. Mary said Aby often talked of that black shawl and wished she had not put it on instead of her hat that particular day of all others. She wondered at herself, for coming out in that shawl. I told her there was nothing to be ashamed of, it was a very good shawl and became her extremely well. When I went away she put her little hand into mine and wished me Goodbye.

Monday, 16 October

Up at 4.30. Breakfast at 5.30. It was hardly fully light when the old mare whirled us* through the village towards the There
*The diarist and his father.

Cocks, the first instalment of our journey to St David's. The morning was warm grey and cloudy, with a soft S.W. wind after a night's rain and a yellow dawn over the dim grey dark mountains. We reached the station in good time thanks to the brave old mare.

[*He visits St. David's Cathedral with his father and returns to Clyro.*]

Sunday, 29 October

Visiting in the evening. William Pugh said the day the railway was opened to Brum as the first train was going up a bull took exception to it and came roaring down the line full charge to attack the train. However the train went on its way and sent the bull flying. The engine knocked him all to pieces. 'So much the worse for the Coo', as George Stephenson said.

Monday, 30 October

Clyro Petty Sessions, and the Magistrates abolished the New Inn, a happy thing for the village.

Tuesday. Llanhollant Eve. All Hallowmas Eve. Hallowe'en. November Eve.

A wild wet night for the girls to go out to sow the hemp seed and pitch dark. They can hardly see their phantom lovers mowing after them to-night.

This is in Welsh, 'Nos Calan Gauaf' . . the first night of winter.

I was sitting with Hannah Whitney this evening telling her of our pilgrimage to St David's and the wonderful things we had seen. 'Dear God,' said the old woman solemnly. 'How many strange things there are in the world.' She was very angry with people who had the means and not the inclination to travel and see the wonders of the earth.

She said she wore a high Welsh hat in Clyro 40 years ago. Then it wore out and she did not get another as they went out of fashion.

When she lived by Whitney's brook three Cardiganshire women used to pass by the house every March walking to London to weed gardens.

Wednesday. Llanhollantine. All hallowmas. November Day. Wind Monat I

And true to its old Saxon name the month has come in howling. A wild wind is blowing to-night over valley and mountain. The wind is unquiet. It cannot rest.

Mrs Venables wrote to me yesterday. She is terribly bothered again about Gibbins'* affairs. Young Lewis, the Hay tailor, has once more suddenly appeared on the scene and all is ablaze again when we thought the attachment had died away at least on her part and been forgotten.

Mrs Venables wants some reliable information about the young man. So I had to consult Evans the schoolmaster yesterday and to go to Hay this morning to the Castle to ask Mrs Bevan's advice.

The old soldier Morgan sent me by his wife a basket of Quince apples, the only ones that grew on his tree this year.

Saturday, 4 November

I went to call at the White Ash where I found Mrs Meredith at home, a handsome dark-eyed rosy girl with a hearty cordial manner and plenty to say for herself. She told me how the salmon came in the great floods up to the little fall below the larger one and how the men would get into the brook up to their arm pits and spear the salmon in the pools. And then she told me the old story of how the fairies used to feed the ploughmen of Penyshaplwyd till the wicked boy stole the silver knife.

Sunday. Gunpowder Treason and Plot

Thank God for this beautiful bright morning, this brilliant frost in this dark time of the year. The first frost forest laced the windows this morning.

*'Gibbins', Miss Gibbins, in service with Mrs Venables. For the sequel, see page 281.

Monday, 6 November

Such a happy day. Thank God for such a happy day. I have
seen my love, my own, I have seen Daisy. She was so lovely and
sweet and kind and the old beautiful love is as fresh and strong
as ever. I never saw her more happy and affectionate and her
lovely Welsh eyes grew radiant whenever they met mine. . . .

She was looking prettier than ever and the East wind had
freshened her pretty colour and her lovely hair was shining like
gold. She wore a brown stuff dress and white ribbons in her hat.

Charlotte went out on to the lawn with me to get a rose bud
for my coat. I never saw such a place as Llan Thomas for roses.
They are blooming now red and white as if it were
summer. There is no last rose of summer at Llan Thomas. . . .

Presently Daisy was left alone with me for a minute. 'It's a
long time since you have been over to see us,' she said, 'I suppose
you have been busy.' 'Yes,' I said, 'but it's not only that. I
should like to come very often but I musn't.' Fanny Bevan went
to her lessons. Daisy sighed. 'I wish', she said, 'that I had lessons
to do.' She cannot bear to be idle.

As we walked to Hay we discovered that I carried off Mr
Thomas' walking stick instead of mine. I asked her if I might
come over to Llan Thomas and change the sticks. 'Yes,' she
said, 'and come *very soon.*'

She gave me a warm kind clasp of the hand at parting. It was
dark when we all sallied out again, that is the Llan Thomas
party and myself, and parted at the Blue Boar.

I wonder if Daisy and I will ever read these pages over together. I think we shall.

Saturday, 11 November

Bitterly cold, north wind and snow on the mountain. The
Venables came home from Llysdinam to-day. Mr George
Venables sent me a brace of Llysdinam pheasants and a rabbit.
Baskerville shot 3 woodcocks this afternoon near the Llainau.

This morning Catherine Price of the New Inn was married to
Davies, a young Painscastle blacksmith, before the Hay registrar.

What I call a gipsy 'jump the broom' marriage. I saw them going in four gaily dressed couples, and they were back again in a very short time. Marianne Price said, 'God Almighty didn't approve of people being married before registrars, that was no marriage at all. He liked them to be married in Church'. The wedding feast was at the New Inn which is now shut up as an inn and abolished. As I passed the house I heard music and dancing, the people dancing at the wedding. They were dancing in an upper room, unfurnished, tramp, tramp, tramp, to the jingling of a concertina, the stamping was tremendous. I thought they would have brought the floor down. They seemed to be jumping round and round. When I came back the dance seemed to have degenerated into a romp and the girls were squealing, as if they were being kissed or tickled and not against their will.

I dined at Cae Mawr. Morrell asked me if it were true that I was going to leave Clyro. I told him I was not at liberty to say. But the secret cannot be kept much longer.

Sunday, 12 November

In the evening as I was sitting by my fire thinking, just after I had lighted the candles came a tap at the door and Mrs Venables. She sat down and put her feet up on the fender and we had a long cosy talk together about Daisy, and Gibbins' love affairs. She says she and Mrs Henry Venables consulted together about the expediency of the step and then she read aloud to Gibbins my letters about her lover young Lewis. I asked if Gibbins did not hate me for what I had said, for I had no idea that she would ever hear the contents of the letter or know that I had written on the subject. No, Mrs Venables said, not at all. Gibbins thought it very kind and friendly of me to take so much trouble about the matter. I must give her a copy of *Stepping Heavenward*. I think it will do her good.

Monday, 13 November

'What a fine day it is. Let us go out and kill something.' The old reproach against the English.

The Squire has just gone by with a shooting party. A line of gentlemen walking first followed by the keepers carrying the guns and a posse comitatus of beaters and boys and dogs and hangers on. They went up the hill by the Brooms to shoot Potts' beat at the Bronith.

Tuesday, 14 November

Tom Williams of Llowes, Pope and Clouston dined with me this evening. Mrs Venables sent some soup from the Vicarage and we had a leg of mutton roasted and a couple of boiled chickens and bacon and a brace of pheasants from Llysdinam, an apple pie and an apricot jam tart.

Thursday, 16 November

Yesterday Mr and Mrs Venables drove to call at Llan Thomas. This morning Mrs Venables told me that Mr Venables likes Daisy very much. He thinks her very nice-looking and admires her nice open face. Mrs Venables was very much disappointed to see so little of Daisy. Mrs Thomas sent her on an errand out of the room and she did not come in again.

Sunday, 19 November

At the school this morning I had a grateful word and glance and clasp of the hand from Gibbins in return for the book I gave her, *Stepping Heavenward*.

Friday, 24 November

This afternoon I took up my musical box for the blind child at Whitty's Mill. The mountains were veiled in mist and a cow was roaring in the valley.

Calling at Bethel. The young widow and her child were wading across the miry fold through pools of water trying to find a bit of dry wood to heat the oven. All the wood was soaked. The house was wet, dirty, cheerless and cold with a low fire and an

open door. A boy of 14, the only servant of the little farm, came
to the door and hung some sacks on the railings. They had half
done their wheat sowing. The poor young widow had gone
through great hardships, trials and struggles and ruinous losses.
Her last horse died in the winter. Now she has none and a
neighbour does the ploughing for hire. Price of Great Wern y
Pentre.

Saturday, 25 November

I went up to Cwm Sir Hugh. A heavy dark mist from the East
brooded over the country and the trees dripped drearily in the
fading light.

A screaming romp with Lucretia who in rolling about upon
the bed upset the candle on to the coverlet and burst into peals
of inextinguishable laughter while a strong smell of burning rose
from the singed woollens and I snatched up the candle in a way
which redoubled Lucretia's mirth.

Sunday, 26 November

A dark dismal day, scarcely any daylight. I preached in the
morning on the High Priest of Humanity from the Second lesson
for the evening's service. Hebrews ii, 17, 18. I went to Bettws. A
drizzling rain came on. The afternoon grew dark and darker.
The darkness in Chapel was fearful. I have seldom been so hard
put to it to read. Before I began the lessons the darkness became
appalling and it seemed as if night were coming on all at once. I
asked Wilding in despair if there were a candle in the Chapel.
'No,' he said. So with the courage of desperation and a wild
beast at bay, I went at the lessons and scrambled through somehow, stumbling and blundering frightfully. Then it grew lighter.
I preached extempore with great satisfaction to myself, better
than I have ever done before, on citizenship.

Monday, 27 November

Busy all day getting ready for the Penny Readings this evening.

There were 167 people present and we took at the doors £1 1s. 6d. I recited some passages from the Deserted Village, the Village Ale House, the Village Schoolmaster and the Village Clergyman. I did not do it well and broke down several times, but I got through more than 100 lines with the help of Mr Venables who had the book and prompted me. Afterwards red herrings for supper at the Vicarage.

Advent Sunday, 3 December. My birthday

Holy Communion. Sadly few communicants. Almost the smallest number I ever saw here. . . .

Champagne at dinner at the Vicarage and a capital plum pudding in honour of my birthday.

Monday, 4 December

The sun went down behind the dark round of the Old Forest filling the air with a strange yellow splendour and brightness as of the colour of shining brass. Visited the Irish girl, Mrs Evans, in the half deserted squalid weedgrown row of cottages at the Bronith by the broken-down cider inn and Methodist Chapel. The baby in the cradle was asleep breathing fast and heavily with a dangerous cold. The clock in the next house struck at least 20.

Called on Hannah Whitney. I told her of the tomb of Walter Whitney.* She had never seen the tomb and did not know of it, but she said she thought it must be the tomb of her grandfather's cousin. 'You are of a better family than many of the gentlemen round here,' I said. 'I know it,' said the old woman proudly. 'If I were any the better for that,' she added with a half sigh. 'Thank God for my bit of breed,' she said cheerfully.

She was sitting at her frugal tea at her little table by the fire in her humble cot, this descendant of a line of squires. I told her I could see her good blood in her face. She replied that she had no cause to be ashamed of her family. The old woman was daily, hourly, expecting a load of club coal from Hay for her scanty

*See Page 135

Views towards Clyro (centre) from the Black Mountains

store was nearly exhausted and the weather is sharp.

While I was dressing this morning the string of nine horses from the stables of Maesllwch Castle went by to exercise with a long steady tramping trot and it appeared to be Talgarth Fair, one of the many, for the farmers went past in troops and squadrons in the early morning dusk betwixt the moonset and sunrise, their horses' feet ringing hard and sharp on the frosty road.

Knocked all to pieces to-day with face ache, feeling miserable. stiff, sick and nohow.

Thursday, 7 December

Mrs Venables gave me to keep a dear little note she had just received from Daisy, thanking her for a book on knitting which she had sent her.

Still hard frost, and the Wye frozen across above Glasbury Bridge. The mountain covered with snow and glittering in the afternoon sun.

The Wye is frozen across above Glasbury Bridge.

Friday, 8 December

News came to Hereford to-day that the Prince of Wales is much worse, dying it is thought.

Sunday, 10 December

The blue mountains were silver ribbed with snow and looked like a dead giant lying in state – a Titan.

Hodgson was at Chapel. The Prince, the Prince is in every one's mouth. We went into Wall's farm house after Chapel and I stayed there till dusk, then home by the upper road crazy with face ache, weak and wretched, and the road never seemed to be so long. As I passed Whitty's Mill in the dusk the mill seemed to be at work. After dinner and four glasses of port I felt better.

Thursday, 14 December

The anniversary of the Prince Consort's death ten years ago, and people were very anxious about it for it was said the Prince

of Wales was conscious of the day, but to-day the Prince is
better. Thank God. Thank God. 'Why', said Mrs Watkins of
Saffron Hill, dropping a deep curtsey and looking reprovingly
at her daughter who was handing me my hat as I was leaving
the house last night, 'why', she asked severely, 'did not you
curtsey to him when you gave him his hat?' I walked to Glasbury
this afternoon to wish the Alfords 'Goodbye'.

At Glasbury I had to ask the way to the Vicarage twice, never
having been there before. The road let me across the village
green and along the low river wall. The broad noble reach of
the Wye shimmered quivering under the last cold gleam of the
setting sun. The old vicarage, the Wye Vicarage, stands close to
the river wall upon the river bank. It is a poor tumble-down
ramshackle old place and unhealthy I should think, damp and
infested by rats which once gnawed a living baby, but the good
little parson and his family cling to it and the memories of 24
years which are not to be lightly broken.

Friday, 15 December

The mountain was veiled in a tender gauze of green mist and a
sudden burst lit the country with a strange violent glare. Called
at the old soldier's and took him a screw of 'rag' tobacco and
Morrell's ticket for some Christmas beef.

Sunday, 17 December

Before he began his sermon this morning Mr Venables read
from the pulpit the latest telegram from Sandringham which is
very comfortable. 'The Prince has passed a tranquil day and the
symptoms continue to be favourable.' Dated last evening. What
a blessed happy contrast to the suspense and fear of last Sunday.
How thankful we all are.

> *Men met each other with erected look,*
> *The steps were higher that they took,*
> *Each to congratulate his friend made haste*
> *And long inveterate foes saluted as they passed.*

I love that man now, and always will love him. I will never say a word against him again. God bless him. God bless him and keep him, the Child of England.

In the afternoon I alluded to the Prince's illness in an old Advent sermon on John the Baptist from Matthew xi, 10 and nearly broke down.

Monday, 18 December

Came from Clyro to Langley.

My father met me at the Chippenham Station.

[*During his stay at Langley he goes to London to stay with his sister Emmie. While there he visits several picture galleries where he particularly admires the Zurbarans and Murillos, also some striking nudes in what Plomer describes as 'precarious but romantic situations'.*]

1872

Saturday, 13 January

Left Langley for Clyro by the usual early beastly train, the up express 8.42, which necessitates in the winter breakfast in the dark. Pouring rain driving to the station and all day. . . .

I hear Daisy came out at the Hereford Hunt Ball last Tuesday, looked very pretty and danced a great deal and was very much admired.

Monday, 15 January

The old soldier was working in his garden at the edge of dusk but came in as I entered the house. We were talking of Maria Williams. I said I thought the tree had better lie where it falls. 'Ah,' said the old soldier, 'I've heard many old people talk about that. When death do call upon we it don't matter what becomes of our bodies.'

He said when he first saw the moon this year it was a very keen moon. Old-fashioned folk used to take great notice of the first moon of the New Year.

Dined at the Vicarage.

Tuesday, 16 January

Lucretia and I had a splendid romp.

Called on Lewis the policeman. His wife has lately been suffering from a dreadful quinsy. They told me their version of the fearful faction fight between Clyro and Hay on the day after Christmas. The general impression seems to be that the Hay people were as much or more in fault than the Clyro people but got off scot-free.

Lewis was in a difficulty to know what to do with some Clyro boys who had been playing football on Sunday.

Sunday, 21 January

Went to Bettws. Down the Roman road below Penrheal the children of Pentwyn were singing 'Ding dong bell'. Perhaps they saw the parson coming up the hill. Then the Chapel bell tolled out sharp and sudden through the white mist to give notice of the service a quarter of an hour beforehand. The hedges were hoary with rime and frost and the trees were hailing large pieces of ice down into the road.

Few people in Chapel. I preached the New Year sermon about the three divisions in the Life of Moses from Deuteronomy xxxiv, 7, with some satisfaction to myself. I thought the markers in the Bible and Prayers had suddenly become very short, and after service Wilding the Clerk told me the Church mice had eaten them off.

Monday, 22 January

Pouring rain. Went to Wye Cliff to see Crichton about the Penny Readings to-morrow. Showed him my coin of Augustus, the denarius found on Boatside Farm.

Found Boosie Evans of the School practising on the piano in the School parlour. A caress and kiss brought a sunny delighted smile rippling over her fair sweet face. She *is* a darling.

The brook at night roaring under the high moon.

Tuesday, 23 January

Visited Edward Evans, old Price the paralysed keeper, Mrs Lacy, Catherine Ferris, James Smith, and Mrs Price of the Swan who showed me preserved in a box part of one of Price's whiskers pulled out by the Clyro women in the late row at the Swan.

Price told some one at the time that he had one of his whiskers in his pocket.

The Penny Readings to-night went off admirably, one of the very best we have ever had. A crowded room, nearly 250 people.

Wednesday, 24 January

Visited John Morgan. The old soldier had another epileptic fit on Sunday. Came home in a wild storm of rain. Will the land ever be dry again? All the low-lying meadows are wastes of wan waters and dreary pools. The land is sodden with wet. A water-spout of rain burst in the night about midnight and the Dulas and Cwmbythog brook are in full roar, rushing through the dark with a wild strange stormy foam light.

Friday, 26 January

Mrs Parker was better to-day. The poor little black dwarf Emily was at home from school with a bad cold. Her mother told me how some of the village children laughed at Emily and called her 'dwarf'. Poor child. I called her to me and she came and nestled to my side and a beautiful delighted smile flitted over her face as I caressed and kissed her and bade her not to mind. It is a beautiful noble spirit caged in a poor deformed stunted body. Mrs Parker told me how deeply attached Emily is to me and how shocked the child is to see the other children sometimes dishonourably looking slyly at their neighbour's books when saying lessons by heart, or offering their books and tempting those who are saying their lessons to look.

Old William Price (old Laver) sat in his filthy den, unkempt, unshaven, shaggy and grey like a wild beast, and if possible filthier than the den.

I read to him Faber's hymn of the Good Shepherd. He was much struck by it. 'That's what He has been telling me,' said the old man.

Saturday, 3 February

The whole of the beautiful Cwmgwanon woods are to be felled,

Hay village as in Kilvert's time

the Castle wood and all that exquisite wooded bank up the dingle to the 'tufted copse' and Bryn y garth.

The trees have been doomed, measured and numbered. The sale is to take place next week. And then the axe will be heard in the sacred dingle.

The cottagers say that these woods are to be felled to pay De Winton's gambling debts.

Monday, 5 February

At Newgate an urchin 3 feet high was swinging a gate. 'Well,' said I, 'and how are you?' 'Pretty well, thank you,' shouted the urchin, 'how's yourself?'

Wednesday, 7 February

I walked to Hay. The afternoon was brilliant in its loveliness.

The sun was under a cloud from behind which streamed seven broad rays on to the variegated mountain and valley, river and meadow, striking out brilliant gems of sunlit emerald green on the hill sides.

Teddy Bevan walked with me to Pont Vaen. In the street we met Mrs Allen's carriage with Mrs Allen and Mrs Oswald. Mrs Allen was dressed as I told her like a duchess in a magnificent ermine cape. The Bridges were at home, gave us tea and showed us all their poultry, the white Brahmas, the golden-pencilled and silver-spangled Hambros, and that ferocious wild beast the silver pheasant who has at length been tamed by having his long spurs cut, and has at last consented to allow his wife of the period to live. He killed all the rest. There is a story that when the man servant had to feed this wild beast he always wore a coalscuttle reversed on his head by way of a helmet for the pheasant flew straight up into the air, descended on the man's head and spurred at his eyes. . . .

Home across the river roaring in the dark.

Before I settled down for the evening I went into old Hannah Whitney's and sat awhile with her.

She spoke of the two extraordinary sermons she heard preached in Llanbedr Church by 'Parson Button', Parson Williams of Llanbedr. 'He was a good Churchman but he was a very drunken man.' 'How then being a very drunken man could he be a good churchman?' 'Oh, he read the Lessons very loud and he was a capital preacher. He used to say to the people in his sermons, "My brethren", says he, "don't you do as I do, but you do as I say".'

He was very quarrelsome, a fighting man, and frequently fought at Clyro on his way home from Hay. One night he got fighting at Clyro and was badly beaten and mauled. The next Sunday he came to Llanbedr Church bruised black and blue, with his head broken and swollen nose and two black eyes. However, he faced his people and his sermon glorified himself and his prowess and gave a false account of the battle at Clyro in which he was worsted, but in which he represented himself as having proved victorious.

The text was taken from Nehemiah xiii, 25. 'And I contended

with them and cursed them and smote certain of them and plucked off their hair, and made them swear by God.'

Another time he was to preach a funeral sermon for a farmer with whom he had quarrelled. He chose this text. Isaiah xiv. 9. 'Hell from beneath is moved for thee to meet thee at thy coming.'

Hannah says her 'clock to go to bed' is the horses coming down the lane from the Swan to water at the brook. They come down about 8 o'clock every night. A sort of 'eight o'clock horse'.

Her clock in the morning to get up is the light as soon as it is strong enough to show her her clothes.

Thursday, 8 February

To-night there is a dinner party at Llan Thomas. Some officers from Brecon are to be there, but all married men, as Mrs Bevan pointedly informed me. I wonder if she suspects anything. Sat up late writing some blank verse in honour of Daisy.

Monday, 12 February

This is Boosie Evans' birthday and at 6.30 eight of the children came to tea at my rooms, for I had arranged my yearly children's party to-day to celebrate the event.

There were Gussena Anthony, Mary Eleanor Williams the clerk's daughter, who came from Cusop on purpose to attend the party, Sarah Cooper, Mary Jane and Boosie Evans, Lizzie Jones of the Harbour, and Louie and Tillie Jones of the Clogan.

The children were a little shy when they first came in, and were standing together at the opposite side of the room. 'Come round here and warm yourselves. You needn't be afraid of me.' 'No, Sir,' replied Sena Anthony quickly and frankly, 'we're too fond of you to be afraid of you.' How easy it is to amuse children and make them happy. They were overwhelmed with admiration of one of the attar of rose bottles which Emmie brought from Hyderabad. Then they were seized with awe at the sight of a lock of hair which I cut from the mane of the great lion at the Clifton Zoological Gardens when he was asleep, in August 1865. But one of the things which amused and interested them most was an old letter lock off my hat box.

I offered a sovereign to whoever could open it. They tried a long time, but the reward was not claimed. They were very indignant and angry with themselves for not being able to open it when I told them the cabalistic word was 'pat'. 'And you were patting your pussy all the while, if we had only thought about it and noticed it,' said one of the children, alluding to my tabby cat who was lying in my arm chair beside me. First came buns, bread and butter, and tea poured out by Boosie amid great fun. Crackers and looking at picture books. They played bagatelle and the Race Game. Then came a grand fiery snap dragon.* And lastly I told them tales till midnight, the story of Faithful Eric and the wolves, and the story of the fright Emmie had in the night at Hyderabad. Dear children, what a pleasure it is to have them. I am never so happy as when I have these children about me. And they behave so nicely, like little gentlewomen, much better than most young ladies. I should be very sorry to spend six hours in the company of many young ladies of my acquaintance, whereas to-night I was as sorry when 12 o'clock came as the children, and missed them sadly when all the bright faces trooped out into the dark night together to their homes in the village, with Goodnight and thanks and courtesies, and left me alone in my silent room.

Wherever I may go I shall never find such children again.

Shrove Tuesday, 13 February

Dined at the Vicarage at 5.30 and at 7 drove with the Venables and Crichton to the Rifle Volunteer Concert in the National Schoolroom at Hay. We had tickets for the first row, and in the third row I immediately espied Daisy and Charlotte. I had the good fortune to get a chat with Daisy before the seats were filled up, and she was so nice and I was so happy. . . . 'It's a long time since you have been over to Llan Thomas. I suppose you have been very busy. If you come over you will find some of us at home. We don't usually go out till half past three.' 'I am afraid,' I said, 'that you have all quite forgotten me.' 'Oh, no,' she said. She told me they had lately been photographed in a family

*Picking raisins out of a dish of burning brandy and eating them.

group. I told her I had seen one of the photographs at Clyro Vicarage. Mrs Venables bought one of the whole family in a group. I did not add that Mrs Venables gave me this very morning a photograph of the six Llan Thomas ladies grouped by themselves, in which Daisy comes out best of all.

I was so happy talking to her. I had been hoping and thinking all day that I might meet her at the concert this evening. But now the seats began to fill. Fanny Bevan her great and inseparable friend sat on one side of her and her father on the other. I sat in the row before them. Henry sang.

Oh Daisy.

When the concert was over rain was pouring and there was a long way to go to the carriages. Daisy took Lechmere's arm but they had no umbrella and were standing in the porch waiting for one of their party to come back with an umbrella. She was dressed entirely in white, a white dress and long white cloak, and she looked so pretty standing there with her fair golden head uncovered. I ran back into the room, got Cooler's umbrella for them and accompanied them to the carriage. '*Thank you*', she said gratefully.

When we reached the door of the school yard their covered waggonette was standing in the middle of the road. It was very dark. 'Where's Fanny?' said Henry. 'Oh here you are, I was just coming back for you. I'll carry you to the carriage.' 'Can you?' she said. 'Yes, put your arms round my neck.' She clasped her arms round her brother's neck, and he took her up in his strong arms and carried her safe and dry to the carriage. It was the prettiest sight in the world and reminded me irresistibly of Huldbrand carrying Undine through the flood.

Monday, 19 February

Went to Langley. Morrell gave me a large wicker cage with a pair of turtle doves or ring doves to take home.

Tuesday, 27 February

The National Thanksgiving for the recovery from desperate illness of Edward Prince of Wales.

Leap Thursday, 29 February. March Eve

There is a general belief amongst the Clyro and Langley people that I cannot travel from Radnorshire to Wiltshire without going over the sea.

Friday, March Day

Villaging. Edward Evans stated that his 'inside was all in an uproar'.

In to-day's paper there was an account of the miserable attack on the Queen at Buckingham Palace as she returned from her drive, by the wretched boy Arthur O'Connor with his unloaded rusty and broken pistol. Fool.

Sunday, 3 March

Supper at the Castle and home under the clear sky brilliant flashing moving with the quick lights of the stars and the bands of Orion, the sweet influences of the Pleiades and Arcturus with his sons.

Monday, 4 March

What a superb day it has been, almost cloudless, brilliant, hot as late May and the warm south wind blowing sweet from the Black Mountains.

Cwmgwanon Wood is being murdered. As I walked along the edge of the beautiful dingle and looked sadly down into the hollow, numbers of my old friends of seven years standing lay below on both banks of the brook prostrate and mutilated, a mournful scene of havoc, the road almost impassable for the limbs of the fallen giants.

At the Homme the door was unlocked but the downstairs rooms empty and the only sounds in the silent house were the scratching of a little fox terrier shut up in a closet and the horrible moaning and growling of the madwoman upstairs. Presently Meredith her brother came in and in some trepidation invited me upstairs to see her. She was in bed, very quiet. 'Read to me about God and Jesus, please, dear,' she said in a whining voice. When I had read five minutes, 'You may go now dear,' she said, 'I am tired, I want to sleep. But you may pray for me first.'

She was in service more than twenty years as a housemaid at Kensington with some people named Collinson I think, an agent of Lord Bute's. In their service she saved £500 and came home to her own country to *enjoy* her money. This is how she is enjoying it.

Wednesday, 6 March

The night was superb, glittering with stars in a cloudless sky.

As I came down the Long Lands Pitch I met a man in the dark coming up. It was old Richard Meredith the land-surveyor who stopped and began to talk about all things in heaven and earth, planets and fixed stars, philosophers and heretics, Mahometans and their creed.

Amongst other things he asked me if I considered that animalculae had the power of suffering. He was inclined to think not.

Friday, 8 March

At the Scripture Lesson at the School this morning asking Eleanor Williams of Paradise, 'What happened on Palm Sunday?' she replied, '*Jesus Christ went up to heaven on an ass*'. This was the promising result of a long struggle to teach her something about the Festivals of the Church.

Sunday, 10 March, Mid Lent. Mothering Sunday

And a fine day for the young people to go Mothering.

Monday, 11 March

In the afternoon I walked over to Llan Thomas. Mrs Thomas better but not downstairs. Mr Venables came soon after me, then the Bridges, and then Mr Allen.

I had a good deal of talk with Daisy. The coming of the other visitors created a confusion and diversion in our favour and being screened and our voices drowned in the Babel of tongues we were not noticed so much. She said that she and her sisters had been looking for birds' nests. 'I hope you didn't take any,' said I. 'Do you *think* we would?' answered she indignantly with a pretty flash of spirit.

She told me that three of the six bells of Llanigon Church were stolen by dissenters who carried them away across the mountain and put them up in their own chapel. She was going for a walk with her father and sisters and said it was 'Such fun'. Rest, happy child, content with a few simple innocent delights. Rest, happy child, guileless and unspoilt. God keep thee, dear. When I got home I found some fresh flowers on my table. The children had brought me some more primroses and the first wood anemone.

Tuesday, 12 March

Called on Esther Rogers. Speaking of Tom Williams the Vicar of Llowes she said he was 'as mild as a dove and as humble as the grave'. . . .

Mary Jones the Jockey told me that Caroline wanted to see me. So I went to Gipsy Castle and Caroline gave me two eggs which her hen had laid and which she had saved for me. She had nothing else to give. I was very much touched and told her I valued them more than if they had been made of gold. At the same time I wished for her sake that her hen would lay golden eggs.

Wednesday, 13 March

Rain was creeping over the hills from the west and blotting out the mountains. Below lay the black and gloomy peat bog, the Rhos Goch, with the dark cold gleam of the stagnant water among its mawn pits, the graves of the children.

This place has always had a strange singular irresistible fascination for me. I dread it yet I am drawn to it.

As I returned I paused at the stonen stile above Llanshifr to look down upon the strange grey dark old house lying in the wet hollow among the springs, with its great dismal solitary yew and the remains of the moat in which the murdered Scotch pedlar was buried.

Sunday, 17 March

At school this morning the children loaded me with wild flowers, primroses, violets and cuckoo flowers. . . .

After dinner Mr Venables told me that I must write next week to the Bishop to give notice that I mean to resign the curacy of Clyro on July 1. He asked me what I should do if the living of Clyro were offered to me. 'I should refuse it,' I said. 'Then you would be mad,' he said. But I don't want the living of Clyro, I don't want to be vicar of Clyro.

Tuesday, 19 March

I called on my old friend Richard Meredith of Colva, the land measurer, who lives in Bridge St, just above Hay Bridge. I used to go there and talk to him very often but I have not been now for a long time. He seemed very glad to see me, for he was much exercised in his mind as to the errors and heresy of the Nicolaitans and as to what Hymenœus and Philetus meant by the Resurrection being already past. I am ashamed to say that I knew as little as he did, and cared to know less, but I promised to try to find out for him and tell him next time I called. Richard Meredith is a great philosopher, the greatest philosopher I know.

Wednesday, 20 March

By the great oak of Cross Foot and the green lane to Cwmpelved Green, where the idiot girl Phoebe sat laughing by the fire while her grandfather was groaning in bed and a black cat rushed in and out through a broken window pane, through which also the keen E. wind rushed in upon my head.

Saturday, 23 March

I had a long talk with Mrs Venables this morning about my prospects. Pointing to a letter on the mantelpiece she said smiling, 'From your father-in-law'. She thinks I am quite right in wishing to decline the living of Clyro if it is offered to me. I devoutly hope it will not be. She says what is quite true, that I could scarcely keep the poor old vicarage in repair. Carpenters and masons are almost always there now to prevent its falling down.

Palm Sunday, 24 March

A snowy Palm Sunday. Snow on the Palms. Mr Venables went to Bettws in a dense snowstorm. In the afternoon I had the happiness to have all the poor people to myself. None of the grand people were at Church by reason of the snow. So of course I could speak much better and more freely.

After service I went up to the Bird's Nest to see old Meredith.

Further up I stopped and turned to look at the view. I saw what I thought was a long dazzling white and golden cloud up in the sky. Suddenly I found that I had been gazing at the great snow slopes of the Black Mountain lit up by the setting sun and looking through the dark storm clouds. It was a sublime spectacle, the long white rampart dazzling in its brilliancy and warmed by a golden tinge standing high up above the clear dark line of the nearer hills taking the sunshine, and bathed in glory. Then in the silence the Hay Church bell for evensong boomed suddenly out across the valley.

Tuesday, 26 March

This morning when the sun rose the trees were still laden thick with snow, but gradually the fairy forest all melted away.

To-day I wrote to the Bishop of St David's to give notice that I intend to resign the Curacy of Clyro on the 1st of July next, 'when' (I added by Mr Venables' advice, but against my own wish) 'I shall have been a licensed curate in the same parish in your Lordship's diocese for seven years and a half.'

I went up to the Homme by New Barn. The New Barn meadows are fearfully cut up by the timber carriages which are hauling away the fallen giants, ash and beech. The shouts of the timber haulers were ringing hollow and echoing through the wasted murdered dingle. My beautiful favourite Cwm is devastated and laid waste.

Good Friday, 29 March

I went down to the Chapel Dingle to see sweet Emma Griffiths and to give her a cross Bun I had brought up for her. There was a smile in her sweet sky-blue eyes as she came to the door, but her voice and manner were very sad and quiet and I soon found she was suffering from face-ache. She said she should so much have liked to come to Chapel but her child kept her at home. She was scarcely ever able to leave home and went nowhere and heard nothing. She could not go to Chapel to-day because her husband Evan was at work at Llwyn Gwillim. Emma told me she was married when she was between nineteen and twenty, nineteen and a half. 'Too early,' she said, 'too early,' with a sad shake of the fair young girlish head, wise by sad experience before its time, that sorrowful touching thing, a grey head on green shoulders. 'It was much too early,' she repeated. 'I've often been sorry since that I married so young. I have been at service ever since I was ten years old. I have not been in a sight of places. My first place was at Bron Ddu at Mr Williams'. One morning all the men were away and the two missises were in bed and I had to fetch the cows in to be milked. There was a bull with the cows. I left the bull in the field with one cow and brought the other cows on to the gate. I saw the bull coming after me. He had come after me before but he had never caught me. I saw him now coming on towards me through the cows. I tried to get through the gate, but the bull caught me and struck [me] down. I felt no pain then or afterwards though he had me down on the ground punishing me for half an hour. I know it was half an hour the bull had me for I had looked what time it was when I went out and they told me what time it was when I came into the house afterwards. No one came to help me

View from Clyro

or to drive the bull away. No one knew about it. He "punned" me with his head mostly, but he ran his horn into my side and into one of my legs. After he had knocked me about on the ground a long time he got me up and pushed me through a pleached hedge that had been newly tined. He did not come after me. Many folk wondered he didn't come through the hedge after me and kill me. When I came to myself and stumbled into the house I was bruised all over and covered with blood, almost naked, with my clothes torn nearly off me, and the doctor couldn't tell whether I had any eyes or not for they were quite closed up. I was half unconscious all the time the bull had me on the ground and I felt no pain, at the time. But I have never been so strong or well since. I have gatherings on my side and the bull hurt something within me. I was at home for three months but after I got well I went back to Bronddu and finished my time till the May Fair though my friends tried to persuade me not to. But I always finished my time if I could. I never liked to break my time. I was not afraid of other cattle after-wards, but I was afraid of that bull. He was a two year-old. Master fatted him and killed him.

'It was a great mercy the bull did not kill me, but my time was not come. The Lord was very merciful to me and saved me from him,' said the girl reverently and humbly. 'The Lord had something else for me to do.'

And this was one of the sorrowful and hard experiences in that her young life. A child between eleven and twelve years old.

We had some talk about Good Friday. She had forgotten why we kept the day holy. I read to her some hymns and Luke xxiii. When I came in she was trying, poor child, to spell out a word here and there in a hymn, trying to do the best she could for herself. She nearly made me cry by the touching way in which she said she was no scholar, she wished she could read, but she went to work so early, when she was only ten years old, that she never had any schooling except a little on Sundays at 'Llandewi's Church' where Mr Williams the Vicar used to hold a little school every Sunday before service.

When I rose to go we found I had been there more than an hour. 'The time hasn't seemed long to me. I feel so much light-ened. I am so much obliged to you for coming and reading to me,' said the poor girl gratefully, with a beautiful and touching smile and the tears standing in her eyes.

An election of a Guardian for the parish is coming on and the place is all in an uproar of excitement. Church versus Chapel and party feeling running very high. The dissenters are behav-ing badly.

Easter Eve, 30 March

At four o'clock the people were already moving about in the Churchyard with baskets of flowers, and the children were especially busy in flowering the graves. I found one little girl with her brothers flowering two little twin graves, the graves of their little sisters, and showed them how to make primrose crosses upon the turf. While I was in the Churchyard among the people it thundered heavily, and the air was warm and sultry.

Later in the evening heavy rain came on but still the people were coming to the churchyard with their baskets of flowers.

Easter Monday, April Day, All Fools' Day, 1872

I dined at Wye Cliff with the Crichtons. They were alone and the evening was exceedingly pleasant.

Crichton said when he lived at Boughrood Castle with his uncle Mr Clutterbuck, old Boughrood Church was a most miserable place. The choir sat upon the altar and played a drum.

Friday, 5 April

I dined at the Vicarage at 6.30 and went with the Venables to the ball at Clifford Priory at 8. We stopped at Hay Castle to pick up Fanny and Willie Bevan. There were 52 people at the party. . . .

We danced in the drawing room and all sat down together to supper in the dining room. After supper about midnight that endless Cotillon was danced, but there was plenty of dancing afterwards.

Daisy promised to dance the 5th dance – a quadrille – with me and gave me her card and pencil to write her name.

Morrell and Miss Child were vis-a-vis to us, but I am afraid we did them out of their fair share of dancing, for Daisy and I were soon absorbed in conversation and each other – I at all events was absorbed in her – and became quite oblivious of the figure and the whole thing.

'You never come to Clyro,' I said, 'and it is such a pretty place.'

'Talking of flowers,' I said, 'do you remember once last September giving me some flowers out of your own garden?' 'Yes,' she said blushing prettily and looking down.

'I have those flowers now,' I said, 'I have kept them carefully ever since, and I prize them more than I can tell you.' 'I am sure,' she said, 'they can't be worth keeping now. They must be withered long ago.' 'No,' I said, 'I kept them in water a long time and then I dried them, and they are as sweet as ever, especially the mignonette. I shall keep them until you give me some more.' She blushed and smiled and I don't think she was displeased. I ought not to have said so much, but I could not help it. She was so pretty and sweet and kind and she made such gentle and kind allowance for my awkwardness and mistakes in dancing, and I did love her so.

She was dressed in white almost entirely, with a faint sweet suspicion of blue, a white flower in her bright hair and a quantity of dainty frilling and puffing almost hiding her fair shoulders. I thought I had never seen her look prettier.

When the quadrille was over – much too soon – she took my arm and we went out into the cool hall. I found her a comfortable chair screened from general observation by a beautiful azalea. She sat down and we began to talk again. But alas, 'the course of true love never did run smooth'. We had not been talking long, when our seclusion was broken in upon and our happiness marred – at least mine was – by hearing her father's voice behind us. As soon as she heard his voice she rose, I thought in a slight and pretty confusion. Then he called to her to know if she were engaged for the next dance, and I saw she was obliged to go. So we went back together to the ball room and I scarcely saw her to speak to her again the whole evening, except once in the gallery when we were drinking claret cup and we had a few words together about the Wen Allt. I should have dearly liked to ask her to dance again, but I was afraid of getting her into a scrape and attracting people's attention, and she was much too kind to refuse if she were not engaged, and much too honest to pretend to be engaged when she was not. . . .

I was quite prepared to walk home, but at the last moment it appeared there was room in Crichton's omnibus so we went home all together, a merry noisy party. Crichton and his friend Mr Lucas, a Ch. Ch.* man, the heir of Sir Harford Brydges and Colonel Scudamore, Morrell, Willie Bevan and myself. When I got out to knock up the man at the turnpike gate going into Hay, the gate was icy with rime and the night was very cold. 'It isn't late, is it?' I said to the turnpike keeper. 'No,' he said in a meaning voice, 'it's early.' It was about 3.30.

*Christchurch College, Oxford.

From Wye Cliff gate Morrell and I walked home. I got to bed at 4.30 just as dawn was breaking.

Saturday, 6 April

To-day I feel good for nothing, from the reaction after the excitement of the ball last night and seeing Daisy. All the old feelings of last September have revived again as keenly, as vividly, as ever. The old wounds are all open and bleeding again and I can rest nowhere in my misery.

In the afternoon I went to the Vicarage. Mrs Venables seeing in a moment what I wanted – God bless her – came out into the garden with me and sitting under the great double-headed fir tree we talked over the evening of yesterday with reference to Daisy and myself. She told me I owed it to myself to speak to her father again before I left the country, and get something settled. But my position is no better now than it was 6 months ago and I cannot humiliate myself before him again for nothing. I don't know what to do. Mrs Venables asked me if I saw any one I liked better should I still consider myself bound in honour to Daisy.'Yes,' I said, 'but I don't think I shall ever see any one I like better. I daresay I shall never marry, but if I do marry I shall marry her.'

Sunday, 7 April

Colonel Pearson has been fishing for the last week in the Llysdinam water. He lost one salmon of 30 lbs, but he brought down with him to Clyro yesterday an excellent 15 lb fish, part of which we had for dinner to-day. . . .

Colonel Pearson gave us some of his Crimean reminiscences. Most of the English officers could speak French. Hardly one of the French officers could speak English. The Russian officers could speak both French and English fluently. Colonel Pearson was on Sir George Brown's staff. The old General was not much of a linguist and knew but little French. One night an Aide de Camp came from Marshal Canrobert with a message about an attack that was to be made or expected in the morning. The

French officer was grinning, bowing, scraping, grimacing and gesticulating. Sir George could not understand a word. He used some strong language and turned to Colonel Pearson. 'What does he say, Master Dick? Give him a glass of sherry and tell him to go away.' *Tell him to go away!* As if he had been an organ-grinder! 'And,' said Colonel Pearson with an expressive shrug, 'perhaps next morning a hundred lives might depend upon that message.'

Wednesday, 10 April

Immediately after breakfast I hurried up to Cross Foot to consult Mrs Watkins about her father, old Price, who is lying ill in his wretched hovel in a most filthy state of dirt and vermin with no one to look after him. She promised to do what she could but said her husband, old Watkins, would not have her father to stay in his house, where she might see to him, nor would he permit her to give her father anything if he knew of it.

Friday, 12 April

In the hot unclouded afternoon I went slowly up the hill by Wern y Pentre and Sunnybank. I called at Crowther's Pool with a picture book about the pilgrim children for Selina. Charles was sitting at tea, having just come in from plough. His mother, the true old-fashioned tall dame with high cap and short petticoats, eagle face and nutcracker nose and chin, was moving about the cabin with a high staff and making pellets of food for the 'gulls'. The old patriarch of 90 sat in the huge dark chimney corner feeling rather unwell for the first time in his life. He is as upright as a larch and has never taken medicine.

The old man was very angry with William Jones, late brickmaker and tenant of the 'corner house' at Crowther's Pool, for 'tarring' (i.e. quarrelling) with the Squire (Hodgson of Cabalva). 'What good is it for a poor man to "tarr" with a gentleman?' he asked scornfully. 'Let him "tar" with some poor mean fellow like himself, not with gentlemen.'

The mountains flushed red and purple, then faded into dark cold clear blue. The clerk who was like everyone else working in his garden this beautiful evening said he feared thunder.

When I went to bed there was a splendid sight. The great service was going on in the North. The crescent was setting in brilliant splendour up the dingle and all the stars were standing still in their courses, to watch the sight. They seemed like hand-maidens waiting on their mistress as she retired to rest.

Saturday, 13 April

I woke early and looked out. The sight was too magnificent to be described. There was not a cloud in the sky. Night was still in the dark West, but all the Eastern horizon was brilliant with light and colour – crimson, orange and yellow bands gradually shading into each other and melting into the splendid blue. It was half past four o'clock. The sun was coming up rapidly and the air was full of the singing of birds. The time of the singing of birds had come. The windows were slightly stained with frost. Not a soul was yet stirring in the village and all was quiet.

I went to see old Price who is in a miserable state and it is almost impossible to get any woman to look to him even for a day. That miser, curmudgeon and villain and beast, Watkins of Cross Foot, his son-in-law, has left him to his fate and will not let his wife come near her father or help him in any way. The Lord reward him according to his works.

The poor old man was lying alone this afternoon parched with thirst. 'I'm very droughty,' he murmured feebly. I went home and got him some brandy and water and gave it him. His gratitude for the little attention was very touching. 'I hope,' said the old man solemnly, 'you will be remembered in heaven.'

The two old women Hannah Jones and Sarah Probert were both lying in bed and groaning horribly. I gave them some money and their cries and groans suddenly ceased.

A man at work with his team in the Cwm was singing Auld Lang Syne.

Sunday, 14 April

The beauty of the view, the first view of the village, coming down by the Brooms this evening was indescribable. The brilliant golden poplar spires shone in the evening light like flames against the dark hill side of the Old Forest and the blossoming fruit trees, the torch trees of Paradise blazed with a transparent green and white lustre up the dingle in the setting sunlight. The village is in a blaze of fruit blossom. Clyro is at its loveliest. What more can be said?

Monday, 15 April

Westhorp was waiting for me at Killay Station with his pretty new waggonette and drove me to Ilston.

[*On 15 April he goes to stay with his friends the Westhorps at Ilston, and returns by train on April 20.*]

Saturday, 20 April

A business man named Small from Swansea travelled with us. He told us that when Matthew Richards was elected member for Merthyr the dissenting voters were brought down in cart-loads and before they went to the poll they were driven like sheep to the chapels and preached to for half an hour. The burden of the addresses was always simply this, 'You'll all go to hell if you don't vote for Matthew Richards'. Talk of being priest-ridden, 'tis nothing to being ridden by political dissenting preachers.

Sunday, 21 April

Preached on the story of Balaam extempore this afternoon from Numbers xxii, 22 and made a miserable exhibition, very nearly breaking down. The Church was almost empty and when I looked along the waste of empty pews and saw two or three

The house where Kilvert lodged in Clyro

people at the end of the Church and the two Mrs Venables sitting directly below there was no more spirit left in me. The thing was a failure.

I hear that Houseman* at Bredwardine wishing to drape the Communion table with black on Good Friday and having no black drapery suitable for the purpose was misguided enough to put over the Table the old filthy parish pall. Everyone was disgusted and shocked at what they considered a piece of indecency. It is the talk of the country and Miss Newton is up in arms.

Monday, 22 April

Held a consultation with Mrs Venables about my love affairs, plans and prospects. I see how it will all end. Alas, who could have believed that I could be such a villain?

*Houseman was vicar of Bredwardine.

> *Alas for the breaking of love*
> *And the lights have died out in the West,*
> *And, oh, for the wings of a dove,*
> *And, oh, for the haven of rest.*

Wednesday, 24 April

I went up the Cwm this afternoon. The road was cut to pieces by the ponderous timber carriages dragging timber down from the Cwm dingle, and old James Jones the stone breaker was in despair. The dingle resounds with rattling of chains, holloing, cracking of whips, cutting and slashing, and the poor horses plunge and struggle, often going down upon their knees in their frantic struggles, almost tearing their hearts out.

I went to Fairlands to see the sick blacksmith Bayliss. He said his son the wantcatcher was very good to him. There were 5 dozen of prepared moleskins hanging up to the cratch, to make somebody a waistcoat.

Wednesday, May Day

I stayed to dinner* and Armine and Helen played very nicely. The night was cool and pleasant as I walked home under the stars. About midnight I passed over the Rhydspence border brook, and crossed the border from England into Wales. The English inn was still ablaze with light and noisy with the songs of revellers, but the Welsh inn was dark and still.

Holy Thursday, 9 May

Visited old Price as usual. He was lying on his bed which has been moved downstairs. He invited me to sit down. I was afraid to because of the lice. I read to him Psalms cxxi and cxxx. . . .

On my favourite green sloping bank above the road between the Lower House and the Bronith, there grew a luxuriant green

*At Whitney Rectory.

hawthorn covered with the white buds of the May blossoms, and looking as if the tree were hung with pearls. A gin fastened to a post by a chain had been set on the top of the post to catch some marauding bird. It had caught a poor blackbird by both legs between its cruel teeth. The bird in its struggles must have dragged the gin off the top of the post and there hung 'the ouzel cock so black of hue with orange tawny bill', the poor ouzel cock silent for ever, quite dead, the blue film over his bright dark eye and his orange tawny bill closed never to open again. He had not I think been dead long. And what a death, the slow agonies of hunger amid the agonies of two crushed and broken legs. I felt sick and sorrowful as I went on. 'The whole creation groaneth and travaileth in pain together until now.' Somehow the suffering creature reminded me of the Saviour upon the Cross. I felt as if some sin of mine had brought him there.

Friday, 10 May

Luncheon tête à tête with Mrs Venables and afterwards I walked with her up the Cwm.

The dingle was full of timber fellers and women peeling bark, the ringing of axes, shouts of the men and rattling of chains as the horses dragged the trees up the steep dingle side. The rain storm had made the parched and trampled ground very greasy and slippery and the horses could hardly stand. Every now and then they came to a dead stop. They could scarcely keep their feet and one horse went down head over heels on his side. In a moment however he was up again, struggling, tearing and plunging away a great tree which was slowly coming up the dingle side till the end of it struck irretrievably in the bank.

Above Pentwyn old James Jones the sawyer was breaking stones. We fell into discourse. He said the ground ivy or Robin-run-in-the-hedge is called Hay Maids in Herefordshire. 'That's hemlock,' said he severely, taking the white blossom from me. 'That's poison for Christians'. He said wild garlic, called Jack-in-the-Bush, is a famous pot herb. The old man's work was done, he put up his tools, took me home with him, and lent me Culpeper's *Herbal*.

Saturday, 11 May

This is the bitterest bleakest May I ever saw and I have seen some bad ones. May is usually the worst and coldest month in the year, but this beats them all and out-herods Herod. A black bitter wind violent and piercing drove from the East with showers of snow. The mountains and Clyro Hill and Cusop Hill were quite white with snow. The hawthorn bushes are white with may and snow at the same time.

Late in the afternoon walking from the Lower House to the Bronith I met Morrell returning from fishing his water at Cabalva. His keeper Whitcombe was carrying with justifiable pride a beautiful 9½ lbs salmon, the first he has killed. Morrell asked me to dine with him and we discussed part of the salmon which was delicious, a bottle of port, and some fine strawberries from Cabalva as well flavoured as if they had been ripened out of doors.

Saturday, 18 May

Hay Fair still going on. To get out of sight and sound of it I went up the unfrequented path from Penllan to the Wern below Gwernfydden to look for bog beans to give to Mrs Venables on Whitsun Day. The marshy ground was thick with the trefoil bean leaves, but not a blossom had yet opened. I found a gate beside a sheltered hedge, in a sunny nook convenient for reading, and returning to the village I climbed Penllan again with that charming book *Lettice Lisle** and established myself in my sunny corner on the gate sheltered from the East wind by the high green hedge and secure from intrusion on a path that led to nowhere and therefore sacred from the folks returning from the fair. It was a quiet peaceful beautiful place. There was no sound to be heard but the singing of the birds, and nothing to be seen but the blue mountains rising over the sunny golden green oaks of Penllan Wood and the blue sky above all. No living thing seemed to be moving except a rising lark and a small blue butterfly which fluttered along the sunny side of the hedge. Presently

*By Frances Parthenope, Lady Verney, a sister of Florence Nightingale.

as I sat perfectly still upon the gate reading I heard a sharp little rustling in the hedge close by me as if some small fourfooted animal were bustling busily about. In a minute or two afterwards came out of the bank on to the open path before the gate a beautiful little creature coloured a deep rich chestnut red except its throat and belly which were pure white. It carried in its mouth a mouse or a young rat. Apparently it did not see me. At all events he took no notice and was not the least startled. He passed under the gate carrying the mouse and went into the hedge on the opposite side of the path. But he did not seem to know what to do with the mouse and soon came out again, still carrying it in his mouth. I made a slight noise on purpose and the weasel dropped his prey on the path and retreated into the hedge. I got down off the gate, picked up the mouse and placed it a few feet further off in front of the gate and then resumed my seat to watch the result. The weasel was not at all abashed. He came to the mouth of the hole in the hedge, rested his little forepaws upon a bit of stick, stood up, and looked round him with his quick brilliant watchful eyes to see what had become of his mouse. Then the beautiful slender creature came out upon the path and began darting about like lightning trying to discover his prey by scent. I never saw any living thing move with such extraordinary swiftness.

The mouse was only 3 or 4 feet from him, but the weasel could not see it, and as I had lifted the mouse from the ground he could not follow it along the earth by scent. So he was completely at fault. He must have been extraordinarily blind or shortsighted. After darting about on the path close by the gate for a few minutes the weasel gave up the search and went back into the original hedge to hunt another mouse and I heard him bustling about in the bank for some time after.

Whitsun Monday, 20 May

To-day I came to Langley.

[*He stays in Langley (and London) until 31 May. During this period he hears from Mr Venables.*]

Thursday, 23 May

This evening I had a letter from Mr Venables written yesterday (his birthday when he was 63) saying that he had decided not to resign the living of Clyro till the end of 1872, and offering me £160 a year to stay on. I decided to keep to my former plan and to leave Clyro at the beginning of August.

Friday, June Eve

Left Langley for Clyro for the last time, and for the last time 'I went back to my lodgings'. To-day is Minna Venables' birthday and I went back to Clyro on purpose to celebrate it.

Flags were flying at Clyro School and children were swarming in and out like bees. Over the school gate the schoolmaster and mistress had made a pretty triumphal arch of greenery and flowers with 'Long live Miss Venables'. As we dashed up to the Vicarage door the bells pealed out. They had been ringing since early morning and the ringers had dined at the Vicarage. The blacksmiths also had been firing anvil cannons since 5.30 a.m.

The children had their tea on the lawn between 5 and 6 o'clock and then went to play on the Lower Bron.

It seemed as if the night would never get dark and we could not begin the fireworks till nearly ten. They were the first fireworks ever seen in Clyro and the village and the Bron were swarming with people.

Saturday, June Day

I went up to the Wern below Gwernfydden this afternoon to see if the bog beans were yet in flower. Since I looked for them a fortnight ago to-day and found none they have come and almost gone. But I found a few here and there standing with their feet in the water and with their delicate lace-like flowers shining like stars about the swamp.

I think it is one of the loveliest flowers that grows, the exquisite fret and filigree work of the white lace blossom surrounded by the cluster of bright pink buds.

A pheasant whirred up from the swamp out of a clump of rushes, and in the dingle orchard above the Cwm the yaffingale was laughing loud.

Monday, 3 June

A letter from my Father asking if I should be very much surprised to see him walk in to-day. . . . at 1.30 the omnibus and my Father drove up to the door. He went out fishing at Cabalva immediately.

Tuesday, 4 June

The news of my leaving Clyro is spreading through the village. These people will break my heart with their affectionate lamentations.

Wednesday, 5 June

Rode Mr Venables' pony to Bredwardine and called on the Housemans. At luncheon there was Mr Williams, Vicar of Bridge Sollars. When I saw him in the garden at first I took him for a beggar.

The Vicarage lawn is very pretty, gay with flower beds terraced steeply sloping down to the Wye, and a river reach and Bredwardine Bridge are seen through the boughs of a cedar. The kitchen garden lies across the river and for every herb wanted in the kitchen the cook has to send round over Bredwardine Bridge half a mile.

Saturday, 8 June

A pouring wet morning. Nevertheless my Father and I started in the rain for the Vale of Arrow, he riding the Vicarage pony sheltered by two mackintoshes and an umbrella and I on foot with an umbrella only. The weather looked desperate. The sky lowered heavily without a break. But we plodded on doggedly through the wet for 6 miles, casting wistful glances at all the quarters of the heavens to catch any gleam of hope. Hope however there seemed to be none. The rain fell pitilessly.

The Harbour below us in the Vale of Arrow was a welcome sight, a haven of refuge.

In spite of the wild weather on the open mountain we could not help noticing the beautiful effect produced upon the steep slopes by the vast sheets of brilliantly green young fern spreading amongst the old black heather. The mountain ashes were still in full blossom in the Fuallt fold and the meadows round the old farm house and the graceful trees were covered with the bunches of white bloom.

We reached the Harbour more like drowned rats than clergymen of the Established Church.

The boy took the pony to the stable and Mrs Jones came to the door. And now here is a fine specimen of Radnorshire manners. She was in her working dress and in the midst of her Saturday cleaning but quite unconscious of herself and her dress she simply and naturally came forward at once and welcomed us to the Harbour with her grand courteous manner as if she had been a queen in disguise or in full purple and ermine. Then at the time when the work was done the mistress of the house took her place at the head of her table with all the natural grace and simple quiet dignity of a woman in the best society.

Mrs Irwine came down and Watkeys Jones, the master of the house, appeared like a wounded soldier with his head bound up in a red handkerchief.

The good people were most kind to us, providing us with dry coats, hats and leggings and hot brandy and water and when the rain had a little abated we went down to the little river to fish under the guidance of the master of the house. The stream was too muddy for the fly and too clear for the worm. But the water was rising fast. We crossed a swampy meadow to the Glasnant above the meeting of the waters, a little stream flowing swiftly under alders. Then we followed the Glasnant down to its meeting with the Arrow. Some willows grew here and there was a likely hole with deep smooth still water under a bush sheltered by a sudden curve in the bank. Out came two trout. From the next pool four trout came out fast one after another. 'Well done, well done!' cried the good farmer with delight, clapping my Father on the back, 'I've never seen better work than that.'

Sunday, 9 June

I went to see Mrs Prosser at the Swan, a young pretty woman dying I fear of consumption which she caught of her sister, Mrs Hope of the Rose and Crown in Hay. It was a sad beautiful story. She was warned not to sleep with her sister who was dying of decline and told that if she did she herself would probably be infected with the disease. But her sister begged her so hard not to leave her and to go on sleeping with her that she gave way. 'What could I do?' she said. 'She was my only sister and we loved each other so.'

'I have been married seven years,' she said, 'and now my first child has just come, a little girl, and it does seem so hard to go away and leave her. But if it is the Lord's will to take me I must be content to go. My left lung is quite gone,' she said looking at me with her lip trembling and her beautiful eyes full of tears.

'Mrs De Winton came and broke it to me that I never could get better and she put it to me in this way, "Wouldn't I like to go and be with my dear sister again?" Mrs De Winton has been like a mother to me, but I should like to live a little longer if I might now for the sake of the child.'

Margaret Griffith, speaking of Mrs John Vaughan of Llwyn Gwillim, who has just been confined with her fourth child, said, 'Mrs Vaughan will have a good family soon. Her children come fast. But the harder the storm the sooner 'tis over. Every one will have her number.' She described how she had washed and cleaned Old Price and how she had 'combed out of his head a score platefuls of 'bocs' (lice).

[*On 17 June he goes to stay with his friends in Bockleton Vicarage, and then spends three days in Liverpool.*]

Wednesday, 19 June

Left Bockleton Vicarage for Liverpool. . . .

At Wrexham two merry saucy Irish hawking girls got into our carriage. The younger had a handsome saucy daring face showing splendid white teeth when she laughed and beautiful Irish eyes of dark grey which looked sometimes black and sometimes blue, with long silky black lashes and finely pencilled black eyebrows. This girl kept her companion and the whole carriage laughing from Wrexham to Chester with her merriment, laughter and songs and her antics with a doll dressed like a boy, which she made dance in the air by pulling a string. She had a magnificent voice and sung to a comic popular air while the doll danced wildly,

> *A-dressed in his Dolly Varden,*
> *A-dressed in his Dolly Varden,*
> *He looks so neat*
> *And he smells so sweet,*
> *A-dressed in his Dolly Varden.*

Then breaking down into merry laughter she hid her face and glanced roguishly at me from behind the doll.

Suddenly she became quiet and pensive and her face grew grave and sad as she sang a love song. And then up went the doll dancing furiously again and the Dolly Varden song accompanying his antics while the girl's white teeth laughed as she sung and her merry grey eyes sparkled as she watched the doll's gambols with her pretty head on one side amidst the inextinguishable laughter of the company. The tower of Chester Cathedral came in sight. 'Now we are in Cheshire,' exclaimed Irish Mary. 'Excuse me, my dear,' said the elder girl politely, 'you are in Flintshire yet. There's the river and the bridge and there's the Roodee.'

The two girls left the carriage at Chester and as she passed the younger put out her hand and shook hands with me. They stood by the carriage door on the platform for a few moments and Irish Mary, the younger girl, asked me to buy some nuts. I gave her sixpence and took a dozen nuts out of a full measure she was going to pour into my hands. She seemed surprized and looked up with a smile. 'You'll come and see me,' she said coaxingly. 'You are not Welsh are you?' 'No, we are a mixture of Irish and

English.' 'Born in Ireland?' 'No, I was born at Huddersfield in Yorkshire.' 'You look Irish – you have the Irish eye.' She laughed and blushed and hid her face. 'What do you think I am?' asked the elder girl, 'do you think I am Spanish?' 'No,' interrupted the other laughing, 'you have too much Irish between your eyes.' 'My eyes are blue,' said the elder girl, 'your eyes are grey, the gentleman's eyes are black.' 'Where did you get in?' I asked Irish Mary. 'At Wrexham,' she said. 'We were caught in the rain, walked a long way in it and got wet through,' said the poor girl pointing to a bundle of wet clothes they were carrying and which they had changed for dry ones. 'What do you do?' 'We go out hawking,' said the girl in a low voice. 'You have a beautiful voice.' 'Hasn't she?' interrupted the elder girl eagerly and delightedly. 'Where did you learn to sing?' She smiled and blushed and hid her face. A porter and some other people were looking wonderingly on, so I thought it best to end the conversation. But there was an attractive power about this poor Irish girl that fascinated me strangely. I felt irresistibly drawn to her. The singular beauty of her eyes, a beauty of deep sadness, a wistful sorrowful imploring look, her swift rich humour, her sudden gravity and sadnesses, her brilliant laughter, a certain intensity and power and richness of life and the extraordinary sweetness, softness and beauty of her voice in singing and talking gave her a power over me which I could not understand nor describe, but the power of a stronger over a weaker will and nature. She lingered about the carriage door. Her look grew more wistful, beautiful, imploring. Our eyes met again and again. Her eyes grew more and more beautiful. My eyes were fixed and riveted on hers. A few minutes more and I know not what might have happened. A wild reckless feeling came over me. Shall I leave all and follow her? No – Yes – No. At that moment the train moved on. She was left behind. Goodbye, sweet Irish Mary. So we parted. Shall we meet again? Yes – No – Yes.

[*He stays in Liverpool for three days.*]

Saturday, 22 June

When I reached Clyro about 5 o'clock I found on my table a red leather case containing a beautiful gold watch and chain with two most kind letters from Mr and Mrs Venables saying in the nicest way that the watch was from him, the chain from her, and the little chain supporting the Braquet Key from the baby. Alas, Alas, how utterly undeserved at all and on this day of all others. I went immediately to the Vicarage to thank them as well as I could, for my heart was full.

They were going out for a walk along the Llowes road, so I joined them and dined with them afterwards.

Monday, Midsummer Day

The cuckoo was still singing this morning. As I was getting up I heard the drone of the Italian bagpipes advancing and two men with dancing children, poor little wretches, came playing through the village.

In the afternoon Tom Williams came and carried me off to Llowes to dine with him.

At dinner he told the following story. A soldier who did not want to go to church told his officer that he was neither Catholic nor Protestant, Church of England nor Presbyterian, nor Dissenter. The officer asked what he did belong to. The soldier said he belonged to the Yarmouth Bloaters. He meant the Plymouth Brethren.

Thursday, 27 June

Mrs Baskerville sent me a kind letter this evening saying that she and her daughters wished me to carry away some remembrance of them and begging me to take my choice of an oaken stationery cabinet, a large musical box, a time piece or a fitted travelling bag, or to mention anything else that I liked better.

Friday, 28 June

I promised Mr Venables in answer to his request that I would

stay here through August till September 1st inclusive and go
home for July if my Father wants me. I hope this will be the last
of the many changes and postponements that have been made
in our plans. Anyhow I must give up the seaside this year and I
fear Dora will be away at Hawkchurch all July. Going down the
village I fell in with old James Jones the sawyer. 'I hear you are
going away,' he said in a broken trembling voice. And he walked
down the village with me weeping as he went.

Saturday, 29 June

Called at Hay Castle and went with the four pretty girl archers
to shoot and pick up their arrows in the field opposite the
Castle.

This evening I went out visiting the village people. The sinking sun shone along the Churchyard and threw long shadows of
the Church and the tombstones over the high waving grass. All
round the lychgate and the churchyard wall the tall purple
mallows are in flower and the banks and hedges about the
village are full of them. Old Hannah Whitney was sitting in her
cottage door at work as usual with her high cap and her little
red shawl pinned over her breast, her thin grey-bearded nutcracker face bent earnestly upon her knitting till she glanced
sharply up over her spectacles to see who it was that was passing.

Wednesday, 3 July

Tom Williams of Llowes and I had long been talking of going
up to Llanbedr Hill to pay a visit to the eccentric solitary, the
Vicar, and we arranged to go this morning. The day promised
to be fine and after school at 10.30 I walked over to Llowes.
When the postman, who followed me closely, had arrived we
started up a steep stony narrow lane so overgrown and over-
arched with wild roses that it was difficult for a horseman to
pass, but a lane most beautiful and picturesque with its wild
luxuriant growth of fern and wild roses and foxgloves. The
foxgloves were wonderful. They grew on both sides of the lane,
multitudes, multitudes in long and deep array.

Tom Williams was on horseback, I on foot. As we mounted

the hill, beautiful views of mountains and valley opened gleaming behind us, and Tom Williams pointed out to me some of the Llowes farmhouses scattered over the hills. The road seemed deserted as we went on our pilgrimage. All the folk were busy in their hay fields. Here and there my fellow pilgrim from his point of vantage in the saddle spoke to a labourer or small farmer over the hedge.

As we went up the steep hill to Painscastle the huge green Castle mound towered above us. A carpenter came down the hill from the village. I asked him where the grave of Tom Tobacco lay upon the moor, but he shook his head. He did not know.

In the village, a Post office had been established since I was last here and the village well, the only one, which was formerly common and open to ducks and cattle had been neatly walled and railed round. We went to Pendre, the house of the Mayor of Painscastle, but the Mayor was not at home.

At last Mr Price the Mayor was discovered in the centre of a group of village politicians before the alehouse door where

While village statesmen talked with looks profound
The weekly paper with their ale went round.

Tom Williams talked to the Mayor about quarrying stone for the Painscastle school while the blacksmith leaned over the wall taking part in the conversation and the rest of the village statesmen lounged in the inn porch. The Mayor came up with us on to Llanbedr Hill to show us the best quarry.

He said Painscastle was an old broken borough, one of the Radnorshire boroughs, and they still went through the form of electing one of the chief men of the village as Mayor. Sometimes the office ran in one family for some time. Williams asked the Mayor if he had any power. 'No,' answered that dignity, 'I dinna think I have much power.' We stopped to look at the stone of the ruined village pound. With a touch of dry humour the Mayor told us that at the last Court Leet the village authorities and tenants of the Manor had made a present to the Lord of the Manor (Mr de Winton) of the pound, the stop gate and the village well, that he might keep them in repair.

Hay Castle

Pointing to one of his fields, whose boundary had lately been moved and enlarged, he said with a merry twinkle in his eye, 'Because the Lord had not land enough before I have taken in a bit more for him off the waste'. The Mayor said there was a small school kept near Llanbedr Church by an old man, who taught the children well. 'But I do consait he do let them out too soon in the evening, he do,' said the Mayor disapprovingly.

The Mayor took us to the quarry and discoursed without enthusiasm and even with despondency on the badness of the roads, the difficulty of hauling the stone and the labour of 'ridding' the ground before the stone could be raised. After some talk at the quarry about ways and means, we parted, the Mayor returning to his mayoralty which had no emolument, no dignity, and no powers, he 'didna think', and we going on over the hill towards the abode of the hermit.

At length we came in sight of a little hollow, a recess in the hills at the foot of Llanbedr Hill, a little cwm running back into the mountain closed at the end and on both sides by the steep hill sides but open to the South, and the sun and the great valley of the Wye and the distant blue mountains. A sunny green little cwm it was, secluded deep among the steep green hills, and until you came close to it you would not be suspecting the existence of the place. A well-watered little cwm with sweet waters from the upper and lower springs which welled up through the turf and peat and fern and heathers, and joining their rills trickled away in a tiny stream down the cwm to form a brook.

In this green cwm stood a little grey hut. It was built of rough dry stone without mortar and the thatch was thin and broken. At one end of the cabin a little garden had been enclosed and fenced in from the waste. There was one other house in sight where the cwm lay open to the west, Pen common which used to belong to Price, the old keeper, who died lately in Clyro Village. Not a soul was stirring or in sight on the hill or in the valley, and the green cwm was perfectly silent and apparently deserted. As we turned the corner of the little grey hut and came in sight of the closed door we gave up all hope of seeing the Solitary and believed that our pilgrimage had been in vain. Then what was my relief when I knocked upon the door to hear a strange deep voice from within saying, 'Ho! Ho!' There was a slight stir within and then the cabin door opened and a strange figure came out. The figure of a man rather below the middle height, about 60 years of age, his head covered with a luxuriant growth of light brown or chestnut hair and his face made remarkable by a mild thoughtful melancholy blue eye and red moustache and white beard. The hermit was dressed in a seedy faded greasy suit of black, a dress coat and a large untidy white cravat, or a cravat that had once been white, lashed round his neck with a loose knot and flying ends. Upon his feet he wore broken low shoes and in his hand he carried a tall hat. There was something in the whole appearance of the Solitary singularly dilapidated and forlorn and he had a distant absent look and a preoccupied air as if the soul were entirely unconscious of the rags in which the body was clothed.

The Solitary came forward and greeted us with the most perfect courtesy and the natural simplicity of the highest breeding. 'And now,' he said thoughtfully, 'how shall we do? My landlord promised at 2 o'clock to meet me in an hour's time on the hill with a gambo* to bring home my mawn.' It was now 3 o'clock.

I asked if he would allow us to accompany him up to the mawn hill. 'Would you like it?' he said eagerly. 'Would you like it?' Then he went off with Williams to Pencommon to stable 'the mare' begging me to wait and sit down in his house till he returned. 'The house' was a sight when once seen never to be forgotten. I sat in amazement taking mental notes of the strangest interior I ever saw. Inside the hut there was a wild confusion of litter and rubbish almost choking and filling up all available space. The floor had once been of stone but was covered thick and deep with an accumulation of the dirt and peat dust of years. The furniture consisted of two wooden saddle-seated chairs polished smooth by the friction of continual sessions, and one of them without a back. A four-legged dressing table littered with broken bread and meat, crumbs, dirty knives and forks, glasses, plates, cups and saucers in squalid

*Gambo, a kind of sledge.

hugger-mugger confusion. No table cloth. No grate. The hearth foul with cold peat ashes, broken bricks and dust, under the great wide open chimney through which stole down a faint ghastly sickly light. In heaps and piles upon the floor were old books, large Bibles, commentaries, old fashioned religious disputations, C.M.S. Reports and odd books of all sorts, Luther on the Galatians, etc.

The floor was further encumbered with beams and logs of wood, flour pans covered over, and old chests.

All the other articles of food were hung up in pot hooks some from the ceiling, some in the chimney out of the way of the rats.

The squalor, the dirt, the dust, the foulness and wretchedness of the place were indescribable, almost inconceivable.

And in this cabin thus lives the Solitary of Llanbedr, the Rev. John Price, Master of Arts of Cambridge University and Vicar of Llanbedr Painscastle.

Presently I heard the voices returning from Pencommon where they had stabled 'the Mare' which was a horse. We had not gone many steps before Williams called the attention of the Solitary to a man with a horse and cart moving along the top of the hill high above us and standing out clear against the sky. 'It is my landlord,' said the Solitary. 'He is as good as his word.'

The hermit told us the name of his house was Cwm Ceilo, and that he had been much perplexed and exercised in mind about the meaning of the latter word. He was Welshman enough to know that there was no such word in Welsh as Ceilo. But in a dictionary which he took up one day in a farm house he found that the word 'Ceilio' meant a retreat or enclosure, or shelter or pen for cattle. 'And indeed', said the Solitary plaintively, 'when I first came to live here I did find that all the sheep and cattle took shelter in my garden as if they had always been used to retreat there, to that very place in a storm. So I called it "the Shepherd's Dingle".'

By this time we had reached the crest of the hill side which was almost as steep as the wall of a house and at a little distance we saw waiting a horse and gambo and a peasant whom the

Anchorite described as his landlord and addressed as 'Mr James'. On the whole the landlord was better dressed than his tenant. Some low conical heaps of peat turf were scattered about among the heather. They were large flat thin pieces skimmed off the surface with the heather upon them. The Solitary and his landlord and a little boy, the son of the landlord, began loading and piling the peats upon the gambo first removing the outer turves which had been thrown over the rest to keep them dry. I helped the hermit in loading his mawn while Tom Williams looked on with a benevolent smile.

When the gambo was loaded heavily enough for the steep descent the Solitary sent it down to the cabin of Cwm Ceilio in charge of his landlord while he walked further over the hill with us to show us the famous Rocks of Pen Cwm and Llanbychllyn Pool. Suddenly we came in sight of the pre-cipitous grey rocks which are so like the Rocks of Aberedw and which were the last haunt of the fairies, the last place where the little people were seen. Then there was a gleam of silver over the dark heather stems and Llanbychllyn Pool lay in its hollow like a silver shield. The view was beautiful and we all lay down upon the dry heather just budding into pink blossom to enjoy the fair and 'delicate prospect' in full view of the grey rocks and the silver lake. And the curlews called and the plovers whistled with their strange wild whistle about the sunny hill. The Solitary was infinitely pleased to learn that the grey rocks which looked at us across a cwm from the opposite hill side had been observed and admired by other people than himself. 'I said to myself', he observed, 'that those were very beautiful rocks.'

He told us that he had been very ill with internal inflam-mation, whether of liver or lungs he did not know. He had gone to Builth for some medicine which he thought he had chosen very judiciously, camomile pills, and he believed they had done him much good. It was touching to hear the Solitary man say rather mournfully and despondingly, 'And I thought I was as strong as ever again, but when I walked to Hay and back yesterday I found my mistake.'

To be ill and to grow old in that lone hut without a soul to care for him or to turn his head. How wretched a prospect for the poor Solitary.

It was touching too to find that in his loneliness the hermit had been employing his time in inventing without help or sympathy, and perfecting, two new systems of shorthand which he had published in Manchester and London. 'I said to myself,' he remarked, 'that I thought I might find out a new way.'

The Solitary told us that he had two little bounty farms in Llandeilo Graban. He kept a few fields in his own hands and occasionally went over the hill to see his land. The Anchorite and the Mayor of Painscastle had both heard of Tom Tobacco's grave, but neither knew the mysterious story of the lonely grave on the open hill, and only the Mayor could tell me the place of the grave, on the top of the ridge where Llanbedr Hill marches with the Hill of Llandeilo Graban.

When we came down from off the hill the Solitary compelled us to come into his hut again and sit down for a while. The gambo stood at the door with its load of mawn but the landlord and his horse and son were gone home. At our request the anchorite hunted among his piles of rubbish with a candlestick covered with the thick grease of years, trying unsuccessfully to find one of his shorthand pamphlets in print. But to give us an idea of his system he drew to the table a flour pan covered with a board, and sitting down on it he produced a pencil and a piece of paper and for our benefit wrote in shorthand the following verse which he had seen in a sampler lately in a farm house and which had taken his fancy:

A little health,
A little wealth,
A little house and freedom,
And at the end
A little friend
And little cause to need him.

This verse the Solitary wrote with extraordinary rapidity and conciseness. A dozen strokes and the thing was done. He said he had no opportunity of trying the new system of shorthand he had discovered except by writing his sermons in it.

Looking round his habitation it seemed suddenly to occur to

him that it was not just like other people's. 'I am afraid', he
said, 'that I am not very tidy to-day.' A little girl, he told us,
came to make his bed and tidy up, four days a week.

Going to a dark corner he routed out three wine glasses
which he washed carefully at the door. Then he rummaged out
a bottle of wine and drawing up his flour pan to the table and
taking his seat upon it he filled our glasses with some black
mixture which he called I suppose port and bade us drink.

The Solitary accompanied us to Pencommon to get the
horse and then showed us the way down the lanes towards the
Church. The people who met him touched their hats to his
reverence with great respect. They recognized him as a very
holy man and if the Solitary had lived a thousand years ago he
would have been revered as a hermit and perhaps canonized as
a Saint. At a gate leading into a lane we parted. There was a
resigned look in his quiet melancholy blue eyes. The last I saw
of him was that he was leaning on the gate looking after us.
Then I saw him no more. He had gone back I suppose to his
grey hut in the green cwm.

The evening became lovely with a heavenly loveliness. The
sinking sun shot along the green pastures with a vivid golden
light and striking through the hedges here and there tipped a
leaf or a foxglove head with a beam of brilliant green or purple.

Down the steep stony lane by the ruined Church of Llanbedr,
a team of horses came home to Llandeviron from plough with
rattling chains.

I crossed the Bach Wye by the short cut at Trewilad leaving
Williams to ride round the longer way by Rhyd Ilydan and to
cross the brook at the Broad Ford lower down. I stood upon
the stepping stones at Trewilad to watch the little herd of cows
undriven coming lazily through the brook home to Trewilad to
be milked. The water, darkly bright, came flowing down and
filling the cool shadowy lane, and the red and white cows
loitered slowly down to the brook, standing still often in the
shallow water as they forded the stream, and the air was full of
sunshine and the honey scent of the charlock, and the hedges
were luxuriant with the luscious sweetness of woodbine and the
beauty of the stars of the deep red rose.

Sunday, 7 July

Last night there was a fearful storm of thunder, lightning, rain and hail. All night the rain poured, not like rain, but as if streams of water were being emptied out of buckets. Once there was such a flash followed immediately by such a roar and crack of thunder that I feared the Church or one of the poplars had been struck. At 6 o'clock a.m. the Dulas was raging red and furious and I thought the bridge might be blown up, but the current is so swift and the fall so steep that the water escapes quickly without doing harm . . .

This afternoon at 5 o'clock there was the highest summer flood that there has been ʾfor exactly 19 years when Mrs Lawrence's house at Aberdihonnwy was washed away with herself, her daughter and her servant, all killed.

Monday, 8 July

Reports coming in all day of the mischief done by yesterday's flood. Pigs, sheep, calves swept away from meadow and cot and carried down the river with hundreds of tons of hay, timber, hurdles and, it is said, furniture. The roads swept bare to the very rock. Culverts choked and blown up, turnips washed out of the ground on the hillsides, down into the orchards and turnpike roads. Four inches of mud in the Rhydspence Inn on the Welsh side of the border, the Sun, Lower Cabalva House flooded again and the carpets out to dry. Pastures covered with grit and gravel and rendered useless and dangerous for cattle till after the next heavy rain.

Tuesday, 9 July

To-day I have been much moved. Just after we had finished lessons at the school at noon, the children deputed little Amy Evans the schoolmaster's daughter (of whom they know I am very fond) to present to me a little box in which I found a beautiful gold pencil case to hang at my watch chain. My own precious lambs. They had of their own will saved up their money to give me this costly and beautiful present. They would not go to the fair and spend the money upon themselves. It was all to be 'for Mr Kilvert'.

I tried to speak to tell them what I felt, but my heart was full. 'Please not to forget us,' said the children.

Dear children, there is no danger. I did not want this to help to keep you in mind.

Mrs Evans told me afterwards that some one asked little Polly Nash if she were not going to the fair. 'No,' said Polly scornfully, 'I'm going to do something better with it than that.' Someone gave the child sixpence. 'Now,' she said triumphantly, 'I shall have a shilling to give for him.'

Thursday, 11 July

Took 3 bottles of Attar of Rose to Clyro Court for the three Miss Baskervilles with a note addressed to Miss Baskerville.

'There is great mourning for you at Pen y cae,' said Mrs Harris. 'Why, do the children really care so much?' 'Ay, that day they gave you the pencil case the girl was crying and dazed all the evening. We could do nothing at all with her, and the boy is worse than her. "There'll be no one to come and teach us now," he says, "Mr Kilvert do come and tell us about all parts." ' I showed her the beautiful pencil case. But oh, Gipsy Lizzie dear, my own love, it doesn't make up to me for losing you.

Friday, 12 July

Rode the pony to Llan Thomas to wish Lechmere and Walter Thomas goodbye. They sail July 25 before I return from Langley. They were however both away at the Sheep Shearing feast of Abergwesyn.

Daisy gave me a rose.

Sunday, 13 July

Left Hay by the 8 o'clock train. Reached Langley at 3 o'clock.

Monday, 5 August

Left Langley and came to Clyro. Rain poured all day. I missed the mid-day train from Hereford to Hay as usual.

I dined at the Vicarage and received a present of a magnificent writing desk, which I am writing upon now, the most beautiful and perfect I ever saw, of coromandel wood bound with brass, fitted with polished mahogany and containing two most secret drawers.

Tuesday, 6 August

The Venables moved to Llysdinam this morning with Minna and Juno and all the servants but Mrs Pring, now Mrs Rogers, who will keep the Vicarage during the autumn and winter. This is Mrs Venables' last day in her old house, the house she came to when she was married. She will never return to it.

Thursday, 8 August

This afternoon Thomas Beavan of Bryn yr hydd came to call, and directly he was gone a servant came from Clyro Court with a magnificent present from the Baskervilles, a travelling bag beautifully fitted, accompanied by a most kind and cordial letter from Baskerville himself.

Then I went over to Gilfach yr rheol. It was perhaps my last journey over the Little Mountain to the sweet Vale of Newchurch and the dear village on the Arrow and Emmeline's grave. Seldom have I seen more lovely the beautiful hills and vales which I shall now see no more. I paid a last visit to the storm blown hawthorn on the mountain top, 'the little lonely tree', among the fern and carved upon the trunk about two feet from the ground a little cross on the Eastern side of the tree looking across Arrow Vale towards Kington.

At the dear old farm house Janet let me in with a radiant smile laying her soft round cheek against my hand fondly, and she and Matilda moved about the house in their black dresses preparing tea.

Presently the Vicar came in and we had tea in the sunny cheerful kitchen and a long talk. It was nearly 8 o'clock when I rose to go. It was hard to say good-bye to my kind friends. Mrs Vaughan thought of old times, in happy years ago, when Emmeline and David were with us, and burst into tears. Janet whispered shyly to her mother to ask for my picture. Then the dear child came to me to say Good-bye and put up her sweet mouth to be kissed. Tilly was gone down into the meadow to help the servant milk the cows. Dusk was falling and the evening air blew sweet and cool over the hills from the North west. The Good Vicar accompanied me over the Mountain to the gate into the lane, where we parted. I cut a cross in remembrance on the stem of one of the silver birches near the Great Cayan, the next tree but one to Newchurch.

Saturday, 10 August

This afternoon I went up the Old Forest road bidding the people Farewell. At the Well Cottage an old spinning wheel stood in the bow window, one of the few spinning wheels that are to be seen at work now.

Dear Sophy Ferris, the warm-hearted Carmarthenshire woman at the old Forest farmhouse, overwhelmed me with bitter lamentations at my departure. 'If gold would keep you with us,' she said, 'we would gather a weight of gold.' She asked me if I had received the present which the Court servants were going to give me, and said she should come down and see me off however early I might go. When I went away she said with tears in her voice, 'You will pray for me?' I will indeed. What have I done? What have I done? What am I that these people should so care for me? How little I have deserved it. Lord requite these people ten thousand fold into their bosom the kindness they have showed to the stranger.

Monday, 12 August

This morning came an envelope by post containing a Bank of England note for £5 and an anonymous line on a scrap of paper

'For the Rev. F. Kilvert's private use'. I don't know who sent it.

Emily and Jenny Dew gave me a most kind and beautiful present, *Wordsworth's Complete Works*.

Friday, 16 August

The stories about the baboon of Maesllwch Castle grow more and more extraordinary. It is said that when visitors come to the Castle the creature descends upon their heads, clambering down the balusters of the staircase. He put Baskerville and Apperley to flight, routed them horse and foot, so that they clapped spurs to their horses and galloped away in mortal fear, the baboon racing after them.

He carries the cats up to the top of the highest Castle Tower, and drops them over into space, and it is believed that the baboon seeks an opportunity to carry the young heir up to the top of the Tower and serve him in the same way.

Saturday, 17 August

Once more for the last time I skirted the dear old Common carrying a great bunch of the purple heather blossoms to take to Wye Cliff to-night for Mrs Crichton. The sun shone hot and bright down into the little valley among the hills, upon the wild white marsh cotton and the purple heather and the bright green Osmunda ferns with their brown flower spikes, and upon the white shirt sleeves of the peat cutters working amongst the mawn pits on a distant part of the Common. It is a bad mawn harvest this year in consequence of the wet summer and what with the dear coal and bread and meat and the diseased potatoes, I don't know what the poor people will do.

The hillsides were purple and glorious with heather as the sun sank low and the mountains and the valley were glowing blue and golden in the evening sunlight. Above Pen y llan a crowd of purple thistles stood in fatal and mischievous splendour among the waving oats.

Monday, 19 August

To-day I went to Llysdinam to spend a week.

Saturday, St Bartholomew's Day

This morning I left Llysdinam for Clyro with Mr Venables. As soon as we got to Clyro we were in the full swing of the School feast. My last in the dear old place. It all seemed very sad. And in the midst of the tea drinking on the Vicarage lawn the new curate Mr Irvine arrived in the omnibus from Hay. It gave me a bitter pang, but I went down to Mrs Chaloner's at once to see and welcome him. He preferred naturally remaining at home and not joining us, though he promised to dine at the Vicarage.

After the usual sport in the Cae Mawr Crichton sent up a most successful fire balloon which curiously enough went home again, descending in the garden at Wye Cliff, though to us watching its course from Cae Mawr the balloon seemed to have crossed the river and to have travelled at least as far as Llydyadyway.

After the balloon had gone up I received a hint to go to the school which immediately after was thronged with people gentle and simple. Wall the Churchwarden mounted the schoolmaster's desk platform and made an admirable speech presenting me in the name of the parishioners with a testimonial of a magnificent silver cup.

Then Holding, the butler at Clyro Court, came forward. He also made a very nice speech and gave me a beautiful inkstand from the servants and workmen at Clyro Court. I was deeply touched. I tried to say a few words, but my heart was full and I could not speak what I would.

Along with the inkstand was given me a short written address followed by the autograph signatures of the subscribers, and with the cup was presented a thin green leather book with my initials stamped in gold on the cover. On the title page Mrs Crichton had painted an exquisite picture of Clyro Church and School and illuminated an address after which came the as far as possible autograph signatures of the subscribers to the testimonial.

Sunday, 25 August

I read prayers in the morning. Irvine preached and Mr Venables sat in his pew.

Irvine and I walked to Bettws. It was my last visit to the dear old Chapel. Every tree and hill and hollow and glimpse of the mountains was precious to me, and I was walking with a stranger to whom it was nought, and who had no dear associations with the place.

I took the whole service and preached a farewell sermon from Philippians 1.3.

'The Prisoner of the Lord.'

'I thank my God upon every remembrance of you.'

It was for the last time. I could not help it. I burst into tears.

After Chapel I went to the Chapel Farm and Llwyn Gwilliam and to the Forge and sweet Emma of the Chapel Dingle to say Good-bye and then to Whitty's Mill, the dear old Mill, to see sweet dying Margaret.

It was a sad sad day.

Wednesday, 28 August

Dined at Hay Castle. Mrs Bevan and the girls gave me a splendid photograph album, and Cousie had painted me with kind and beautiful thoughtfulness a garland of heartsease encircling this text from Exodus xxxiii. 14:

'My Presence shall go with thee and I will give thee rest.'

My last evening at Hay, a home to me for nearly 8 years, and its inmates like brothers and sisters.

Good-bye and God bless and keep you all.

Thursday, 29 August

Hannah Jones told me yesterday that she lost a hen some time ago. It was stolen from her hen house at night by a woman.

They tracked her home in the morning by her footmarks in the snow. It was Jane Phillips who lives now at the Little Hendon.

I asked why Hannah did not prosecute the thief. 'She was an old neighbour,' said Hannah, 'and I would not persecute the carrion.'

Villaging.

Sunday, September Day

My last day at Clyro.

I read prayers in the morning and Irvine preached. Holy Communion. Irvine went to Chapel in the rain and would not put on leggings as I advised him. He came back wet and weary, saying there were a man, a woman and a boy in Chapel. In the afternoon I preached my farewell sermon at Clyro, the same that I preached at Bettws last Sunday. Though the afternoon was so rainy there were a good many people in Church. I don't know how I got through the service. It was the last time. My voice was broken and choked by sobs and tears, and I think the people in the Church were affected too. Richard Brooks in the choir was crying like a child.

The last round through the village in the evening.

'To-morrow to fresh woods and pastures new.'

Monday, September Morrow

Left Clyro for ever. A chapter of life closed and a leaf in the Book of Life turned over. The day I came to Clyro I remember fixing my eyes on a particular bough of an apple tree in the orchard opposite the school and the Vicarage and saying to myself that on the day I left Clyro I would look at that same branch.

I did look for it this morning but I could not recognize it. All the dear people were standing in their cottage doors waving their hands as I drove away.

As the train went down the valley of the Wye to Hereford I waved my handkerchief to all the old familiar friendly houses, to Mrs Bridge at Pont Vaen, to Annie Dyke at Upper Cabalva, to Rosie Hodgson at Lower Cabalva, and to Louisa Dew at Whitney Rectory.

[*From now on, until June 1876, Kilvert is mainly in Langley Burrell, acting as curate for his father. He pays occasional visits to Wales, the first in March 1873.*]

1873

Monday, 3 March

Returned to Clyro to take charge of the parish for three weeks, two Sundays for Mr Venables.

Reached Hay at 1.18 and going to the Castle joined the Bevans at luncheon. As I walked over to Clyro I overtook Mrs Williams of Little Wern y Pentre hobbling home with her stick, and Hannah. She was almost overcome and besought me to stay with them and never to leave them again. 'You know what we want,' she said. 'We want you to live at the Vicarage.' Alas, it is not in my power. At the school the dear children were on the look out for me. Afternoon school was just over and they were clustering in the playground and some walking along the road towards the Hay – such exclamations of delight and smiles of loving welcome and faces lighted up and flushed with pleasure.

It was very touching to be so welcomed back.

Mrs Rogers (Pring) makes me most comfortable at the Vicarage and quite spoils me.

Tuesday, 4 March

I have the bedroom at the Vicarage looking towards the south and the mountains.

How sweet once more to see the morning spread upon the mountains.

Mrs Chaloner says I must put myself in a cage to-day or the old women will tear me to pieces for joy. I have been villaging all day. The welcome of the people is very touching.

There are changes in Clyro since I left. Six or seven of the

Wye Cliff; Mrs Crichton and child

old familiar faces have passed away in those six months. Dear little Lily Crichton, aged 7 years, and the patriarch William Williams of Crowther's Pool, aged fourscore years and ten, William Price of the Stocks House aged 85 years, and sweet Margaret Gore of Whitty's Mill in the bloom of her youth and 20 years.

Edward Evans has left us, having just fulfilled his three-score years and ten. The troubles of poor mad Margaret Meredith (entered in the Burial Register of the Parish as Margaret Mulready) have ended in her 62nd year.

There are changes too in the landscape of Clyro for the trees have all been felled on the Castle mound which now looks bare and dreary.

Wednesday, 5 March

After Church I went to see Hannah Whitney and she received

the Holy Communion for the first time at the age of fourscore years and ten. I am very happy and thankful about this. I feared at one time that she would never soften and give way.

After luncheon I started to walk to Gilfa. At the Brooms I turned in to see Jenny Sackville and while I was there the Radnorshire and West Herefordshire hounds and the whole hunt came down the steep pitch from the hills where they had killed their fox. The country was in a fearful state, the roads almost under water and the snow still lying about the hills in deep beds.

As I descended the steep hillside, and came in sight of the farm yard of Gilfa, the good Vicar* came up from folding his sheep in the field and catching sight of me ran forward to meet me with both hands outstretched and his face beaming with smiles. He took me into the cheerful sunny kitchen and we sat and talked there till the three beautiful sisters came in from the village school, Marion, Tillie and Janet, all blushing radiant and lovely in their rich golden brown curls.

Friday, 7 March

In the afternoon I drove to Whitney Rectory in the dog-cart to dine and sleep. . . .

After dinner Henry Dew told us some of his old hunting reminiscences of the days when he rode with the Maesllwch fox-hounds.

Charles Lacy was out with the Radnorshire and West Herefordshire foxhounds when they met at Cabalva last Wednesday. He gave an amusing description of the run. Old Tom Evans, the tailor, of Cwm Ithel on Clyro Hill, was once a running huntsman with the Clyro harriers, and very keen after the sport. When he heard the hunting horns along the hill on Wednesday the old hunting instinct in him awoke like a giant refreshed. He scrambled on to his old pony and rode furiously into the middle of the pack hat in hand hooping and holloing and laying the hounds on to the scent as of yore. Colonel Price the M.F.H. was greatly enraged. 'Man! Man!' he shouted. 'Where are you

*Vaughan.

going, man? Come from those hounds!' But the tailor mad-
dened with the chase was deaf to all entreaties and commands.
He careered along among and over the hounds, hooping, holloing and waving his hat till the enraged M.F.H. charged him
and knocked tailor and pony head over heels. Nothing daunted
however the tailor scrambled on to his beast again and he and
his pony were second in at the death, close at the heels of the
M.F.H.

Charles Lacy said the bag fox had been kept in a dark cellar
so long that he was dazed and half blind, when he was turned
out. After they had killed the bag fox they tried for a wild one
at Dolbedwyn, where some poultry had been stolen by a fox.

The day before the hunt little Rosie Hodgson 'let the fox out
of the bag' to one of the guests. 'Papa has got a fox in a bag
down in the cellar,' said the child innocently.

Saturday, 8 March

At eleven o'clock the dog cart came for me with the chestnut
old Rocket, and I returned to Clyro.

Amelia Meredith tells me that at Llanhollantine people used
to go to the Church door at midnight to hear the saints within
call over the names of those who were to die within the year.
Also they heard the sound of the pew doors opening and shutting though no one was in the church.

Tuesday, 11 March

Last night Sir Francis Ford's harriers came from his place at
Cathedin Court to Clyro Court Farm to put up for the night,
and this morning there was a meet above Gwernfydden. The
morning was stormy and there was a tearing wind on the Vicar's
Hill. The mad March hares of Clyro Hill were too many for
the Breconshire harriers and though they had one or two good
runs they killed nothing and there was no need for currant jelly.
These Breconshire harriers have always been used to be hunted
in Welsh. But when Sir Francis Ford took to them he had no

Welsh and the hounds had no English except one or two of the
pack who understood a little English. Sir Francis could make
them understand him and the rest of the hounds followed their
lead.

To-night was the last Clyro Penny Reading of the season.

The programme was fair but the attendance small, only 14/5
taken at the door. Charlie Powell had proposed to sing two
songs, one perfectly unobjectionable and even nice, the other
low and coarse. To the latter I objected strongly, refused to sit
by and hear it sung, and threatened to leave the choir and the
platform. Charlie Powell turned rusty and sulky when I proposed that he should substitute another song for the objection-
able one and refused to sing either. Not only so, but he tried to
raise a disturbance at the Readings by calling out, romping,
and making insulting remarks. John Vaughan very properly
went down the room to the policeman who very quietly and
ignominiously put Master Charlie out of the room and now
Charlie is the laughing stock of the village.

Friday, 14 March

When we rose this morning the ground was white with snow.

Today I went over to Newchurch to see the Vaughans again
and took with me in a little basket all the primroses the children
had gathered for me to flower Emmeline's grave. The air was
raw and cold but good for walking. I stopped for a few minutes
at the Brooms.

Next I went to Little Wern y Pentre and the snow covered
the trees with fantastic and beautiful forms.

I went on to Newchurch by Dolbedwyn Mount and Tynycwm.
I gathered some ferns in the lane and as I came in sight of the
little Church spire snow began again to fall heavily in large
flakes. The little village was very quiet. The Rectory was apparently deserted. The school held there had probably just broken
up. I was alone in the Churchyard and no one was in sight. As
I stooped over the green grave by the Churchyard gate placing
the primrose bunches in a cross upon the turf the large flakes of
snow still fell thickly upon us, but melted as they fell, and the

great yew tree overhead bent weeping upon the grave.

I left the Churchyard, crossed the rushing Milw with its hazels by the plank footbridge and climbed the steep slippery snowy bank once more and reached the old house of Gilfa at 1 o'clock. The good Vicar came to the door with a hearty welcome, brought me into the kitchen where was a joint of meat roasting before a roaring fire, gave me some dry warm slippers and bade me take off my wet boots. There we sat and talked for some time. Then he showed me upstairs with a jug of hot water. The narrow steep staircase was perfectly dark and the landing was divided from the girls' bedroom only by a low and almost transparent screen which I could have looked over and behind which the three pretty girls were dressing and undressing.

When they came down I kissed Matilda in mistake for Janet at which Miss Tillie was considerably abashed, surprised and amused.

Janet nothing loth came and stood by me to show me some photographs while I stole my arm round her waist and looked up in her beautiful face. 'Kiss, dear.' She bent her sweet face and mouth and smiled at the shower of kisses that followed. Then she moved about between the kitchen and parlour helping to get the dinner and every time she left the room the beautiful saucy girl shot a brilliant Parthian glance.

For dinner we had fowls eaten with pork and what was best of all a kind and hearty welcome.

After dinner Janet came and sat by me, and the girls and their mother made a circle round the fire and I told them stories of Indian life while the good Vicar went to look after his ewes and lambs.

Then Janet brought the draught board and played five games of draughts with me. After tea, between 5 and 6 o'clock, I came away.

Saturday, 15 March

I caught a chill yesterday in the snow at Emmeline's grave and tossed all night in a fever.

I had heard that William Meredith of the Tump just above

Whitty's Mill was very sick, and going to the house I found him dying.

As I sat talking with the dying man and as we knelt round the bed the tempest shook the old house and roared in the roof so as almost to drown my voice, and the dying man rolled his eyes wildly in the darkness of the curtained bed. It was a stormy day to go.

A bitter east wind blew furiously over the hills as I stood at the exposed door of Llwyn Gwillim.

At the lone cottage in the Chapel Dingle my dear friend sweet Emma Griffiths* was almost beside herself with delight when I opened the door. But her joy was soon turned into sorrow. I had not many minutes to stay and when I rose to go poor Emma clasped my hands in both of hers, gave me a long loving look and turned away with a burst of weeping, in a passion of tears. What is it? What is it? What do they all mean? It is a strange and terrible gift, this power of stealing hearts and exciting such love.

At the new Chapel Farm I found Wall and his wife at home and little Nellie lay lovingly in my arms.

I ran down to Cabalva and called at Whitcombe's at the Bronith. Saw Mrs Watkeys and kissed her two beautiful grandchildren as the girls sat together by the fire.

Found Mrs Potts the keeper's wife among the tubs surrounded by naked girls and boys whom she was washing and putting to bed. Spent a quarter of an hour, my last, with the old soldier John Morgan and his wife Mary, and reached home just in time for dinner at Cae Mawr with the Morrells, almost worn out with running, talking, and different emotions. I had been obliged to run almost all the way between the various houses.

Sunday, 16 March

At Gipsy Castle I found Sally Whitney sitting with Mary Jones and Caroline Price. Sally said she remembered the old Clyro stocks and whipping post which stood by the village pound in front of their door. She had often seen people in the stocks and

*See p. 212.

once she saw a sweep whipped by the parish constable for using foul language at the Swan. When people were put in the stocks it was generally for rioting and using bad language at the Swan, and fighting. Sally does not remember if the sweep was stripped naked to be whipped.

Monday, 17 March

Old James Jones the sawyer of the Infant School told me that he remembers a reprobate drunken fellow named James Davies, but nicknamed 'Jim of the Dingle' being put in the stocks at Clyro by Archdeacon Venables and the parish constable. This Jim of the Dingle had a companion spirit as wicked as himself. And both of them belonged to the Herefordshire Militia. So when the Archdeacon and the Constable had gone away leaving Jim in the stocks, Jim's friend brought an axe and beat the stocks all to pieces and let the prisoner out. The two worthies fled away to Hereford to the militia and never returned to Clyro. But the Clyro people, seeing the stocks broken, demolished and burnt the stocks and the whipping post, and no one was ever confined or whipped at Clyro after that.

Wednesday, 19 March

I drove to Llan Thomas to dine and sleep. . . .
    Daisy was very good to me all the evening. She taught me to play Commerce, and thinking the lamp hurt my eyes as I shaded them a moment with the cards to look across the table she rose at once and brought the lamp shade. She asked anxiously if my cough hurt me and whenever I coughed she seemed to suffer pain herself.

Saturday, 22 March

Left Clyro again at 11 o'clock.

    [*He returns to Langley, but pays a brief visit to Llysdinam and Whitney in August. He does not return to Wales until March of the following year, 1874, for a fortnight.*]

1874

Monday, 16 March

Started for Llysdinam by the 8.30 express. . . .

At Three Cocks we waited some time and I fell into talk with one of the Bridgwaters of one of the Porthamal farms who told me about the elections and how at Talgarth Mr de Winton of Maesllwch had been insulted by men kicking round him as a football a rabbit stuffed with bran, in allusion to his propensity for ruining his tenants by keeping vast hordes of rabbits on his estate.

When the train came in from Brecon a tall girl with a fresh colour dressed in deep mourning got out of the train and came towards me. It was Daisy, and her brother John was with her. There was a half sweet, half sad look, a little reproachful in the beautiful kind eyes as she said in a low voice, 'I have been looking out for you such a long time.' Poor child, my poor child.

Saturday, 21 March

Left Llysdinam at 12.27 and came to Whitney Rectory.

On the platform at Whitney I found Henry Dew and Walter waiting for me and Louisa was lying in wait for me in the bushes in the Rectory grounds and came bounding up the steep bank to be kissed. She is growing a tall and pretty girl.

Monday, 23 March

I rode with Henry Dew senior to Clifford Priory to see how Haigh Allen was.

We had a scamper back to Whitney Rectory to catch the
1.8 train which was to take me to Hay to stay at Hay Castle.
I was just in time to scramble into the train streaming with
perspiration after the hot ride. . . .

Then we drove to Clyro. As we passed along the old familiar
road that I have journeyed over so many times a thousand
memories swept over me. Every foot of Clyro ground is classical
and sacred and has its story. When we reached the dear old
village the children had just come out of school. I kissed my
hand to them, but they seemed as if they could hardly believe
their eyes and it was not till after we had alighted at the lodge
under the old weeping willow and were walking up the steep
drive to Cae Mawr that a ringing cheer came up from the
playground. . . .

As we walked down the drive to the carriage renewed cheers
came ringing from the school. Mrs Bevan was much amused
and Baskerville said to me, 'It is a pity you don't stand for the
county. You would have the suffrages of every one here.'

The dear children crowded round the school door. They were
a little shy and much grown since I saw them this time last
year, but my sweet little Amy was unmistakable and so were
the frank sweet eyes of Eleanor Hill.

When we returned to Hay I walked to the almshouses beyond
the Brecon turnpike with Mrs Bevan, Alice and Cousie.

The daffodils were nodding in bright yellow clumps in the
little garden plots before the almshouse doors. And there a great
ecstasy of happiness fell upon me. It was evening when I met
her and the sun was setting up the Brecon road. I was walking
by the almshouses when there came down the steps a tall slight
beautiful girl with a graceful figure and long flowing fair hair.
Her lovely face was delicately pale, her features refined and
aristocratic and her eyes a soft dark tender blue. She looked at
me earnestly, longingly and lovingly, and dropped a pretty
courtesy. Florence, Florence Hill, sweet Florence Hill, is it you?
Once more. Thank God. Once more. My darling, my darling.
As she stood and lifted those blue eyes, those soft dark loving
eyes shyly to mine, it seemed to me as if the doors and windows
of heaven were suddenly opened. It was one of the supreme

moments of life. As I stood by the roadside holding her hand, lost to all else and conscious only of her presence, I was in heaven already, or if still on earth in the body, the flights of golden stairs sloped to my feet and one of the angels had come down to me. Florence, Florence Hill, my darling, my darling. It was well nigh all I could say in my emotion. With one long lingering loving look and clasp of the hand we parted and I saw her no more.

Tuesday, 24 March. Lady Day Eve

I went down to the almshouses hoping to see Florence Hill again. Alas, the daffodils were still blowing in the little garden plot, but Florence Hill was gone. . . .

I walked to Clyro by the old familiar fields and the Beacon stile, and when I looked down upon the dear old village nestling round the Church in the hollow at the dingle mouth and saw the fringes of the beautiful woods and the hanging orchards and the green slopes of Penllan and the white farms and cottages dotted over the hills a thousand sweet and sad memories came over me and all my heart rose up within me and went out in love towards the beloved place and people among whom I lived so long and so happily. . . .

I saw a number of the old people. Hannah Whitney was going to the well as of old in her rusty black bonnet tilted on to the top of her head. Mrs Richard Williams was in the churchyard. She had come down from Paradise to trim Mr Henry Venables' grave. Poor Lizzie Powell, a wreck and shadow of the fine blooming girl she was when I saw her last, was crouching up in the sunny window opposite the Vicarage, pale, wasted, shrunken, hollow-eyed and hollow-cheeked, dying of consumption, but with the sanguine and buoyant spirit of that mysterious and fatally deceptive disease, hoping still against hope even with the hand of death upon her. She seemed pleased to see me. She was amusing herself by watching the men at work at the Vicarage building the new garden wall and her brother Charlie among them.

I went to the school to see Evans and his wife and the

children. 'We will never forget you,' said one of them, Elizabeth Anne Evans.

Then I went to Cae Mawr, found Mrs Morrell at home and had luncheon there. 'I wish,' said Mr Higgins of Clyro Court Farm to me, 'I wish to goodness you were going to stay amongst us. We all love you. We do indeed.'

Thursday, 26 March

I slept at Whitney Rectory last night and came to Hay this morning with Henry Dew by the ten o'clock train.

I walked over to Llanthomas to luncheon with Captain John Thomas. Howarth Greenly was there at luncheon and they played quoits after lunch while I walked to the gardens with Charlotte and Fanny.

I went back to Whitney Rectory to sleep as Mr Venables is staying at the Castle. My poor, poor Daisy. When we parted the tears came into her eyes. She turned her face away. I saw the anguish of her soul. What could I do?

Friday, 27 March

After breakfast I walked with Jane and Helen Dew for a charming walk.

We walked along Wordsworth's Terrace where he was taken once to see the view. He was staying at the Stow Farm at the time with his friend and relation, blind Mr Monkhouse. It was Sunday and the poet had been at Whitney Church in the morning and came up to the Rectory to luncheon. Henry Dew took him the same walk along the side of the hill, which is now called 'Wordsworth's Terrace', and when the great poet saw the river below winding down through the beautiful valley and the hill ranges rising one above another and the blue mountains behind crowning the whole, Clifford, Castleton Hill and the Wye, he was enraptured and said that though he had travelled through many countries he had never looked upon a more beautiful scene.

We loitered through some lovely woods and dingles starred

thick with primroses, and across a rushing brook upon the stepping stones. There was a sweet stirring of new life among the woods and a dawn of green upon the larches and hawthorns. On the outskirts of a little wood stood three white-haired children, babes in the wood. 'I scratched my arm in yonder wood,' said one flaxen-haired urchin. We passed by a cottage inhabited by the peasant descendants of the famous and ancient family of De La Haye. The wife of the present De La Haye came to the garden gate to speak to us, a pleasant comely woman.

Farewell to pleasant kindly Whitney Rectory and dear Louisa. To Hay by 1.8 train, a wet afternoon.

Saturday, 28 March

Left Hay Castle and returned to Langley after a very pleasant holiday.

[*He is at Langley almost continuously (with a brief visit to Wales in September 1874) until April 1875, when he goes to Monnington to stay with his sister Thersie, who is married to the rector, William Smith.*]

1875

Monday, 5 April

Left Langley for Monnington-on-Wye with Dora. At Hereford Station I fell in with Higgins of the Court Farm, Clyro, who told me that poor dear old Clyro is all at sixes and sevens and the church and school nearly empty. He himself goes to Llowes Church. The new Vicar (Prickard) seems to have been unwise in introducing several changes suddenly and so alienating and disturbing the people.

William met us at Moorhampton with the dog cart and chestnut horse Paddy, and drove us to Monnington. I like the look of the place very much. The house is large and comfortable and the situation pretty, roomy and pleasant. One great feature of the place is the famous 'Monnington Walk', a noble avenue of magnificent Scotch firs bordering a broad green ride, stretching from Brobury Scar (a red sandstone precipice beetling over the winds of Wye) to Monnington Court House, where the aunt of Owen Glendower lived.

Tuesday, 6 April

When I awoke a woodpigeon was crooning from the trees near the house and the early morning sunshine glinted upon the red boles of the gigantic Scotch firs in Monnington Walk. I rose early and went out. The morning was fresh and bright with a slight sunshiny shower flying.

Hard by the Church porch and on the western side of it I saw what I knew must be the grave of Owen Glendower. It is a flat stone of whitish grey shaped like a rude obelisk figure,

The River Wye near Monnington

sunk deep into the ground in the middle of an oblong patch
of the old grey church the strong wild heart, still now, has
smashed into several fragments.

And here in the little Herefordshire churchyard within
hearing of the rushing of the Wye and close under the shadow
of the old grey church the strong wild heart, still now, has
rested by the ancient home and roof tree of his kindred since
he fell asleep there more than four hundred years ago. It is a
quiet peaceful spot.

In the afternoon Thersie, Dora, Florence and I called at
Monnington Court and were kindly received by the worthy
Churchwarden farmer and his wife, Mr and Mrs James,
who showed us the fine old oak carving and the banqueting
room. In the garden of the Court House was dug up a few
days ago a huge silver coin which Mr James showed us and
which looked to me like a crown of Charles I. On one side
of the coin was a king crowned, armed and mounted. Mr

James went with us to the Church which is light and pleasant and cheerful within and seemed well cared for. He told us that in the great flood of February 6, 1852, he and the present Sir Gilbert Lewis of Harpton (then Rector of Monnington) had punted in a flat-bottomed boat across the Court garden, in at the Church door, up to the Nave and into the Chancel. The flood that day rose as high in the Church as the seats of the benches.

Thursday, 8 April

Mrs Bryan had told her daughter of a sad accident that had lately befallen the poor strange Solitary, the Vicar of Llanbedr Painscastle.* He was sitting by the fire in his little lone hut at Cwm Cello that lies in the bosom of Llanbedr Hill when he either dropped heavily asleep or had a fit and fell full on the fire. Before he could recover himself his stomach, bowels, and thighs were dreadfully burnt, and he has had to stay away from Church for three Sundays. Yet he will let neither doctor nor nurse come near him. The poor solitary.

Mr Bishop, the curate of Moccas, dined with us this evening.

Saturday, 10 April

Yesterday Bishop promised to meet me at noon to-day at Moccas Church and shew me over it. As I crossed Moccas bridge I heard a chime of deep melodious voices and at the next lodge I came upon four men, wandering singers, with voices matched like bells, singing in harmony and exquisitely melodious, but I could not understand what they said.... The thing that interested me most in the Church was the beautiful tomb of Sir Reginald de Fresne (Fraxinus = Ashe) the Crusader, perhaps an ancestor of my own.

He lay very still and quiet with his legs crossed and his feet resting against his faithful hound. There was a look of deep calm upon his face as if his soul were at perfect peace. The Great Crusade, the Battle of Life, was over, and now no

*See p. 237.

Saracen or Infidel vexed the warrior Crusader's rest. The shield upon his arm was pure. His good sword slept in its sheath by his side and his hands were clasped in silent prayer. And so in the dim light of the choir of the old Norman Church he had lain silently praying night and day for seven hundred years.

Requiescat in Pace.

Monday, 12 April

I went up to Llysdinam by 1.18 train, and my spirits rose as we passed up the beautiful valley amongst the old familiar scenes.... Then Aberedw, the Rocks of Aberedw. What more need be, can be, said? How pleasant and happy it was once more to be in the midst of the throng of the kindly merry Builth market folk in the sunny afternoon home returning, the pretty smiling fair-haired girls coming in with their heavy market baskets, the good-humoured crowding, the courteous apologies and giving way, the lively animated talk, how different from England. Wales, sweet Wales. I believe I must have Welsh blood. I always feel so happy and natural and at home amongst the kindly Welsh.

Tuesday, 13 April

Oh, Aberedw, Aberedw. Would God I might dwell and die by thee.... Once more I stand by the riverside and look up at the cliff castle towers and mark the wild roses swinging from the crag and watch the green woods waving and shimmering with a twinkling dazzle as they rustle in the breeze and shining of the summer afternoon, while here and there a grey crag peeps from among the tufted trees. And once again I hear the merry voices and laughter of the children as they clamber down the cliff path among the bushes or along the rock ledges of the riverside or climb the Castle Mount, or saunter along the narrow green meadow tree-fringed and rock-bordered and pass in and out of Llewellyn's cave, or gather wood and light the fire amongst the rocks upon the

Hardenhuish Church, near Chippenham

moor, or loiter down the valley to Cavan Twm Bach and cross
the shining ferry at sunset, when the evening shadows lie
long and still across the broad reaches of the river.

Oh, Aberedw, Aberedw.

[*He leaves Llysdinam on April 17. After this stay at Monnington,
Kilvert does not visit Wales again for a year. During this period he
has fallen in love with one of the bridesmaids at a wedding he attends
(Kathleen Heanley) whom he calls 'Kathleen Mavourneen'; but this
sentiment is obliterated by a 'coup de foudre' in the shape of Ettie
Meredith Brown.*]

6 September

Etty Meredith Brown is one of the most striking-looking
and handsomest girls whom I have seen for a long time.
She was admirably dressed in light grey with a close fitting
crimson body which set off her exquisite figure and suited
to perfection her black hair and eyes and her dark Spanish
brunette complexion with its rich glow of health which gave
her cheeks the dusky bloom and flush of a ripe pomegranate.
But the greatest triumph was her hat, broad and picturesque,
carelessly twined with flowers and set jauntily on one side of
her pretty dark head, while round her shapely slender throat
she wore a rich gold chain necklace with broad gold links.
And from beneath the shadow of the picturesque hat the
beautiful dark face and the dark wild fine eyes looked with a
true gipsy beauty.

[*There is a break in the diary from September 1875 until March
1876, for some of the notebooks were lost. Kilvert seems to have met
Ettie quite often and to have fallen deeply in love. In April 1876
however, he goes to stay with his sister Thersie in Monnington and we
see how the affair ends.*]

1876

Thursday, 20 April

This morning I received a long sad sweet loving letter from my darling Ettie, a tender beautiful letter of farewell, the last she will ever be able to write to me. With it came enclosed a kind friendly little note from young Mrs Meredith Brown, so friendly and so kind, saying she is afraid Ettie and I must hold no further communication by letter or poetry or any other way. I know it. I know it. She is right and I have been, alas, very very wrong. She says she knows I care for Ettie too much to wish to cause her needless unhappiness. It is true. She does me justice and yet no more than justice. I will not make my darling sorrowful or cause her to shed one unnecessary tear, or tempt her to do wrong. The best and only way left me of showing my love for her now is to be silent. But oh, I hope she will not quite forget me. She says she never will. Yet perhaps it is selfish of me to wish this, and it may be better for her that she should. I hope, I hope, I have not done her any harm or wrong. She says, God bless her, that I never have. How kind and gentle she has always been to me, how sweet and good, how patient and forbearing, how noble and generous, how self-sacrificing and devoted, how unselfish and loving. Ettie. Ettie, my own only lost love, yet not lost, for we shall meet in heaven. Ettie, oh Ettie, my own dear little girl.

As I walked round the Rectory garden at Monnington this morning thinking of Ettie's last letter and all the wild sweet sorrowful past the great everlasting sigh of the majestic firs, as mournful and soothing as the sighing of the sea, blended with my mood and sympathized with the sadness of my heart. The beautiful weeping birch too wept with me and its graceful drooping tresses softly moving reminded me with a strange sweet thrill of Ettie's hair. This afternoon I walked over to Bredwardine going up Monnington Walk through the majestic avenue of Scotch firs evermore sighing overhead, and over Brobury Scar.

Saturday, 22 April

A lovely summer morning which I spent in sauntering round the lawn at Monnington Rectory watching the waving of the birch tresses, listening to the sighing of the firs in the great solemn avenue, that vast Cathedral, and reading Robert Browning's 'In a Gondola' and thinking of dear Ettie. To-day there was a luncheon party consisting of Andrew and Mary Pope from Blakemere, Mr and Mrs Phillott from Staunton-on-Wye, Houseman, and Mr Robinson from Norton Canon. After they had left William and I walked up to the top of Moccas Park, whence we had a glorious view of the Golden Valley shining in the evening sunlight with the white houses of Dorstone scattered about the green hillsides 'like a handful of pearls in a cup of emerald' and the noble spire of Peterchurch rising from out of the heart of the beautiful rich valley which was closed below by the Sugar Loaf and the Skyrrid blue above Abergavenny.

We came tumbling and plunging down the steep hillside of Moccas Park, slipping, tearing and sliding through oak and birch and fallow wood of which there seemed to be underfoot an accumulation of several feet, the gathering ruin and decay probably of centuries.

As we came down the lower slopes of the wooded hillside into the glades of the park the herds of deer were moving under the brown oaks and the brilliant green hawthorns, and we came upon the tallest largest stateliest ash I ever saw and what seemed at first in the dusk to be a great ruined grey tower, but which proved to be the vast ruin of the king oak of Moccas Park, hollow and broken but still alive and vigorous in parts and actually pushing out new shoots and branches. That tree may be 2000 years old. It measured roughly 33 feet round by arm stretching.

I fear those grey old men of Moccas, those grey, gnarled, low-browed, knock-kneed, bowed, bent, huge, strange, long-armed, deformed, hunchbacked, misshapen, oak men that stand waiting and watching century after century, biding God's time with both feet in the grave and yet tiring down and seeing out generation after generation, with such tales to tell, as when they whisper them to each other in the mid-summer nights, make the silver birches weep and the poplars and aspens shiver and the long ears of the hares and rabbits stand on end. No human hand set those oaks. They are 'the trees which the Lord hath planted'. They look as if they had been at the beginning and making of the world, and they will probably see its end.

Monday, 24 April

This morning came a letter from Mr Venables saying that Archdeacon De Winton, the Archdeacon of Brecon, had written to him to ask if I would entertain the idea of going to St Harmon's should the Bishop of St David's offer me the Living. The old Vicar, Bowen Evans, is just dead. I wrote to the Archdeacon to ask for a few days' grace till I could go to St Harmon's from Llysdinam and see the place. I think I would accept the living. I am not sure that I should be justified in refusing it, as it will be worth between £300 and £400 a year when the lease on one or two old lives falls in, but it would be a great sad wrench to leave Langley.

Tuesday, 25 April

This morning William drove to Hereford with Mr Phillott of Staunton-on-Wye to the Bishop's visitation. At ten o'clock I started in an April shower to walk to Peterchurch. I went through Moccas Park and up a deep wild picturesque lane beyond the Bredwardine Lodge. The noble spire of the fine

Norman Church rises grandly in the midst of the valley, the white houses of the village are gathered round it and hard by are one or two poplars rising with golden green spires against the blue sides of the distant hills. The Church is approached over a broad rude stone pitched causeway, quaint and ancient, which borders and then bridges the broad fair stream of the Dore which flows close beneath the churchyard and the great steeple of St Peter's Church. The Church has been well restored but I was disappointed to find the old picture of the Peterchurch Fish gone from the interior wall.

I went home another way, over the hill to Blakemere. A wild storm of hail swept down the valley but I took shelter under a hawthorn bush and the sun still went on shining. When the wild storm and white squall were over I went on up the steep lane between the dripping glancing glittering hedges, till across a dingle which separated it from the lane I saw an old man at work in a cottage garden. We exchanged greetings and gave the time of day across the dingle, and I asked him about the picture of the Peterchurch Fish. 'The Church', said the old man, 'was restored three years. I cannot justly say whether the picture of the Fish is on the wall now or not. I have only been to Church once since the Church was restored. There was a collection at the Church and I went. I don't go to Church a lot. I don't remember seeing the Fish on the wall then. The picture of the Fish was on the wall furthest from the door as you do go in. They do say the Fish was first seen at Dorston and speared there, but he got away and they hunted him down to Peterchurch and killed him close by the Church. He was as big as a salmon and had a gold chain round his neck. They do say you can see the blood now upon the stones at Dorston where the Fish was speared first.'

Wednesday, 26 April

This morning I bade farewell to sweet kind hospitable beautiful Monnington and came to Clyro. I stopped at Hay and went to the Castle to luncheon and to wish Couzie many happy returns of her birthday. The first Clyro person I saw was

William Davies, the road man, who gave me a hearty welcome, but not a more hearty or kindly one than I received from my dear friends with whom I am staying at Cae Mawr.

Thursday, 27 April

This morning I called on Mrs and Miss Chaloner and on Mrs Thomas the blacksmith's wife. Then at the Browns' I had a grand romp with Polly Sackville, but poor old Jinny was ill in bed. As I went over Clyro I called at Pen y Cae. Old Harris the farmer had actually forgotten me and I was obliged to tell him my name. I asked for Lizzie and he went to look for her. I followed him into an inner room and there was my gipsy beauty as beautiful and shy as ever. Once more I kissed that pale sweet lovely face shadowed by the soft dark curling hair. 'Do you remember me? Do you love me?' 'Yes,' she said with a shy sweet sorrowful smile. I sat awhile in the kitchen talking to Harris and another man as they sat eating their luncheon. Meantime my gipsy beauty had stolen out silently and when I rose to go she was nowhere to be seen. Her grandfather went out into the yard to seek her calling, 'Lizzie, Lizzie!' How familiar the old grey group of buildings looked with the ancient yew tree in the west. But there was a new slate roof on the old house. 'Lizzie, Lizzie!' called her grandfather. 'She is gone away by herself to cry, I doubt,' he said. At length the girl came from one of the outhouses with a sad smile on her pale sweet beautiful face. 'Goodbye, dear,' said I, kissing her again. 'Don't forget me. Write to me sometimes.' We parted, and she went away again to cry alone. Too fond, too faithful heart.

Friday, 28 April

At Llan Thomas some of the girls were playing croquet on the bright sunny lawn with a Miss Ravenscroft who had come to spend the afternoon with them. Lady Hereford, who had brought her from Tregoyd, was out fishing with her eldest son Robert Devereux and Mary Thomas. In the drawing room

I found Mrs Thomas looking well, bright and cheery. She has got through this winter better than usual. Daisy came into the drawing-room, shy, confused and blushing painfully, but looking very nice and well.

After the game of croquet was over Charlotte and Edith Thomas took me to the Church by my request to see their Easter decorations. Then we came back to afternoon tea and found the fishing party returned with empty baskets. Edith showed me her beautiful drawings of wild flowers and fungi. No sooner had Lady Hereford and her party gone than I found she had taken my umbrella and left me a much better one, a fine silk umbrella in place of my zenilla. Edith and Daisy took me to the garden and were very kind to me, Daisy giving me a sprig of sweet verbena, and we had a nice long talk together. When I went away they sent me half a mile or more along the road and we had a merry laughing walk. It was so pleasant, just like the dear old times, and the girls were so nice and cordial and friendly, I do like those girls. They half expected to meet their sisters coming home from a walk or pretended to, but as Mary and Grace did not appear they were obliged to turn back with a pleasant affectionate 'Goodbye'. After we had parted Daisy turned and called back with a bright sweet loving look, 'Please give my best love to your sister'.

As I went back I called at the almshouses again and knocked at Mrs Michael's door. 'Come in, Sir,' she said, 'Florrie's* come. She is in the other room.' 'Florrie, Florrie!' she called. The door of the inner room opened gently and Florrie entered. I never saw anything so lovely. A tall beautiful stately girl with an exquisite figure, a noble carriage, the most lovely delicate and aristocratic features, gentle loving blue eyes shaded by long silken lashes, eyebrows delicately arched and exquisitely pencilled, and beautiful silky tresses of golden brown hair falling in curling clusters upon her shoulders. And the loveliest part of it all was that the girl seemed perfectly unconscious of her own loveliness. Well, I thought, you will make some hearts ache some day.

*Florence Hill.

She was indeed as Mrs Vaughan said 'beautiful and wild and stately, a true mountain child.' I was dazzled by her beauty and almost overcome with emotion. The girl dropped a pretty courtesy and smiled. I took her little slender hand. 'Do you remember me, Florence?' 'Oh yes, Sir,' she said, opening her blue eyes wide with a sweet surprised look peculiar to herself. She had a quick timid almost breathless way of speaking in a low undertone, half frightened, half confiding, which completed the charm. I asked after my old schoolgirl pupil, her sister Eleanor. 'Eleanor will be sure to be very sorry not to see you, Sir,' said Florence in her quick sweet timid voice and manner. 'I am going home to-morrow for a few days,' she added breathlessly. I resolved instantly to pay a visit to the Upper Noyadd and see her and Eleanor and the kindly people at her dear home, the mountain farm. I was obliged to tear myself away from her. I could scarcely part. One more look, one more clasp of the tiny slender hand. 'Good-bye, darling.' Good-bye, Florence, sweet lovely beautiful Florence, rightly named 'The Flower', the Flower of light and sweetness and loveliness. Good-bye, dear, dear mountain child. Until to-morrow. To-morrow we shall meet again. Meanwhile angels ever bright and fair watch over thee, and happy be thy dreams.

Saturday, 29 April

A day of unceasing hopeless rain. I spent the morning in the village. Amongst other people I went to see the old wizard James Jones and his wife.* The poor old dame was still struggling amidst deafness, blindness, weakness, age, poverty and friendlessness to keep her poor little infant school to-gether. She was sitting in the dark gloomy kitchen getting her humble meal between school hours while the children were gone home. The wizard lay upstairs in bed very weak and ill, perhaps dying. I went up to see him by his own request. He seemed very peaceful and happy and quite content. The days of magic and necromancy had gone by and he had emerged from the atmosphere of charms, incantations, astrology and witch-

*See p. 128.

craft a simple humble childlike Christian man. The old wizard took my hand lovingly and most tenderly, touchingly and affectionately he gave me his blessing, and bade me Godspeed. 'You have done great good in this place,' he said. 'You have been a blessing to this place.' Then lifting his withered shrunken hand and arm and raising his eyes solemnly to heaven the dying necromancer called to God to witness that he died in charity with all men. 'I wish no one any harm,' he said. 'I am at peace with all the world.' And so we parted, never perhaps to meet again in this world. May we meet in heaven.

After luncheon I walked to Wye Cliff in heavy rain. At the top of the Longlands Pitch, just before I reached the Cross Roads and the lane leading to Boatside, I saw a tall slight girl coming towards me dressed in a long grey cloak. In another moment I recognised the clustering curls of golden brown hair falling upon her shoulders and the gleam of those lovely innocent blue eyes, and once more I was dazzled by the beauty of Florence Hill. Flushed with the rain and the wind she was walking alone wrapped in her long grey cloak but with no umbrella to shelter her lovely head from the driving storm. And thus she was going to walk through Clyro all the way to the Upper Noyadd. I wanted her to take my umbrella but she gently yet firmly refused saying she should take shelter with her aunt at Clyro. Se we parted for a little time, I knowing, though she did not, in how short a while we should meet again. . . .

I passed through the village and went up by Ciluni Dingle sides in search of the Upper Noyadd. Up and up I went past Moity and the chapel, the road growing narrower, steeper and stonier, till at length from a lane it threatened to become a watercourse and the rain growing harder till I seemed to be amongst the clouds.

I had come a mile out of my way up the steep stony hill in the pouring rain, but I soon dropped down again upon the little wayside sheltered Chapel by the dingle brookside and heard the welcome clink of the anvil from the blacksmith's forge at Moity. Fortunately there was at the forge a boy named Greenway from the Parkey at Clyro who had come to the blacksmith's with some ploughshare points. He was going home past the Upper Noyadd and offered to show me the way. At Moity the brook was out in such heavy flood that the lane was filled with it and we could only just scramble past along the wall-side. At Tylybyregam a tributary stream was swollen by the ceaseless streaming rain to a raging red torrent and went roaring down the dingle with a voice of thunder. I never saw the brooks out so quickly or roaring so fast and furious in so short a time.

After crossing some upland meadows we came into a mountain lane steep and narrow where we found Mrs Sheldon's donkey cart drawn up under the slender shelter of a thorn bush opposite the Lower Noyadd where its mistress seemed to have taken refuge while the cart was steadily filling with rainwater. The breadth of meadow beyond and a little further up the hillside stood the Upper Noyadd. Here I bade the boy Greenway 'Good evening' with thanks for his guidance, and crossed the yard. It was a new house just finished and the débris of stone and masonwork yet lay fresh about the place. I knocked at the door rather hesitatingly and shyly for I had never been to the house before and I felt that I might be a stranger and intruding upon the family. But I need not have doubted nor feared for my reception. The kindly farmer Mr Hill came to the door. For one moment he looked doubtful. Then he said eagerly, 'It's Mr Kilvert, isn't it?' and took me heartily by the hand and drew me in. 'Come in, come in,' he said, 'we are just at tea. Mrs Michael and Florrie are come now just.' And he had me into the bright warm kitchen where the family were assembled at their evening meal. Mrs Hill, the mistress of the house, came forward with her beautiful face, gentle manner, graceful courtesy and warm welcome.

'Well, well,' she said, 'to think of seeing you here and on such a day as this. I am so glad. But you are very wet.' So she seated me in the warm corner of the inglenook next to the sofa where old Mrs Michael was sitting at tea and resting after her long wet drive in the donkey cart. The fine old lady's face was beaming with happiness and content to find herself among her own people in her own dear home once more. There was Florence, tall and stately, looking more beautiful than ever in her sweet mountain home, with her lovely golden brown hair still damp from her long rainy walk, there was Colvyn with his something of his sister Florence's beauty in his fair boyish face, and there was dear Eleanor grown a tall fine handsome girl with the same frank sweet truthful look in her clear beautiful eyes that she had as a child. Sweet Eleanor of Noyadd Farm.

The party was made up by a little rosy-faced dark-haired niece of Mrs Hill. I felt at home at once in this dear kind family circle. There was an air of delicate courtesy, refinement and high breeding which I have looked for in vain in many grander homes. All were simple, natural, and at their ease. All were courteous, considerate and attentive, and unaffectedly happy to see and welcome me as a friend of the family. I felt that I was in a congenial atmosphere and was perfectly happy. The hours passed only too quickly. I could gladly have spent the whole evening with my dear and newly found friends. My kind and hospitable hostess Mrs Hill replenished my cup with tea and my plate with sweet home-made cake and Florence shyly whispered to her mother and begged to be allowed to fetch for me to see the sketch of their old house which Mr Vulliamy took just before the old farmhouse was pulled down to make room for the new one. 'The girls have got your poetry which came out in the *Hereford Times*,' said their father smiling. ' "The Rocks of Aberedw" and "Clyro Water". They are very fond of the verses and they often read them. The rhymes all come in so beautiful, and young people are fond of poetry.'

Mrs Hill took me to the window to see the view down the dingle through the blossoming plum trees in front of the house towards the distant mountains, the Wye-side meadows and the shining river, but much of the beauty of the prospect was blotted out by the driving rain. I could stay no longer. I took an affectionate farewell of the beautiful girls, and their kind warmhearted mother, and their father obligingly went with me some distance through the rain to show me the way to Llowes Common.

Sunday. May Eve

I walked up to Bettws Chapel for the 3.30 afternoon service by the desire of the curate and the Bettws people.

At Whitty's Mill* I found dear Hannah (Gore) Price dying. Dying of consumption in the same chair set in the same chimney corner where her sweet sisters Margaret and Mary had sat waiting so long and patiently for death. It was all very touching and pathetic. She was so gentle and patient and resigned. How familiar her face was, reminding me of the girl's long and faithful service at the Swan. She is not long behind her dear old mistress Betty Price.

The Chapel bell struck out as of old when I came in sight round the corner of the Chapel barn. How dear and familiar were the scene and the kind friendly faces grouped about the Chapel door. And within how things were changed and improved. A little vestry under the old gallery, a new harmonium and Annie, dear Annie Dyke, seated at it with her little choir, her brother Willie and her cousins round her. Such nice singing, the Glorias, Canticles and three hymns, one of them 'We love the place of God', and another my favourite 'Lead, kindly Light'. There too were good Mrs Dyke and Mrs Wall, my kind friend, Lucretia and Eliza Wall, my dear old school-girls and pupils, and their father, the honest Churchwarden with his beaming face, sitting in his accustomed place and his fine growing boys opposite. After service I went to Llwyn Gwillim to tea with Annie and Willie Dyke and Lucretia and Eliza Wall, stopping for a few minutes at the Chapel Dingle to see dear Emma Griffiths who has been very ill.

Then all five of us went down to Evening Church at Clyro at 6 o'clock, a merry party at a swinging pace, for we only left Llwyn Gwillim at 5.20. We came into Church in the 1st Lesson. I dashed on the surplice over boots and gaiters and sat within the rails and preached on Mizpah to a very attentive congregation and a much larger one than in the morning.

*See p. 112.

Monday, May Day

Called on Fanny (Gibbins) Lewis. Sat an hour with her and saw her pretty friendly little boy . . . .*

At the Bronith I went up the steep stony lane to see John Morgan, the old soldier and Peninsular veteran. The old man was sitting in his chair, nearly 90 years old, but not looking a day older than when I saw him last. His stalwart wife Mary stood by him. 'I knew your step in a moment,' she said. The veteran was delighted to see his old friend again. 'I have clean lost my shepherd,' he said. Speaking of my Father taking the whole duty at Langley during my absence the old soldier said, 'You have left him a heavy legacy'. 'I do try to oblige the Lord all as I can,' he said with a touching earnestness and humility.

Tuesday, May Morrow

This morning I finished visiting all my dear friends in the village and called on Miss Bynon. 'I was very happy', said the good old lady, 'to hear on Sunday that you had not lost your piety.' . . .

Then through the pear orchard, snowy and sweet-scented with blossom, and by the meadows to the net house where I found the deformed dwarf Emily Parker with her black long hair and humped shoulders, the beautiful spirit confined awhile in its strange misshapen cage. . . .

I was going through the sweet-scented sunny pear orchard of the Court of Clyro enjoying the beauty of the scene, the richness of the foliage and the fragrance of the snowy blossoms, when beneath the orchard boughs I caught a glimpse of the gleam of golden brown curls shining in the sunlight. A boy and girl were passing along the road from school towards Llowes. There could be no mistaking that tall graceful stately form, that beautiful head and glorious flood of clustering brown tresses. It was Florence and Colvyn Hill. 'Florrie, Florrie!' I called. She turned with that bewitching look of sweet and innocent

*Evidently, in spite of opposition, 'Gibbins' has married the 'Hay tailor' (see p. 189).

surprise in her lovely blue eyes and came back with a glad smile. 'I am going your way,' I said. 'Shall we walk together?' 'Oh yes, Sir,' she said with a happy look. So we three went together up through the steep cherry orchard to the Old Forest and over the sunny green slopes of Llowes Common among the gorse bushes and thymy knolls. Never shall I forget that walk from Clyro to the Upper Noyadd with beautiful Florence Hill and her brother Colvyn. It was a glorious sunny evening, but had there been no sun the presence and beauty and love of Florence Hill would have lighted and glorified the world for me with a light that never was on land or sea, a light far more tender and beautiful than the shining of the sun on the valley and the mountains. 'Shall I tell you a story?' I said. 'Do you like hearing stories?' Both my companions pressed eagerly to my side and Florence glanced up with a swift shy look of pleasure. 'Oh, if you *please*, Sir,' she said in her quick low voice, timid and breathless. So as we walked up the hill under the shadow of the Old Forest and then over the sunny knolls of Llowes Common where the evening air moved sweet among the gorse clumps and the hillocks where the wild thyme grows, I told my dear fellow pilgrims the old stories of the Prince and the Picture and the Virginian Sentinel. Both my hearers walked entranced as the tales beguiled the way, the beautiful girl beside me every now and then lifting her lovely face and soft blue eyes with a grave sweet look, wondering, awe-struck or pitiful, according to the progress and passion of the tale, her sensitive features reflecting as a mirror the swiftly changing emotions of her gentle heart. 'What did the Prince find in the forbidden drawer?' proceeded the story. 'It was a picture,' whispered Florence in a solemn awe-struck voice. 'Well,' I thought to myself though I did not say it, 'and if the picture was only half as lovely as you no wonder the Prince went wandering round the world to find the original or that he died of a broken heart when he found the meaning of that mysterious writing and that the woman whom that picture represented had passed away three thousand years before.'

'And what was it that had killed the sentinel?' concluded the last story.

'It was a wild Indian,' whispered the girl in a frightened voice.

And so the tales and the sweet brief journey and our fellow pilgrimage came to an end and when we lifted up our eyes and looked behold we were close to my dear companions' mountain home, the Upper Noyadd Farm. At the last stile I was going to wish my dear companions 'Goodbye' and return alone to Clyro but Florence would not hear of it. Looking up with a pleading grace in her beautiful eyes and a pretty insistence in her voice and manner and one little hand gently detaining me, 'No, please don't go, please come in,' she persisted lovingly. 'You must come in and have some tea, do come in. Father and Mother and Eleanor and all of them will be so glad to see you.' So the beautiful face and the pleading voice and the loving eyes prevailed, how could I resist, and I went again to the happy home and found as kind a welcome as before. After tea by her father's wish Florence took her concertina and played to me those tender lovely and touching airs 'The Bluebells of Scotland' and 'Home Sweet Home'. I never saw anything more beautiful than Florence Hill as she stood playing by the window with the evening light falling upon her golden head. Her head was slightly turned on one side as she played and there came over her lovely face a rapt far-away look, self-forgetful, self-unconscious, a look as of one divinely inspired. She seemed to me to be the daughter of the Bards. So pure, so heavenly, so perfect in her beauty. I saw her face as it had been the face of an angel.

When she had finished playing she went and fetched Eleanor and the two sweet beautiful sisters, the fair and the dark beauty, standing by the western window and in the evening light sang to me the lovely hymn of the 'Pilgrims of the Night'.

[*He leaves Cae Mawr and goes to stay with the Venables at Llysdinam – partly in order to visit St Harmon's where he has been asked to consider accepting the living; see 24 April.*]

Thursday, 4 May

Breakfast at 8 with the Archdeacon, train at 9, he to Doldowlod to discover if a Welsh service is needed at Llanwrthwl Church (Answer, 'No') and I to look at St Harmon's. Soon after leaving Rhayader the railway leaves the valley of the Wye and enters the sweet vale of Marteg by a wild and narrow gorge which soon opens, broadens and settles down into a winding valley shut in by gentle hills about which are dotted lone white cottages and farms. The little by-station of St Harmon's is kept by a handsome pleasant-faced woman, very stout, who lives in a cottage on the line. The Church stands close to the station on a little mount half veiled by a clump of trees. Across the little river Marteg crossed here by a bridge and on the side of the opposite bank stands the National School, built some two years ago. Two men were leaning idly against the gates where the road crosses the railway, and the younger of them, a pleasant-looking youth, offered to go and fetch the keys of the Church for me from the clerk's house. I found out afterwards that this young man was the clerk's son. He was named Jones, apprenticed to a dentist in London, and home for change of air after illness. Whilst my young friend was gone to fetch the key I fell into conversation with the people who still remained lounging by the gate, and learned what I could about the country. Presently the clerk's son returned and we entered the Church-yard over an iron grating outside the gate which serves to keep sheep out it is said. The church was built in the Dark Ages of fifty years ago and was simply hideous. But ugly as it appeared externally the interior was worse and my heart sank within me like a stone as I entered the door. A bare cold squalid interior and high ugly square boxes for seats, a three-decker pulpit and desk, no stove, a flimsy altar rail, a ragged faded altar cloth, a singing gallery with a broken organ, a dark little box for a vestry and a roof in bad repair, admitting the rain. Such was St Harmon's Church as I first saw it. My cicerone was very courteous and attentive and gave me what information he could about the Church, the school, the parish, the people, the country and the neighbourhood, and played some tunes

(Martin Luther's Hymn among the rest) for my benefit on the broken-winded organ while I pumped away at the wheezing bellows. In the Churchyard he pointed out to me the tombstone of the late Mr Foxton, the Atheist of Bwlch Gwynne, and gave me a Railway Guide to the district. Then he accompanied me to the school. I found 22 children in the long room and the schoolmaster Fancroft soured, disappointed, and complaining of the managers, the people, the school, the schoolhouse and everything. He said he was on the point of leaving for a school in Northamptonshire. However he and his wife were very civil to me. I went next to the little farmhouse of Jones the clerk called Temple Bar. He was busy on the farm, but I found his wife at home, a stout jolly good-natured looking woman with a large family some of whom I had just seen at the school. He told me that her husband was a cousin to Walter Vaughan, the Vicar of Llandegley, who has property in St Harmon's, and that directly the old Vicar Bowen Evans was dead her son wrote to his cousin Walter to tell him of the vacancy and ask him to apply to the Bishop for the living. But she thought Walter Vaughan would hardly move from Llandegley. Shrewdly divining the reason of my visit to St Harmon's she asked me with a favouring eye if I would like to come there as Vicar. I said I could hardly tell till I knew more of the place and the circumstances of the living. On hospitable thoughts intent, the clerk's wife brought out some cakes and ale and pressed me to eat and drink. I was to have returned to Llysdinam to luncheon by the noonday train from St Harmon's but as I wanted to see more of the country and the people I decided to let the train go by, accept the hospitality of my hostess and the cakes and ale which life offered, and walk home quietly in the course of the afternoon. As I was at luncheon thus the children came in from school. Nice children they were too, courteous and friendly. I drew one pretty girl to me, put my arm round her waist and kissed her, whereat a small boy surprised out of his propriety laughed pleasantly. Then my guide of the morning came in with his brother. We had some more talk and producing the ordnance map I read out the names of some of the farms and hills in St Harmon's to the great delight of the children as they recognized the names of familiar places. At length I rose to go and bid farewell to the kindly hospitable family at Temple Bar. When I had shaken hands with the household all round and kissed the pretty girl once more on her blooming cheek and sweet lips, the clerk's family accompanied me on to the sunny road to set me on my way, and the stout good-humoured wife called after me kindly and heartily, 'I hope you will come here and be our Vicar. Do you think you will come?' I said, 'I don't know. It does not depend upon me. I shall not ask for it.' 'Will you not?' she cried sadly. And then I saw them no more.

It was a glorious noonday and I was glad I had decided to walk. St Harmon's had put on a holiday dress and was looking its best. The trees, and especially the oaks, were not yet fully out in leaf, but the larch groves shone brilliant and the graceful weeping birches which stood about the 'banks and braes' had just veiled their slender delicate silvery limbs with their spring robes and fashions of the sweetest freshest tenderest green. The blackthorn was blossoming bright in the hedges, and from the banks a few primroses and blue violets looked at me with a smile of welcome. The farm folks were busy at their field work and the two or three people I met were friendly and courteous. Crossing the mouth of a wild and beautiful little valley and a green cwm or dingle, down which a silvery stream came murmuring softly under scattered birches to pour itself into the Marteg, I came out on the open hillside of short sweet mountain turf strewn with huge grey boulders. Sitting upon a warm and sunny rock on a green knoll commanding a view of the rushing river I ate my sandwiches and enjoyed the prospect. I was entirely alone except for the presence of the mountain sheep. The sun shone, and the stillness of mountain and valley was unbroken save by the bleating of the sheep, the rushing of the river and the calling of the cuckoo from the green hillsides.

Saturday, 6 May

As I lay in bed this morning it suddenly occurred to me to get up early, breakfast alone at 8 o'clock, and go by 9 o'clock train

to Tylwch to see the upper part of St Harmon's parish. I wrote
to Mr Venables stating my intention (the note to be given to
him at breakfast) and promising to be home to luncheon. When
I alighted at Tylwch I found myself amongst the mountains, at
the mouth of a gorge and actually in North Wales, in Mont-
gomeryshire. At Pantydwr, the highest point in the line, I had
crossed the watershed and now all the streams were flowing the
other way and were tributaries of the Severn instead of the
Wye. I had some pleasant talk with the one-armed station-
master who told me a good deal about the country and the
people and much that he said was friendly and favourable. I
asked of him if Mary Evans of Cwmbythog, my dear old
schoolgirl pupil, was not living in service near Tylwch but I
could get no tidings of her. The station-master told me that
upon the mountain above Tylwch peace had been signed
between the Welsh and English in the reign of Edward I, and
that some allusion to this historical fact was preserved in the
word 'Tylwch' which means he thought the 'House of Peace'.

The beautiful little river Clwrdag came rushing down the
gorge on its way to the Severn and in a curiously picturesque
manner it was carried over and across the course of another
stream in a rough wooden trough which conveyed the water to
a mill lower down the valley, the water meanwhile on its way
leaking and dripping from the mossy ferny trough in brilliant
little cascades. This other and smaller stream came wimpling
down a pretty little dingle and running over the yellow pebble
stones as clear as crystal. It was the boundary brook between
the North and South, between Radnorshire and Montgomery-
shire and between the parishes of St Harmon's and Llandinam.
I leaped across it easily and at one bound I was again in South
Wales. I knocked at the door of one of a group of St Harmon's
cottages and a tidy woman with a plaid shawl pinned over her
breast came to the door to speak to me. She also knew nothing
of Mary Evans being in that neighbourhood. She went over all
the neighbouring servant girls in her mind and then shook her
head. In answer to my question she said she sometimes got as
far as her parish church of St Harmon's though it was five
miles off.

I leaped once more across the boundary brook into North
Wales, and took a farewell glance at the picturesque wooden
trough, mossy and fern-fringed, from which the brilliant sparkling little cascades of water streamed and dripped splashing
with a musical sweet murmur into the boundary brook that
rushed below. Then I set my face up the hilly road amongst the
mountains to walk to Llanidloes. Down the mountain road past
the tall chimneys of the lead mines came rushing a flock of
mountain sheep out of North Wales. The sheep were followed
by a dog and a tall handsome young farmer, a man who, with
all the beautiful and native Welsh courtesy, answered my
questions and told me that it was about two miles to Llanidloes.

I was sorry when our roads parted and my kind and courteous
companion with his sheep and dog turned off into a by-lane
amongst the hills. How beautiful is the descent into Llanidloes
and the valley of the Severn as the town lies deeply sequestered,
embosomed by the mountains on every side and lapped so
lovingly amongst those fair blue hills. It was a bright glorious
day and the valley of the Severn was glowing with loveliness.
Llanidloes, beautiful Llanidloes. No wonder that St Idloes
loved the place and built his church by that fair vale in the lap
and bosom of those blue hills by the sweet waters of the Severn.

I had not more than a quarter of an hour to spare before the
return train started, and I hurried down the broad blazing
street, bright and busy with groups of market folk, and through
the cool shade and shelter of the curious quaint old market
house, long, low, and open on all sides, and with its high-
pitched roof supported upon ancient timber pillars. At length I
reached the Church, the old Church of St Idloes. The great bell
was tolling in the low turret for the death or burial of one of
the townspeople. I found some boys in the belfry, and sent one
of them for the church key. I thought the interior very fine,
especially the arches, roof, and sculptured figures which, with
the bells, are said to have been brought away as part of the
spoils from the ruined devastated pillaged Church of
Abbey Cwm Hir. The screen of the Abbey Church is now at
Newtown.

When I returned to Llysdinam I found Mr Venables and

Langley Burrell Church

Mr Dew walking together before the house. 'Well,' cried the former, 'you are an adventurous young man!'

Sunday, 7 May

Preached twice in the beautiful little iron Church. Mr Venables read prayers in the morning and Morgan the curate in the afternoon, when there was a capital congregation.. In the morning I preached upon the Mountain of Galilee and by Miss Higginson's request I put in a little bit specially for Mrs Venables about the duty of not being discouraged at seeing no immediate result of our work. In the afternoon I preached upon 'Mizpah' with another little word for Mrs Venables on the loss of her baby. As I came out of church after the second service I saw a respectable elderly-looking woman with a black and white checked shawl standing near the door. 'You have a very nice Church here,' I said to her smiling. 'Yes,' she said eagerly and enthusiastically catching hold of my arm, 'and you're a very nice man.'

The morning had been dull and cold but the afternoon brightened pleasantly and we had a happy Sunday evening walk with the children in the sunny larch woods.

[*He returned to Langley on 9 May and later made a short visit to Oxford, to his friend Mayhew. After his return to Langley the following entry appears.*]

Trinity Sunday, 11 June

Barnaby Bright.* This morning came a letter from the Bishop of St David's offering me the Vicarage of St Harmon's. I wrote and accepted it. Then it has come at last and I must leave my dear old home and parish and say goodbye to Langley and all my dear kind friends there. It will be a hard bitter wrench and a sorrowful, a very sorrowful parting. It seems dreadful to leave my Father alone at his age and with his infirmities to

*St Barnabas Day. Before the reform of the calendar 11 June was the longest day.

contend with the worries and anxieties of the parish and at the tender mercies of a curate. I hope I have not acted selfishly in leaving him. But at my age I feel that I cannot throw away a chance in life and our tenure of this living is a very precarious one. It is 'the warm nest on the rotten bough'. I have not sought this or any other preferment. Indeed I have rather shrunk from it. And as it has so come to me without my wish or seeking of my own it seems as if the Finger of God were in it and as if I were but following the calling of His Voice and the beckoning, guiding and leading of His Hand.

1877

[There is a break in the diary from June 1876 to December 1877. During most of this time Kilvert has been vicar of St Harmon's. There is no record of his time there. In the latter part of 1876 he went on a tour abroad with his friend Mayhew. In the course of it he met his future wife, Elizabeth Rowland, in Paris. According to her niece, Miss M. A. Rowland, the missing portion of the diary was removed by Mrs Kilvert because it contained references to her.

When the diary resumes he has become vicar of Bredwardine and has been there for a month. His sister Dora keeps house for him, and his sister Thersie's husband is rector of the adjoining parish of Monnington.]

BREDWARDINE VICARAGE, 1877
Monday, 31 December, New Year's Eve

A fine mild spring morning, bright sunshine, the river full, swift and brown, but falling, the cedars and the bright green lawn terraces very lovely in the morning sunshine.

I stayed in all the morning to see Mr Williams of Brobury about the Club coal for the poor people of Brobury, but he did not come. After dinner I went to Brobury Court and saw him.

I called on my tenant at the Rectory Farm, Brobury, Thomas Preece. The old man was in a low way about his wheat which turns out badly. He complained of his liability to parish offices in spite of his small tenure. He took me into the scullery to show me how much the stone tile roof wanted repairing, and proposed to cover it afresh with slates, of which he had 100 to spare, left over from roofing a cottage of his at Letton. As I crossed Bredwardine Bridge I went in to see the Jenkinses who have kept the bridge toll gate for two months. They seem nice old people. They have lately come from Llanigon to which they seem much attached while they feel strange here.

The old woman was full of strange stories of the countryside. She had felt beforehand and predicted the coming of the great rainstorm and waterspout which fell on the Epynt Hills in the summer of 1854 in July, and swept away the Lawrences' house on the Dihonn brook near Builth. She had lived for years at the Holly Bush on the northern slope of the Black Mountain and her husband had kept school in the Baptist Chapel at Capel y Ffin. 'There are strange things about the Black Mountain,' she said, 'but I have travelled the hills at all hours, night and day, and never saw anything bad. One time I had been working late at the Parc on the southern side of the Mountain down in the dingle and I was coming home pretty late in the dark. It was about February or March. As I came over the Bwlch y fingel I was singing to keep my courage up, and I was singing a hymn out of an old book for I thought I wouldn't sing any-thing but what was good then. It was a fine starlight night and just as I got down into the plain I heard beautiful singing overhead, like the singing of birds. They seemed to be some great birds travelling. I could not see them but they sang and whistled most beautiful, and they were just overhead. They seemed to be going away down the mountain towards Caedwgan. And I said to myself, "God bless me from here, there will be a funeral from that house," and sure enough within a month a dead person was carried out from Caedwgan.'

I sat up till after midnight to watch the Old Year out and the New Year in. The bells rang at intervals all the evening, tolled just before the turn of the night and the year and then rang a joy peal, and rang on till one o'clock. After I had gone to bed I saw from where I lay a bright blaze sprung up in the fields beyond the river and I knew at once that they were keeping up the old custom of Burning the Bush on New Year's Day in the morning. From the Knap, the hill above the village masked by the two clumps of trees, the whole valley can be seen early on New Year's Morning alight with fires Burning the Bush, as it can be seen also from the hill at Bettws, Clyro, on which the old Chapel stands.

1878

Tuesday, New Year's Day, 1878

At nine o'clock after breakfast I went to the Old Court to see Mr Evans, the Churchwarden, on parish business. He had not finished breakfast. 'We were up rather late last night Christmassing,' he said with a smile.

At 10 a.m. I went up the hill to Crafta Webb, receiving kindly New Year greetings and good wishes from every one in the road. The sound of the joy bells ringing at Bredwardine Church for New Year's Morning floated sweetly up the hillside from the blue valley. I visited Preece the tailor and Bevan the shoemaker, my tenants, and arranged with Eliza Preece to hold a cottage lecture at her cottage on Winter Thursday evenings till Lent, beginning next Thursday. The shoemaker took me round the little meadows which he holds of me. I visited Kitty Arrowsmith and went down a beautiful wild dingle to the cottage of Ellen Lewis at Little Fine Street. 'The like to you,' said Ellen Lewis in answer to my salutation of 'a happy New Year'. In the cottage gardens the monthly pink roses and the gilly flowers were blooming sweetly. Kitty Arrowsmith told me that Crafta Webb was variously nicknamed Hyde Park Corner, New Town, and Poverty Street.

In the lane between Great and Little Fine Street I met James Davies, my churchwarden. He took off his hat with a profound and courteous bow and 'the compliments of the season' and turning conducted me to his house where I saw his wife and daughter Jane and grandniece, little Bessie Davies from Llanafon in Dorstone. They were all most kind and courteous. 'I should not like to insult you, Sir, this morning,' said the handsome grey-haired grey-eyed churchwarden, 'but will you drink a glass of my home-made cider?' So I did and drank their healths all round, while he signed the paper declaring that I had read the 39 Articles and the Declaration of Assent thereunto. The Churchwarden apologised much for his farmhouse which he said disparagingly was worse than a cottage. Mrs Davies was busy baking and Jane seeing to the house and dinner. He courteously accompanied me on my way as far as the nearest stile and told me that his father and grandfather had rented the same farm of the Cornewall family without a lease, tenants only from year to year, and that it had been in the family for nearly 100 years. I told him that the knight in armour (Reginald? de Fresne) whose recumbent figure rests upon the tomb in the chancel of Moccas Church was an ancestor of mine, and that my forefathers owned the Moccas estate. The Churchwarden opened his grey eyes almost incredulously at first. 'Well,' he said as I went on with the history and the pedigree, 'I have heard the name of Fraxinus, I suppose then you are some kin to Sir George, and he has royal blood.' I said laughing that his ancestors bought the estate from mine or after mine had sold it and that I could not claim blood royal. . . .

[*His father and mother come to stay.*]

Wednesday, 2 January

A thick dark mild morning with a Scotch mist. Showed my father round the garden and over the Church. He was much pleased with everything. The house and garden were much larger and more beautiful than he had supposed. Both he and my mother are delighted with the place. My Father especially admired the old Norman 12th or 13th century work in the Church and more particularly the South doorway arch and the carving over the Devil's Door (the North door). . . .

We had for our early dinner Sir George Cornewall's hare and brace of pheasants.

Thursday, 3 January

The weather was very close and oppressive. At 6.15 I took Arthur's lantern and went up to Crafta Webb to give a cottage lecture at Eliza Preece's house. It was pitch dark and raining, the road very steep and bad, and before I got to the end of my journey I was streaming with perspiration, and wet without and within. Just before I reached Eliza Preece's cottage the paraffin lamp in the lantern went out and left me in the dark so that I had much ado and worried myself to find the garden gate. The room was full of people, there was a cheerful fire, and a lamp bright on the table, and I was glad I had come, for the people seemed glad to see me. I had a hymn first, 'Sun of my soul', then some of the Evening Prayer, and read Hebrews xi. 8, 9, 10, and spoke of our going into the year 1878 as Abraham went out at the call of God into the strange and Promised Land. Just before I ended poor Mrs Jenkins fainted and had to be carried to the door to be revived with fresh air and cold water. She had been turned suddenly out of Bredwardine Bridge Gate house and been obliged to move to a damp, long untenanted cottage which had troubled her much and made her weak and ill. She was violently sick and then better and some of the kind neighbours helped her home. The incident distressed us all and brought our little gathering to a sudden close.

Friday, 4 January

I went up the Hill to Crafta Webb to see how Mrs Jenkins was, who fainted at the cottage lecture last night. She was better. Her darling little grandchild Alice flung her arms round my neck, laid her soft round cheek to mine, kissed me over and over again, and declared that I should not go away and if I went she should come with me. I called next at old John Williams' (Jack my Lord) and read to him and his wife Mary, from John x. The people all seem pleased with the lecture last night and said they should come again next week. It was getting very dark as I came down the hill. I looked in at the Cottage, the organ was sounding in the hall and there sat Holingshed, the blind organist of the Moor, playing while Algernon Bates,

Miss Newton and Mrs W. Newton were standing round singing and Polly Parry was blowing.

I was very glad to see my old acquaintance Holingshed again. He played us some beautiful hymn tunes and gems from the Elijah. 'O rest in the Lord' and 'If with all your hearts'.

In the *Standard* yesterday there was a leading article on the election of John Henry Newman* to an honorary fellowship at Trinity College, Oxford, which interested my dear Father much. He remembers Newman well at Oriel. He told me that some years after he had left Oxford, Uncle Francis, who had letters of introduction to Newman, called upon him when he was Vicar of St Mary's. He spoke to Newman about my Father. 'I remember him well,' said Newman, 'he left a fragrant memory behind him in Oriel.'

Saturday, 5 January

Sarah Lewis who brings our eggs brought a message from her aunt old Priscilla Price that she was ill and would be glad to see me. . . .

I found Priscilla Price and the idiot woman, her stepdaughter, sitting at their tea by the fire. Prissy is 77 and the idiot 55. 'Ar Tader, Ar Tader!' cried the idiot. 'She means "Our Father," ' explained her stepmother. 'She has been wanting to see the clergyman, the gentleman that says "Our Father".' Prissy detailed to me the story of an illness she had suffered, illustrated by a dramatic performance by the idiot as a running accompaniment. Occasionally in addition to the acting of the details of the illness, the bursting of a bloodvessel, the holding the head of the invalid, and yelling to the neighbours for help, the idiot roared out an affirmative or negative according to the requirements of the tale. 'The blood spouted up,' said Prissy. 'Yes!' thundered the idiot. 'She held my head,' explained Prissy. 'Yes!' roared the idiot. 'There was no one here but her,' said Prissy. 'No!' shouted the idiot. 'They say Mr Davies heard her crying for help as far as Fine Street,' declared Prissy. 'Yes!' asserverated the idiot with a roar of pride and satisfaction. 'She

*He was to be created cardinal in the following year.

had to run out into the deep snow,' said the stepmother. The idiot stepdaughter measured the depth of the snow upon her thigh. 'I want to explain to you, if you please,' said Priscilla, 'what it was that I meant when I said to you the day you first came to see me, "God send you to overturn the tables of the money-changers". I meant the tables of sin in this place. When our Saviour was on earth He had His difficulties and you will have yours here at first, but as I took the liberty to tell Mrs Clarke and Mr Houseman so I tell you, don't fret and worry yourself. This Charity interferes with people, and does them harm. Those who get it are discontented and those who don't get it are discontented, but don't you distress yourself.' Speaking of the Jenkinses being turned out of The Bridge Gate and having nowhere to go when they were obliged to leave Prissy said, 'A loaf of bread is a poor provision if there is no roof to eat it under.' I reminded her that our Lord had nowhere to lay His head.

She asked me to read and pray for her. I read a passage from Matthew xvii, the idiot having brought me a fine large-print Prayer Book and Testament. The reading was accompanied by a running fire of ejaculations and devout utterances from Prissy. She put a mat on the floor for me to kneel on and knelt down herself with some pain and difficulty, having sprained her knee. I begged her to be seated. 'No,' she said, 'I will kneel. I must punish the body. Kneel down, my dear,' she said reprovingly to the idiot. The idiot knelt humbly down in front of the fire with her head almost in the ashes. Prissy accompanied the prayer as she had done the reading with a running fire of comment and ejaculation. 'Ay, ay, Father,' she explained when the prayer was ended, and she rose with difficulty to her feet.

Speaking of the blowing of the Holy Thorn and the kneeling and weeping of the oxen on old Christmas Eve (to-night) Priscilla said, 'I have known old James Meredith 40 years and I have never known him far from the truth, and I said to him one day, "James, tell me the truth, did you ever see the oxen kneel on old Christmas Eve at the Weston?" And he said, "No, I never saw them kneel at the Weston but when I was at Hinton at Staunton-on-Wye I saw them. I was watching them on old

Christmas Eve and at 12 o'clock the oxen that were standing knelt down upon their knees and those that were lying down rose up on their knees and there they stayed kneeling and moaning, the tears running down their faces." '

Monday, 7 January

I went to the little farmhouse of Dolfach on the hill to see the Holy Thorn there in blossom. The tree (a graft from the old Holy Thorn at Tibberton now cut down) bloomed on Old Christmas Eve and there were 15 people watching round the tree to see it blow at midnight. I found old John Perry sitting at tea by the cheerful firelight in the chimney corner. His kind daughter gave me a bit of a spray of the Holy Thorn which was gathered from the tree at midnight, old Christmas Eve. She set great store by the spray and always gathered and kept a bit each year. The blossoms were not fully out and the leaves were scarcely unfolded but the daughter of the house assured me that the little white bud clusters would soon come out into full blow if put in soft water. The parent tree is a hawthorn and blossoms again in May. It was the first bit of Holy Thorn I had ever seen. I brought it home as a curiosity. Parry and his daughter were deeply interested by my translation of the Welsh names of the farms and fields about Bredwardine Hill.

Wednesday, 9 January

Afternoon I went to the Cottage and had a long talk with Mrs William Newton walking up and down the drive. She gave me much good kind advice about the management of the parish. She told me it had become a difficult parish to manage and would require much care and judgment and tact.

Monday, 14 January

I found a nice letter from sweet Florence Hill of the Upper Noyadd at Llowes, and one from dear little Mary Pitchford of the Rock House, Pantydown, St Harmon's. Mary says, 'We have lost our shepherd, for you have planted a rose in my heart which I hope I shall never forget.'

Tuesday, 15 January

School at 9.30 and taught the higher standards the history of Hezekiah's illness, and the shadow returning on the dial. Mr Heywood called and went over the gross and net value of the livings with me. They are more valuable than I thought, gross £412, net £375.

Wednesday, 16 January

Gave the upper standards at the school questions on paper on the Catechism. Promised Mr Bates the schoolmaster to read the 1st book of the *Iliad* with his son Henry to help him on in his Greek. He is at the Cathedral School, Hereford.

Gave a cottage lecture at Crafta Webb at 7 o'clock. Esther and Tom Hyde walked up with me and I told them how I had once been lost on the Black Mountain and obliged to eat dock leaves. There were 23 people at the Lecture, all very attentive, the room crowded and some standing. I spoke on 'Wist ye not that I must be about my Father's business'.

Saturday, 19 January

I am glad to hear that Ettie Meredith Brown is to be married in April to Mr Wright, the brother of her brother-in-law.

Thursday, 24 January, Eve of St Paul

Shoolbreds sent in their bill, £230.9.6.

Saturday, 26 January

The people of the three parishes of Bredwardine, Staunton and Letton have a rooted and ineradicable belief that the Trustees

Bredwardine Vicarage

of the Jarvis Charity draw £100 a year each and this is why, they say, there is no money for the poor lately. Nothing will persuade them to the contrary.

Tuesday, 29 January

Mary Matthews had just come from Dowlais. She said the distress there was terrible and pitiful, the people perishing of hunger and the distress in Merthyr worse than at Dowlais.

'You great bear,' said Mrs Harris severely to her black and white cat. Garmin, the Brobury keeper, brought a hare and brace of pheasants from Sir Henry Cotterell.

Wednesday, 30 January

Cottage Lecture at Crafta Webb, the room thronged. 36 people, some standing. Eliza Preece fainted. I spoke on Candlemas and the Purification. 'The Lord whom ye seek shall suddenly come to His Temple.'

Saturday, Candlemas Day

Dear Mrs Lewis of Pen Pistyll sent me to-day from St Harmon's a noble turkey for the Tithe dinner next Tuesday. This kind and loving gift and remembrance from my dear old parish and friends was very sweet to me.

Tuesday, 5 February

To-day was the Tithe audit and tithe dinner to the farmers, both held at the Vicarage. About 50 tithe payers came, most of them very small holders, some paying as little as 9d. As soon as they had paid their tithe to Mr Haywood in the front hall they retired into the back hall and regaled themselves with bread, cheese and beer, some of them eating and drinking the value of the tithe they had paid. The tithe-paying began about 3 p.m. and the stream went on till six. At 7 I sat down to dinner with the farmers. Haywood took the foot of the table. His son sat on my left and Price of Bodcote on my right hand. The other guests were Griffiths of the Pentre, James Davies of Fine St, George Davies of Benfield and young Thomas Davies of the Old House, Edmund Preece, young Parry of Dolfach and Mr Bates the schoolmaster.

The Pen Pistyll turkey boiled looked very noble when it came to table. George Davies of Benfield was so impressed with the size of the bird that he declared it must be 'a three-year-old,' and he did not hear the last of this all the evening. At the foot of the table there was roast beef, and at the sides jugged hare and beefsteak pie, preceded by pea soup, and in due course followed by plum pudding, apple tart, mince pies and blanc-mange, cheese and dessert. It was a very nice dinner, thanks to Dora, and I think they all liked it and enjoyed themselves. After dinner Mr Haywood proposed my health very kindly and I made a little speech. We broke up at 10.30. Thersie came over to help us and spent the night here.

Saturday, 9 February

Burney and Evans of Shrewsbury have at last sent me 5 copies of *Selections from our Poetical Portfolio*. No names given, and many mistakes and misprints in the poems. I gave a copy to Miss Newton . . .

To-day we heard of the death of Pope Pius IX.

Soon after I had gone to bed I heard our cock crow. I knew he always crowed at midnight and I had the curiosity to get out of bed and look at my watch to see if he was true to the time. The hands of the watch pointed to two minutes past midnight.

Thursday, 14 February

To-day I went for the first time into the kitchen garden on the Brobury side of the river. There were some old Espalier pears and apples and some young peach, nectarine and apricot trees against the walls, and one fine fig tree. The garden frames were in a very ruinous state.

Friday, 15 February

A day indoors nursing a bad cold and troublesome cough. Read *The Marquis of Lossie*, the sequel of *Malcolm*, by George Macdonald, but inferior to it, I think.

Arthur went to Staunton in the evening to fetch a bottle of cough mixture for me from Mr Giles. It was a beautiful moonlit night and from my bedroom window I could see the moonbeams shining in the basin of the fountain on the lawn and broken shattering as the water was stirred into little waves by the night breeze. The white house was bathed in a flood of brilliant moonlight, a strange weird contrast to the black solemn cedars.

Saturday, 16 February

Another day indoors nursing against Sunday. A lovely spring day, bright and warm and joyous with birdsinging. The crocuses are beginning to appear in the garden and in the churchyard some of the graves are white and beautiful with snowdrops. Wrote *The Shepherd's Farewell* and part of *The Companion*. Emily walked to Staunton to get another bottle of medicine for me from Mr Giles. It was a beautiful warm moonlit evening. Looking from my bedroom window I saw the moon shining in the river which was streaming as with flakes of fire under the black cedars.

Wednesday, 20 February

Cottage lecture at Crafta Webb. I spoke on the parable of the Good Shepherd and told the people of my own blindness and difficulty in knowing my own sheep by sight and calling them by name. No one fainted, but Mrs Bubb of Wooller had to go out to look after her daughter Sarah who had started from home before her to come to the lecture but had not arrived. Presently she came back with the strayed lamb whom she found lost in a wood.

Friday, 22 February

James Meredith spoke of the seats in Church as if they were fields and of the people as if they were cattle. Each person he said had 'his ground'. 'Mr —— is now coming back to his own ground,' he said. 'That was always the —— ground'.

Tuesday, 26 February

My dear Father's 75th birthday. May it please God to spare him to us yet for many years to come.

At 10 a.m. went on the box of Miss Newton's brougham to the reopening of Mansel Gamage Church after a good restoration. More than 25 clergy in surplices. The Bishop preached in the morning, the Archdeacon, Lord Saye and Sele, in the afternoon. It was difficult to say which was the worse sermon. The former was a screed, the latter a rigmarole, but the rigmarole was more appropriate and more to the purpose than the screed. A nice luncheon at the Stanhopes' at Byford

Rectory. I was with a small party at a table in the study at which Miss Stanhope presided. The large party was in the dining room. Good congregations and the offertories amounted to nearly £50 and cleared off the debt on the Church. The weather dry and the roads good, a satisfactory day. Many people laugh at the old Baron's sermons, but the cottagers like them for he is plain and homely and speaks of names and places that they know. When Moccas Church was restored and re-opened Lord Saye and Sele preached in the afternoon and told the people that Moccas was so called from 'the badgers which came down to the river to eat the fish'. It is supposed he meant otters, and that he had in some strange confused way mixed up together otters, badgers and pigs, for Moccas is so called from the swine (Welsh *Moch*) which used to feed on the acorns in the great oak forest.

Saturday, 2 March

I went on to see Priscilla Price. I saw her over the hedge in her garden below the road leaning her back against the garden gate and sunning herself in the evening light. The old woman took me indoors. 'Rise up, my dear,' she said to her idiot step-daughter, 'rise up and make your courtesy and shake hands with the gentleman.' The idiot sat immovable with her eyes fixed on the fire. Presently as we were talking she rose slowly and solemnly offered me her hand with a strange mechanical motion. 'She wants to shake hands with you now', said Priscilla in a low voice.

I went down the green lane between the orchards and through a gate which brought me under the gable of a small farmhouse picturesquely placed among orchards and crofts on the green hillside sheltered from the west winds, and looking towards the rising sun. A few steps brought me round to the front of the house. In the door stood a tall fair comely girl with a clear fresh open face, kind grey eyes, and golden brown hair, Annie Abberley. She welcomed me in kindly and set a chair by the fire. She was expecting her father in to his dinner, she said. Another girl's footstep sounded overhead and in a few moments pretty Lizzie came down the stair in her russet brown dress with her dark hair and eyes, her quiet demure manner and shy sweet smile. I told Annie I had discovered that Lizzie and I were old friends. 'Yes,' she said, 'when Lizzie came home from school and told me what you had told her I reminded her of what she said years ago, how a gentleman had come into the school one afternoon and found her and Elizabeth Hyde sweeping the room and how he had shown them the way to sweep and told them to put their hats on or they would get their hair dusty.' I had quite forgotten this. Annie said she had been house and parlourmaid at Pont Vaen when I was at Clyro. She had often seen me there and had often heard me preach. Then she was in service as housemaid at Whitney Rectory and one day when she was there she said she heard of my being in the house but she did not see me. She was also nursemaid to the Housemans at Bredwardine Vicarage. And now she keeps her father's at the Upper Cwm. 'It is a wonderful place for birds,' she said, 'the cuckoo sings here all night long. And only the other night I heard a blackbird keep on waking up and whistling through the night. Sometimes when I have [been] up and out early, starting father for Hereford at daylight, I have stood out in the orchards listening to the singing of the birds. On a clear day we can see the steeple of All Saints' Church in Hereford, there I can see it now through that apple bough against the far blue hill.' We were standing out in the fold. 'It is a very quiet place here', Annie went on, 'and we don't see many people passing, but it is very peaceful and a pleasant prospect, and I like to be amongst the fields and orchards and to hear the singing of the birds and we are content.' 'How wise,' I thought, and said, 'to be content and happy with the beauties and the blessings that lie around.' The father who had been looking after his lambs now came in to his dinner, a swarthy peculiar-looking man in a smock frock. He said he had 2 lambs as yet. He had 20 ewes to lamb and he preferred singles to doubles on poor land. As we stood at the door talking a voice floated up from the Lower Cwm through the evening air singing the Canadian Boat Song.

Quinquagesima Sunday, 3 March

As I walked in the Churchyard this morning the fresh sweet sunny air was full of the singing of the birds and the brightness and gladness of the Spring.

Some of the graves were as white as snow with snowdrops. The southern side of the Churchyard was crowded with a multitude of tombstones. They stood thick together, some taller, some shorter, some looking over the shoulders of others, and as they stood up all looking one way and facing the morning sun they looked like a crowd of men, and it seemed as if the morning of the Resurrection had come and the sleepers had arisen from their graves and were standing upon their feet silent and solemn, all looking toward the East to meet the Rising of the Sun. The whole air was melodious with the distant indefinite sound of sweet bells that seemed to be ringing from every quarter by turns, now from the hill, now from the valley, now from the deer forest, now from the river. The chimes rose and fell, swelled and grew faint again.

Saturday, 9 March

I went out for a little while on the terrace this morning and walked up and down on the sunny side of the house. After how many illnesses such as this* have I taken my first convalescent walk on the sunny terrace and always at this time of year when the honeysuckle leaves were shooting green and the apricot blossoms were dawning and the daffodils in blow. But some day will come the last illness from which there will be no convalescence and after which there will be no going out to enjoy the sweet sights and sounds of the earthly spring, the singing of the birds, the opening of the fruit blossoms, the budding dawn of green leaves, and the blowing of the March daffodils. May I then be prepared to enter into the everlasting Spring and to walk among the birds and flowers of Paradise.

Monday, 11 March

To-day I wrote to Mr C. T. Longman, to whom I had received

*Congestion of the lungs.

an introduction from Mrs Middleton Evans of Llwynbarried, to ask him if and on what terms he would publish a small book of poems for me.

Friday, 15 March

This morning came a letter from Mr Longman, very courteous but not encouraging the idea of my publishing a book of poems. . . .

To-day old John Parry came down from Dolfoch to Bredwardine Vicarage and grafted a slip of his Holy Thorn on a hawthorn below the terrace.

Tuesday, 26 March

Called at the Bridge Gate house on the Merediths. Mrs Meredith told me she had seen better days. She once kept the Monmouth Gap Hotel and a coaching establishment of 18 horses, 16 of which died of influenza at one time. Then her husband died and she moved with her 5 children to the shop opposite the hotel, and brought them up. Her second husband was a small timber merchant who was ruined by the failure of a man in the same business. Now they have come down to keep a turnpike gate. . . .

This evening while we were at prayers and singing the hymn 'My God, my Father while I stray' Dora suddenly fell on the floor in a fainting fit. I thought she had only overbalanced herself, slipped and fallen against Florence who was looking over her hymn book, but Louisa rushed forward crying, 'She's fainting, Sir!' and helped me to raise her lay her back in an easy chair while Arthur stood aghast. I called to Emily to run for cold water. Dora soon came round again and drank a glass of sherry. She said she had never quite lost consciousness. She had been singing a good deal and her dress was tight and the east wind made her feel ill and she caught her breath and could not get it again.

Thursday, 28 March

Yesterday Florence was much delighted by discovering in the basin of the fountain on the lawn a fish which she called a carp.

Tuesday, April Morrow

I had long wished to pay a visit to Maurice Richards the woodman's cottage in the wood and as to-day was fine and drying I determined to go.

Mary Jackson showed me my way over the wattled stiles and along the bankside, through the wood to the woodman's cottage. It was a beautiful afternoon, the larches in the sheltered hollows were thickening green and waving their first tender green feathers and the woods were full of the singing of birds. As I went through the wood I heard a sudden sharp rustling and struggling amongst the dry leaves and sticks and then some animal began to scream violently. A little chestnut-coloured creature was darting and struggling about upon the ground with such furious vehemence and extraordinary rapidity that I could not for some time make out what it was. The animal had evidently been caught in a trap by the hind leg. At first I thought from its bushy tail it was a squirrel. Finding that it could not free its leg from the teeth of the powerful gin the little creature after darting about and struggling with the most inconceivable swiftness and furious violence, turned like a wild beast to bay and faced me like a lion with its eyes flaming with fury and its lips drawn savagely so as to bare its teeth. It was a beautiful and graceful little creature with a bushy tail, a body arched like a greyhound, glossy chestnut fur on the back and sides and underneath a pale delicate yellow. I think it was a stoat. I could not help but admire the courage of the little creature and the steadiness and fierceness with which he gazed at me. Then he turned with pathetic curiosity and concern to look at the trap and his imprisoned and wounded leg, and fearing that the leg might be broken or that he might be left there to die of hunger, with one blow on the back of the head I put him out of his fear and pain.

I went on to Maurice Richards' cottage seated in a pleasant nook in the wooded hillside looking towards the rising sun and 'towards Lady Lift' as Mrs Richards said. Her kindly pleasant comely face carried me back to Clyro and reminded me strongly of Mrs Vaughan the shoemaker's wife and widow. The garden was in the most exquisitely neat order and the house beautifully clean. I took a great fancy to the place and the people.

Elizabeth Bubb took me down to the arable field below where Mr Hawkins's (late of the Western Farm) wheat and beans had all been eaten by the birds and failed, and which was being prepared for barley. Two steam engines were at work, one on each side of the field, drawing to and fro between them by a wide chain a scuffle or cultivator with a man riding on it which dragged a harrow behind it.

Wednesday, 3 April

Yesterday morning and this morning after school I went to see James Carver at the Cwm. He is very delicate and suffers from some affliction of the head. His mother said she dreamed when sleeping with him she heard a bubble burst in his head.

Thursday, 4 April

Lady Cornewall called and kindly brought me another bottle of the Syrup of Hypophosphate of lime.

Thursday, 11 April

School. The Confirmation at Eardisley. After the pouring rain of yesterday we had a lovely soft mild day, the sun tenderly veiled, like those soft pure young hearts which today came to make their vows to God. I took a little flock of eleven.

Easter Day, 21 April

I took the three full services. There were twenty guests at the H.C., the largest number I have yet seen in Bredwardine.

Alms 18/9¼. Good congregations at all three services. I was very thankful to be able to do it all myself without troubling anyone. My voice was stronger and clearer to-day than it has been at all since my illness. Some of the graves were very nicely dressed, especially at Brobury. Mrs Williams of Brobury Court and Lizzie Willis dressed the little Brobury Church very prettily, and dear Lizzie had written 'Christ is risen' on the S. window sill in primroses. Mrs Williams decorated the Font with apple blossom.

*Friday, 26 April**

To St Harmon's by 9.10 train to marry David Powell and Maggie Jones of Tylare. Mrs Jones of the Gates had made a triumphal arch of moss over the Churchyard gate and flowers were strewn in the bride's path. Maggie was surprised and delighted to see and be married by her old friend. Fog signals were laid on the line and the wedding party issued from Church just as the noon train came down with the banging of crackers and guns and a great crowd at the station crossing gates. The wedding party and guests went to the Sun where I joined them for a minute to drink a glass of wine to the health of the bride and bridegroom and then walked on to Cwm yr ychen, stopping for a few minutes by the way at Traveller's Rest and Ty Graig, to see Mary and Kate, and for a romp with Emmeline at Tan yr Allt. 'Is the bride in the family way?' asked her grandmother, old Mary Jones, with eager interest. 'I hope not,' I said. I went on to Cwm yr ychen, a glass of wine and a chat with Mrs Meredith and her son Edward, the young squire of Cwm yr ychen, and then back to the wedding dinner at Tylare by the hillside path. I took the head and Jack Evans the foot of the long table to carve for the company. When one set had dined another took their places and we carved them all. Then we went into another room, the parlour (the dinner was in the kitchen), the bride and bridegroom were with some difficulty gathered together and brought into the parlour and made to sit in the place of honour and observation in the window seat

*He is staying at Rhayader vicarage.

and I made a little speech and proposed their healths. Then Jack Evans proposed mine and wishing all my friends 'Good-bye' I had to run to the St Harmon's Station by way of Lingen to catch the 4.45 train.

' 'Tis a pity but what you had stayed here,' sighed the clerk deeply as I carved for him at dinner.

Saturday, 27 April

Neuralgia very troublesome all the week, no sleep at nights.

[*He spends two nights at Llysdinam.*]

Friday, 3 May

After breakfast I went to Lyncam and engaged Morgan's house-keeper, Mrs Price, as our housekeeper at Bredwardine Vicarage. She is to have £14 a year to begin and to come to us Monday, 13 May. Old May Day. She has been having £12 a year from Morgan, who gives her an excellent character and would take her with him to his Glasbury Curacy but he is going into lodgings.

Saturday, 4 May

Left Llysdinam by 12.30 train and returned to Bredwardine.

Monday, 27 May

Showery. Sent Schoolbred and Co. a cheque for £50 on account of a bill of £230.9.6 for furniture.

Wednesday, 29 May

To-day Walter de Winton Esqre of Maesllwch Castle was buried at Glasbury. He died at Maesllwch Castle last Friday, 24 May, aged 46.

Maesllwch Castle, near Clyro

A new lawn mower by Follows and Bates came from Morley's at Hereford in Baynham's cart, price £4.2.6.

Saturday, June Day

Afternoon visited Joseph Gwynne and Sarah Lewis. I found poor unfortunate Bessie Hyde at home alone and spoke to her sadly and solemnly about her dreadful fall. At Priscilla Price's Mary the idiot made signs that she was very ill and going to die. She pressed her hand on her side and said, 'Puff, Puff.' Priscilla interpreted for her. 'That means "die",' she said. 'Bom, Bom,' said the idiot. 'She means the great bell will toll over her grave,' said Priscilla. The idiot rose and curtsied profoundly. 'That is,' said Priscilla, 'that after she is dead she will rise and curtsey to everyone who has been good to her.' 'Yes, yes,' said the idiot. 'She is not willing for me to die before her,' said Priscilla. 'No, no!' exclaimed the idiot. 'Poor Prissy.' 'The will of the Lord be done,' said Priscilla. 'Amen,' said the idiot.

Tuesday, 4 June

To-day Teddy was married to Nellie Pitcairn at St Barnabas Church, Kensington. Teddy and I (his groomsman) left Norris' hotel at 9.30 and drove to 13 Colville Terrace where the brothers Pitcairn have rooms and where the breakfast was given. He dressed there and we drove down to St Barnabas' Vicarage. Wedding at 11.15. My Father performed the ceremony, assisted by Dr F. Hessey. The fees were enormous, £3.3.

Thursday, 20 June

In the morning I weeded the raspberry bed in the lower garden. Afternoon walked to a garden party at Eardisley Vicarage. A very pleasant evening. Palmer took me aside as soon as I came in and offered me from Canon Walsham How the permanent Chaplaincy at Cannes. He thought it might perhaps be desirable to accept it on account of my health. I came home on the box of Miss Newton's carriage.

Friday, 21 June

The longest day. Wrote to my Father, Mr Venables, Spencer and Canon Walsham How about the Cannes Chaplaincy.

Saturday, 22 June

A fine summer's day. Very hot. Walked to Monnington to luncheon. On the way called on Miss Cornewall who has lately come back from Cannes to ask her information about the place. She was very kind and told me much. She said she thought the Chaplaincy must be a very delightful position. Mr Giles came in to see one of the servants. I asked if I ought to go to Cannes on account of my health. He said, 'Go by all means. It is the very place. It may prolong your life for some years.'

Monday, 24 June, Midsummer Day

Edward Awdry came by the last train from Kington St Michael to stay a few days with us. Weather fine and hot. Corresponding and thinking with some perplexity about the offer of the Cannes Chaplaincy.

Thursday, 27 June

Wrote to Palmer and Walsham How to decline the Cannes Chaplaincy.

Friday, 12 July

I called on Mrs Godsall to see her daughter (the wife of Lord Lyons' coachman or steed groom) and the 4 grandchildren, 2 girls and 2 boys, lately come from Paris on a visit to their grand-parents. The coachman's wife told me that her husband drove Lord Lyons into Paris from Versailles on the last day of the Commune troubles. The firing was still going on in the streets and he could hardly drive the carriage for the dead bodies.

Saturday, 13 July

Visited Priscilla Price and took a pudding for her and a pie for Mary the idiot from Dora.

Wednesday, 17 July

Very hot. Afternoon went to Crafta Webb. Visited Jack my Lord, Hancox, Margaret Bowen. Mrs Hancox told me her husband had been an altered man since he heard my Father preach a sermon in Bredwardine Church last January.

Thursday, 18 July

Hotter and hotter. My Father and I drove to Kinnersley Station in Baynham's trap and went by 9.50 train to Talyllyn to fish in Llangorse Lake. About noon we got into a shoal of perch and killed five dozen or more in two hours, not large ones. We pulled them out as fast as we could put the lines in.

Tuesday, 6 August

Afternoon visited Priscilla Price. The idiot had ordered her coffin and paid a halfpenny for it. The carpenter kept the half-penny three months and then returned it without the coffin. The idiot was angry, said he should not make her coffin now, and gave the order to someone else.

Wednesday, 7 August

Saw Price at the Cottage and spoke to him seriously about his fault this week. He expressed penitence and said he had resolved not to drink very intoxicating liquor for six months. To-day Baynham made a lawn tennis ground in Mrs Wall's meadow for the Furlonge girls who are staying at the Lion and fenced it with hurdles.

Thursday, 8 August

Visited the old Merediths at the Bridge Gate. Mrs Meredith said she was very ill. ' 'Tis the dog star,' she said. 'I shall not be better till Saturday when the dog days end. 'Tis an evil star.'

Saturday, 10 August

At 3 o'clock I administered the Holy Communion to Priscilla Price. The idiot Mary had fallen in a fit with her head under the grate a day or two ago, but was not burnt or hurt. Priscilla pulled her out.

Wednesday, 14 August

Went to a garden party at Moccas Court. As I walked by the deer park lodge I heard that the lodge keeper's wife, Mrs Beaven, was ill and went up to see her. I called at the other

lodge and saw Mrs Hicks who said gratefully that the ointment which Dora brought her from Aberystwyth for her exema
was doing her great good. Her husband and sons were shooting
bucks for venison in the Park. She said it was the worst park in
England for killing bucks, and killed the men as well as the
deer. I saw a herd of bucks near the lodge walking about
together with their sides as tight together as herrings packed in
a barrel and their horns going like a forest. They let me come
quite close to them as I had no gun though the keepers could
not get within a ¼ mile. The afternoon and evening and the
river scene at Moccas were enchantingly beautiful. Lady Cornewall was very kind and nice. I had some delicious grapes and a
peach and nectarine. Walwyn Trumper drove me home.

Tuesday, 3 September

I visited Mrs Parry and Mrs Michael at the Alms-houses and
heard from the latter that dear Florence Hill had gone to a
place at Clifton.

Thursday, 5 September

Paid Miss Newton 16/8 for 25 gallons of cider at 8d. a gallon.

Friday, 6 September

A lovely autumn day opening with a slight wind and tender
mist on the river, then ripening into a splendid golden mellow
afternoon. Visited Priscilla Price and was much interested by
her account of her reminiscences of the days when George the
Fourth was King.

I came down by the Upper Cwm and had a long pleasant
talk with nice Sarah Abberley who was neatly dressed, waiting
in a clean bright tidy kitchen to give her father his tea when he
came in. She reminded me of what I have often thought of this
week, that it will be exactly a year tomorrow since John Houseman the late Vicar of Bredwardine was called to his rest on
Saturday, 8 September, 1877. She told me that he had experi-

enced one or two slight apoplectic attacks before and the doctors had forbidden him to use cold baths telling him that it might be fatal to him. He persisted however in taking them and had just had a cold bath before he was struck down.

The Reminiscences of Priscilla Price of the time when George the Fourth was King.

'When George IV was crowned I was living in London at 31 Russell Square in service with Squire Atkinson. I remember seeing the procession but could not see much for the great crowds of people and when I got home safe I would not go out again. Queen Caroline went to the Abbey too in Alderman Wood's Carriage. She was staying at Alderman Wood's house at the time. The King would not let her be crowned with him. They told her at the Abbey door that she might come in if she liked to sit in a back seat, but she would not do that and drove away again. The soldiers were ordered not to touch their hats to her but they all saluted her. That night there was a great illumination. All those who took the King's part put lights in their windows and those who took the Queen's part put none. We did not know what to do but at last we put up lights. But when Squire Atkinson came up from Brighton that night he told us to take the lights down again, saying he wasn't going to light up his house for *him*. Two great crowds were going about all night. One was for the King and the other for the Queen. The King's crowd shouted "Lights up!" and the Queen's crowd shouted "Light's down!" One crowd smashed the dark windows and the other smashed the lighted windows and people did not know what to do. I saw Queen Caroline on a balcony. She came out and made her obeisance on every hand. She was nice-looking, to my mind, with a pleasant face. I saw the King too but not so plain as the Queen. He was riding by in a close carriage. He was a passable looking man, but not so well-looking as the Queen. I thought he was dressed very old-fashioned in breeches and waistcoat and a wig. The King was not very well liked upon. Nine days after the King was crowned the Queen died (?). I was washing and stoning the steps before the front door one morning when I heard a sound that shook the town. I was frightened and ran in thinking something dreadful had happened to London, but they told me it was the tolling of the great bell at St Paul's and that one of the Royal Family must be dead because the great bell only tolled for them. Then we heard that Queen Caroline was dead. There was a great deal of talk at that time in London about the quarrel between the King and the Queen. There was about six for one and half a dozen for the other. Some believed the Queen had done wrong and some didn't. We thought the King was too hard upon the Queen and I favoured the Queen.

'It was a terrible day when Queen Caroline was buried. They would not let the funeral go by the main streets. It was to go by the back streets. But the people blocked up the back streets with carriages, carts and coaches and forced the procession to go by the great streets. There was a great mob and the funeral could not go on. Then there was a disturbance and the soldiers fired upon the people. My sister who was living in service at No. 5 Montague Street was in the crowd that day and the second woman from her was shot.

'I saw the Princess Charlotte once but I don't remember where it was or what she looked like. She was a strip of a girl. The King would not let her see her mother. But once she escaped and ran out into the street and called a hackney coach. "Drive me to Buckingham House!" she cried. "Drive me to Buckingham House!" and I believe she was driven there.

'I saw the first steamboat that ever was in the Thames pass under London Bridge. There used to be a saying that no vessel could pass under the middle arch of London Bridge for there was something in the water that would suck the vessel in. However, the steamboat started from Westminster Bridge with a number of people on board and passed through the middle arch of London Bridge and was not sucked in.'

12th Sunday after Trinity, 8 September

The anniversary of the sudden death by apoplexy of the Rev. John Houseman, late Vicar of Bredwardine and Rector of Brobury. I alluded to this in the morning sermon and also to the Sittingbourne railway disaster and the terrible calamity of

Tuesday last on the Thames near Woolwich when the *Princess Alice*, excursion steamboat, was run down by the *Bywell Castle*, screw collier, and more than 700 people drowned.

Monday, 9 September

Weeding the Churchyard path.

I had a serious talk with Ellen Lewis of the turnpike gate house. She is in great distress and very anxious about herself. She was much terrified by the heavy thunderstorm of Saturday night last. She thought the end of the world might be come and feared she was not fit to meet it.

Wednesday, 11 September

The morning was so lovely in the autumn veil of mist that I was tempted to go to Clyro again. Called at the Whitcombes and went up to see old John Morgan. The old Peninsular veteran was working in his garden digging potatoes. He came indoors and sat down for awhile. 'I have lost my shepherd,' he said. I asked him as Pharoah asked Jacob, 'How old art thou?' 'I am 97,' he said, 'but the Lord has behaved very honourable to me.'

Friday, 13 September

This morning I cut the edges of the Churchyard path between the church porch and the Vicarage. The grass had much over-grown the edges and narrowed the path. Afternoon visited Jack my Lord at Crafta Webb. John told me how he and his family got the nickname of 'Lords' or 'My Lords'. His father when a boy worked for old Mrs Higgins at Middlewood. She was displeased with him one day because he would not do something that she told him, and said scornfully that she supposed he was as great a person as 'My Lord North'*. From this simple circumstance the nickname of 'Lords' or 'My Lords' has clung to this family for 3 generations.

*Prime Minister 1770–82.

13th Sunday after Trinity. 15 September

Mrs Jenkins told me that as she was dressing at her window about 5 a.m. she saw a creature which she thought at first was a calf rush madly into the little stable in the fold and then dash out again, hop over the stone wall into the brook, and away. About half an hour after 2 couple of white hounds and a couple of bloodhounds came hunting down the lane with the keepers riding after them and she learnt from the keeper (Hicks) that the animal she had taken for a calf was a buck. They had rifles with them and they had followed the deer all night over part of the Black Mountain. The hounds lost the scent in the water but struck it again and ran into the buck at Upper Castleton. The deer was taken to Mr Medlicott's farmhouse to be cut up and a cart was sent for it from Moccas. Mrs Jenkins said she went into the stable after the buck had bolted from it and saw by the hoof marks and the mud which the deer had brought in with it that the poor hunted creature in its frantic terror and attempts to escape and hide itself had climbed up into the manger and tried to scramble into the rack.

I asked the children at the School what an embalmed Egyptian body was called. 'A life preserver,' said one, 'A muffin,' said another. 'What is a muffin?' I asked. 'A bird,' said a child.

Monday, 23 September

To-day I received a kind letter from Rosie Meredith Brown saying that Ettie would sail for India on 5 October to be married there. I wrote to both of the sisters.

Thursday, 26 September

Service at 3 o'clock. An overwhelming congregation. The Church crowded and a number of people obliged to remain outside. The decorations* quite lovely.

*For the harvest festival.

16 Sunday after Trinity. 6 October

H.C. 19 guests, the greatest number I have seen since I have
been at Bredwardine.

Tuesday, 8 October

Miss Newton's new brougham came home. A very nice
carriage, dark blue picked out with red, a great improvement
on the last.

[*Kilvert goes to stay with his friends the Westhorps at Ilston Rectory;
thence to Langley, returning to Bredwardine on 30 October.*]

21 Sunday after Trinity, 10 November

Heavy rain in the night, thaw on the hills, snow melting and
river rising fast. People busy all day saving cattle and sheep in
the low river meadows. Torrents of rain this morning. Church
almost empty. When I came home from Brobury at 7.30 the
flood had risen much and was nearly over the road by the
Bridge gate. Mrs Jenkins was wading in the water saving he
fowls from being drowned and Alice lacing up her boots again
prepatory to a flight from the house. Mr Stoke's people were
going about with a lantern in his orchard saving and fencing
round some heaps of cider apples.

Monday, 11 November

School. Flood falling. So far the second greatest flood of this
century. Before breakfast I went down to the bridge to see how
the Jenkins family were. Soon after I passed last night the river
came down with a sudden rush and wave and filled the road
full of water and they had to escape to the trap, carrying their
children on their backs, wading through water kneedeep, and
leaving 3 feet of water in the house, the house also being surrounded by water and the water running in at front and back.
Mr Stokes kindly rode down from the Old Court to see if they
were safe, the water was then up to his horse's girths. Many
people were flooded out of their houses at Letton and Staunton

and spent the night on Bredwardine Bridge watching the flood. A number of cattle and colts were seen to pass under the bridge in the moonlight and it was feared they would be drowned. Some women saw a bullock swept down under the bridge at noon to-day. Mr W. Clarke of the Staunton Store room told me that the Whitney iron railway bridge was carried away last night by the flood and 2 miles of line seriously damaged. No trains can run for 3 months, during which time the gap will be filled by coaches.

Tuesday, 12 November

School. Snow fell in the night. Weather much colder. A letter from Mrs Hilton from Hay Castle says that the flood put out all the gas in Hay and that the church at Hay had suddenly to be lighted with candles for evening service on Sunday. Reports keep on coming in of damage and loss, cattle swept away from the Llowes Meadows. Visited Susan Hancox, Samuel Williams, Jack my Lord, Eliza Preece and Priscilla Price, who told me about the mail coach accident in the flood on Bredwardine Bridge 50 years ago when 3 of the horses were drowned.

Thursday, 14 November

To-day I was unfortunately seized with a painful attack of emerods.† Garmin, the Brobury keeper, brought me from Sir Henry Cotterell, who has been shooting the Brobury Woods to-day, a hare and 4 hen pheasants.

Friday, 15 November

Suffering much and obliged to give up going to the school.

Thursday, 21 November

Still on the sofa all day, but getting gradually better. Reading *Is he Popenjoy?** Mr and Mrs Webb lunched at the Cottage. Mr Webb came to see me and brought me two presents from Mrs

*By Anthony Trollope.   †Haemorrhoids.

Webb, a sketch of Chillon Castle and a lamp-shade ornamented with dried flowers, leaves and ferns, fastened between perforated cardboard and net.

Wednesday, 27 November

I had a letter from Mr Venables proposing that I should take Sam Cowper Coles as a pupil. Wrote to Dora on the subject. I think I shall take the boy. 13 years old at £80 a year.

Advent Sunday. December Day.

Hoarse as a raven.

Saturday, 7 December

Indoors all day with a bad sore throat, very hoarse, deaf, stupefied and stunned. Expecting Mr Giles. He came at evening, and prescribed tannin and glycerine to paint the interior of the throat.

2nd Sunday in Advent. 8 December

Fine and cold in the morning, overcast in the afternoon, glass falling and snow threatening. Good congregations.

In the bright sunny morning the sheep were all dotted white about the green slopes across the river. They were all lying down almost at even distances from each other. It was a peaceful pastoral scene. There is a still green beauty peculiar to a fine winter's morning and afternoon which is not seen in summer.

Monday, 16 December

The ground very slippery and dangerous. Children sliding on the Wye below Bredwardine Bridge where the river is frozen half-across. At Moccas Bridge the Wye is frozen entirely over. Snow began to fall at 9 a.m. and continued to fall till 2 p.m.

Tuesday, 17 December

Sharp frost again last night. The snow clouds cleared off and the day became cloudless and blue and brilliant. The bridge in the sunshine was most beautiful. We have cut down several of the shrubs, evergreen oak, Portugal laurel, and laurustinus under the cedar nearest the house and the laurel garden hedge so as to let in more light and a pretty view of the lawn, river and bridge. Visited Bethell, Cae Perthan, the Lower Cwm and the old turnpike gate house. Mrs Powell of Bethell told me of a dream she had shortly before her daughter's death. She saw a funeral going overhead and her own black dress worn by someone in the funeral procession swept over her face and filled her eyes with dust. Then she saw 12 men sitting round her bed.

As I went up the steep snowy hill to Bethell I pursued the fast retreating and ascending wan sunshine of the still winter afternoon. I overtook the sunshine just before I got to the lone house on the bleak windy hill top. All the valley and plain lay bathed in a frosty rosy golden glow, and just as I got to Cae Perthan the sun was setting behind the lone level snowy blue-white line of the Black Mountain and the last rays were reddening the walls and chimney stack of the solitary cottage.

As I came down into the sheltered hollow of the Lower Cwm in the twilight I heard rising from the cottage in the dingle across the brook a woman's voice addressing a naughty child and uttering that threatening promise which in this form is probably as old as the English language and in some form is perhaps as old as the world. 'I'll whip your bottom!' Were bottoms so formed that they might be whipped? or why since the foundation of the world has this part of the human body been universally chosen to suffer chastisement?

Monday, 23 December

Very hard frost. The Wye froze across below Bredwardine Bridge between the Vicarage garden and the Brobury Shore. It has been frozen over and the ice passable for some time at Moccas. Visited Priscilla Price and took her a pudding and some mincepies for Christmas. Snow deep on the hill.

Shepherds in the Black Mountains

Tuesday, 24 December, Christmas Eve

Very hard frost. Brilliant sunshine on sparkling snow. After breakfast I went to the Old Weston to see the poor Davieses and comfort them concerning their child. On the road I met David Davies the father the shepherd at the Weston on his way to the village to order the coffin and to the Churchyard to mark out the ground for the grave. He told me it was not Andrew as I had been informed and supposed, but little Davie who was dead. The father seemed greatly distressed and indignant because he thought the child's life had been thrown away by some mistake of the doctor. I went on to the house of mourning. Margaret Davies seemed very glad to see me and her humble gratitude for my visit was most touching. She took me upstairs into the room where the dead child was lying on the bed and turned down the sheet from his face. I never saw death look so beautiful. There was no bandage round the chin. The pretty innocent child face looked as peaceful and natural as if the child were asleep and the dark curls lay upon the little pillow. I could hardly believe he was dead. Leaving the face still uncovered the poor mother knelt with me by the little bedside while I prayed for them all. She was deeply touched and most humbly grateful. Before I left the room I stooped and kissed the child's forehead, and the mother did the same. It was as cold and as hard as marble. This is always a fresh surprise. I had not touched death for more than 30 years, and it brought back the sudden shock that I felt when as a child I was taken into a room at Hardenhuish Rectory where our little sister lay dead and was told to touch her hand.

Margaret Davies told me that before Little Davie died he saw a number of people and some pretty children dancing in a beautiful garden and heard some sweet music. Then someone seems to have called him for he answered, 'What do you want with me?' He also saw beautiful birds, and the men of the Weston (who carried him to his funeral). He thought his little sister Margaret was throwing ice and snow on him. (The snow fell on the coffin at the burial.) On the road I overtook Miss Stokes and went into the Old Court with her but before Kate could come and speak to me my nose began to bleed and I was obliged to fly.

Wednesday, Christmas Day

Very hard frost last night. At Presteign the thermometer fell to 2 degrees, showing 30 degrees of frost. At Monnington it fell to 4. Last night is said to have been the coldest night for 100 years. The windows of the house and Church were so thick with frost rime that we could not see out. We could not look through the church windows all day. Snow lay on the ground and the day was dark and gloomy with a murky sky. A fair morning congregation considering the weather. By Miss Newton's special desire Dora and I went to the Cottage to eat our Christmas dinner at 1.30 immediately after service.

Immediately after dinner I had to go back to the church for the funeral of little Davie of the Old Weston who died on Monday was fixed for 2.15. The weather was dreadful, the snow driving in blinding clouds and the walking tiresome. Yet the funeral was only 20 minutes late. The Welcome Home, as it chimed softly and slowly to greet the little pilgrim coming to his rest, sounded bleared and muffled through the thick snowy air. The snow fell thickly all through the funeral service and at the service by the grave a kind woman offered her umbrella which a kind young fellow came and held over my head. The woman and man were Mrs Richards and William Jackson. I asked the poor mourners to come in and rest and warm themselves but they would not and went into Church. The poor father, David Davies the shepherd, was crying bitterly for the loss of his little lamb. Owing to the funeral it was rather late before we began the afternoon service. There were very few people in Church beside the mourners. The afternoon was very dark. I was obliged to move close to the great south window to read the Lessons and could hardly see even then. I preached from Luke ii. 7. 'There was no room for them in the inn,' and connected the little bed in the churchyard in which we had laid Davie to rest with the manger cradle at Bethlehem.

In spite of the heavy and deep snow there was a fair congregation at Brobury Church. I walked there with Powell. The water was out in Brobury Lane. As we came back a thaw had set in and rain fell. By Miss Newton's special wish I went to the Cottage and spent the evening with Dora. The Cottage servants had invited the Vicarage servants to tea and supper and they came into the drawing room after supper and sang some Christmas Carols.

Sunday after Christmas. 29 December

Sudden thaw and break up of the frozen river. Huge masses and floes of ice have been coming down the river all day rearing, crushing, grinding against each other, and thundering against the bridge. A crowd of people were on the bridge looking over the parapet and watching the ice pass through the arches. The ground very slippery and dangerous, people walking along the ditches and going on all fours up Bredwardine Hill and across the Lion Square. Emma Jones' mother came all the way from

Dorstone to Bredwardine in the ditches. Price was obliged to go up the hill from the Cottage to his house on all fours and Jane Davies of Fine Street confessed to Dora that she had to crawl on the ice across the Lion Square on her hands and knees.

1879

Wednesday, New Year's Day, 1879.

I sat up last night to watch the old year out and the new year in. The Church bells rang at intervals all last night and all to-day. At 6 I went to Crafta Webb to begin my cottage lectures there. It was raining fast when I started, but when I got as far as the Common I noticed that the ground was white. At first I thought it was moonlight. Then I saw it was snow. At Crafta Webb the snowstorm was blinding and stifling, and I passed by Preece's cottage where I was going to hold the lecture without seeing it in the thickness of the driving snow. Before the lecture I went in to see old John Williams. On opening the door I was confronted by the motionless silent figure of a person veiled and wearing a conical cap which I presently discovered to be a dead pig hanging up by its snout. John Williams deplored my being out in such a night and said it was not fit for me. There were not many people at the service but the usual faithful few. When I came back the storm was worse and so thick and driving that I was glad I was between hedges and not out on the open hill. The young people at the servants' party seemed to be enjoying themselves with dancing and singing. After supper they came into the dining room to sing to me each with a comical cap out of a cracker on her head. Then there was a snapdragon and they went away about 10.30.

Thursday, New Year's Morrow

Deep snow. A brilliant morning and against the cloudless blue and in the bright sunshine the trees were a glorious sight. The sudden sharp frost had found the trees full of snow and had arrested it there. The land was a snow forest. Every branch was weighed down with its glittering dazzling burden and was as full of frosted snow as of leaf in the summer.

I went up to Crafta Webb after breakfast and took broth, wine and pudding for Betty Jones and Sarah Whiting.

Saturday, 4 January

At noon I went by appointment to Priscilla Price and gave her and Sarah Lewis the Holy Communion. The idiot remained almost bowed to the ground through the whole service till told to rise at its conclusion.

Monday, Epiphany. Old Christmas Day

Last night the slip of the Holy Thorn which John Parry of Dolfach grafted for me last spring in the Vicarage lower garden blossomed in an intense frost.

Thursday, 9 January

Afternoon visited Sarah Gwynne at the Claypits and Margaret Davies at the Old Weston, who gave me some tea and consulted me about a little cross which she wished to put up over Davie's grave. She was very humble and thankful for the visit. I went on across the long snowy fields to see Godsall and take him some books. As I came back through the deep snow and drew near the Old Weston I heard a man's voice calling through the dusk to the sheep and the form of David Davies the shepherd loomed through the twilight carrying a truss of hay. The sheep came running eagerly to him and as he fed them I spoke to him of the Good Shepherd who had gathered his lamb with His arm and carried him in His bosom.

Friday, 10th January

I reached home at 5 o'clock just before my first pupil Sam

Cowper Coles came in Baynham's trap from Kinnersley Station.

Saturday, 11 January

Took Sam for a walk up Bredwardine Hill in the afternoon. Carried Priscilla Price a pudding, etc. Went on to the Old House and saw Thomas Davies. Speaking of the necessity of renting land according to his capital the old farmer said, 'I couldn't cut rumps of beef out of mouse's legs.'

We called at James Meredith's. Jane took a great fancy to Sam. 'You are a beauty,' she said. 'You are the prettiest young gentleman out. Don't you think so?' 'No,' said Sam. 'I do,' said Jane.

We found the snow very deep in places and almost impassable. The sky looked black, heavy and full of snow.

Tuesday, 14 January

Last night the river rose rapidly and at midnight the ice was rushing down in vast masses, roaring, cracking and thundering against the bridge like the rolling of a hundred waggons. By morning the river had sunk and left huge piles of ice stranded on the banks.

Friday, 17 January

I think Sam is getting on with his reading and writing which were very bad. His arithmetic is his strongest point. He is very backward and ignorant.

Saturday, 18 January

Fine afternoon. Walked with Sam to Crafta Webb. Visited Jack my Lord, Betty Matthews, Samuel and Anne Williams. All the people take a great fancy to Sam and his fair pink and white face and light hair. Betty Matthews made a great piece of work over him and his fair head. 'Dear little fellow!' and Jack my Lord asked if he was a parson and if he was my brother.

Tuesday, 21 January

Very cold with bitter E. wind and hard frost. Visited Carver and Davies of the Old House. William Davies of Llanafan came in. The father and son were telling me of the games and sports, the fights and merriments, that went on in old times upon Bredwardine Knap. 'What kind of games?' I asked. 'I wouldn't suggest,' said William Davies, 'that they were of any spiritual good.'

Tuesday, 4 February

School. Visited Harper, Carver and Emily Williams, Priscilla Price and Mary Hyde, all ill. At 7 p.m. the farmers came to dine at the Vicarage. I had ten guests, Haywood, Evans, Stokes, Preece, Price, Parry, Bates, James Griffiths, James and Tom Davies. The dinner was very nice. White soup, roast beef, boiled chickens and ham, curried rabbit, stewed woodpigeons, beef-steak pie, potatoes and stewed celery, plum pudding, custard, plum tart, mince pies, apricot jam tart.

Emily waited alone and managed everything very nicely.

Friday, 7 February

The birds are beginning to sing again by the river after the hard frost and the long winter.

Saturday, 8 February

My verses on 'Little Davie' of the Old Weston, who died on Dec. 23rd and was buried on Christmas Day, were published in the *Hereford Times* yesterday.

Septuagesima, 9 February

The first snowdrops appeared in the Churchyard.

Monday, 10 February

Lunched at Cae Mawr. Went in rain to the Upper Noyaddau

to see dear Florence Hill who is thought to be dying of consumption. She was in bed very weak and ill.*

Wednesday, 12 February

A lovely morning and a heavenly blue day. After lunch Bishop drove me home. A pleasant sunny drive but the roads very bad from the frost. The frost had cracked the parapet of Merbach Bridge from top to bottom. Stopped at Meredith's at Traveller's Rest and ordered a 27 lb tub of salt butter. Confirmation class of girls at 5.

Monday, 17 February

Snow. Dear Margaret Davies was profuse in her gratitude for the lines in the *Hereford Times* on Little Davie and told me she had asked Mr Horden of the Hay to print off some copies on cards to be framed and glazed. We agreed that a monumental cross should be put up in Bredwardine Churchyard to 'Little Davie'.

Thursday, 28 February. March Eve

Walking in the garden in the evening I discovered that the intense frost of last month had caused a slip and settlement of the rail on the terrace walk and caused the wall supporting the terrace to bulge dangerously. A large slice of the Vicarage river bank just below the hydraulic ram has slipped into the river, the churchyard wall has bulged, Brobury Churchyard wall has been thrown down by the frost, the walls all over the place have been strained and shaken, the plaster is peeling and shelling off the house and conservatory, and the steps from the upper to the lower garden are in ruins. This is the work of the frost of 1878–1879.

Wednesday, 12 March

When I came home from Moccas last night Dora showed me a

*She did not die, but lived to a comfortable age.

letter she received to-day from James Pitcairn asking her to marry him. This took me entirely by surprise, but I foresee that she will do so.

Thursday, 13 March

A lovely and cloudless day. Walked with Sam to Kinnersley Station to catch 11.45 train to Hereford. I got out at Credenhill with Mr Fowle and Charlesworth. We three walked to Credenhill Church, then up by Credenhill Court and along the hillside under the wood to Brinsop. Lovely views of the Black Mountain with snow patches, the Gaden Fawr and the Skyrrid, a very striking and picturesque peak. Little Brinsop Church lay peacefully below among the meadows of the Brinsop Vale. Lunch at Brinsop Vicarage, then Charlesworth left for the train to Hereford. In the afternoon I walked with Mr Fowle to the Church and then across the meadows to Brinsop Court. We met a fine old lady walking with a tall staff as high as her shoulder. A young woman in a scarlet cloak was with her. A fine sunset gleam lit up the grand old manor house and the lawn and the two snow-white swans on the flowing water of the Moat. On the lawn grew the cedar planted by William Words-worth the poet. Young Mr Edwards (the tenant of the farm which belongs to the Ricardo family) was carpentering in the greenhouse. He courteously took us into a noble sitting room Turkey carpeted and nicely furnished with a fine painting of the poet over the chimney-piece. And here dear Dorothy Wordsworth spent much of her time.

A grand old Quaker lady with white hair, the mother of the tenant, sat by the fire nursing a little girl, while a dark young lady, vivacious and pleasant, the mother of the child, knelt on the hearthrug by them, a pretty family picture. Mr Edwards showed us the grand old banqueting hall reached by a flight of exterior steps from the courtyard. It is now a granary. Opposite were the Chapel and Armoury. Some of the old men on the farm can remember a waggon load of armour and arms being taken away when the Danseys, the former lords of Brinsop, sold the property and vacated the Court.

Mr Edwards said he had heard his father say that when he first came down to Brinsop out of Radnorshire he rode across the moat over the old drawbridge. Back to Brinsop Vicarage to tea and then I was driven to the Credenhill station to catch the 8.10 train. Walked home from Kinnersley. A sharp frost and the N.W. wind bitterly cold.

The diary ends here.

On 20 August, 1879, Kilvert was married at Wootton in Oxford-shire to Elizabeth Roland. On 23 September he died suddenly of peritonitis and was buried in Bredwardine churchyard.

Kilvert's epitaph

CLYRO WATER
[From the *Hereford Times* 20 March, 1875].

Oh, Clyro Water! ceaselessly
For seven sweet years my lullaby;
My life, my love, my footsteps free
For seven sweet years have been by thee;
And as life stole from year to year
Thy voice still more I loved to hear,
Whether with storms thy roar was high,
Or when thou softly murmured'st by
With summer nights' melodious tones,
And quiet clink amongst thy stones.

And often I, when sheltered warm,
From driving rain and howling storm,
Have listened from the lighted book
To hear the roaring of the brook;
And as it thundered, rising still,
It brought a message from the hill
Of torrent, rain and tempest still.
But when thy waters dimpling smiled
Adown the Cwm some sweet spring day,
Fern-fringed, flower-lighted on their way
By primrose stars that shone on thee,
And many a wood anemone,
How have I watched on the green breast
Of orchards sloping to the west,
In sister groups about the hills
The yellow-coated daffodils
Through all the bright March afternoon
Dance, nodding to thy rippling tune.

On Sunday morns the church bells shook
Sweet music o'er the murmuring brook,

That flowed in chime; and from the hill
The parish folk came wending still
Churchwards from many a mountain ridge,
And loitered, leaning on the bridge
To talk, before the dropping chime
Gave warning of the service time;
And ere had ceased the parson's bell,
A silence o'er the village fell,
For all the churchyard path had trod,
And gathering kneeled to worship God,
And the sole sound the air that shook
Was the sweet tinkle of the brook.

Sweet Clyro Water! oh, let me
Still by thy banks remembered be,
And keep yet as thy grasses green,
The love for me that once has been!
And if 'tis given to me once more
To tread thy well remembered shore,
May I not wander there unknown,
But find a hand to clasp my own,
A voice of welcome, gladdening eyes
And kindly smiles or kindlier sighs,
But, oh, meanwhile, sweet stream, by thee
May many a prayer arise for me,
May kind thoughts, wishes that in heaven
Are counted prayers, at morn and even
From those worn water-steps below
The mountain ash, still heavenward go,
For him who exiled far away
For his dear friends doth ever pray.

EOS GWYNDDWR.

18 March 1875.

SET IN 11 POINT BASKERVILLE TYPE LEADED 1 POINT

AND PRINTED BY LITHOGRAPHY

ON FINEBLADE CARTRIDGE PAPER

BY SHENVAL PRESS LIMITED, HARLOW

BOUND BY W & J MACKAY LIMITED, CHATHAM

USING RUSKIN CLOTH AND PAPER SIDES

PRINTED IN DUOTONE FROM PHOTOGRAPHS

BY TIM STEPHENS

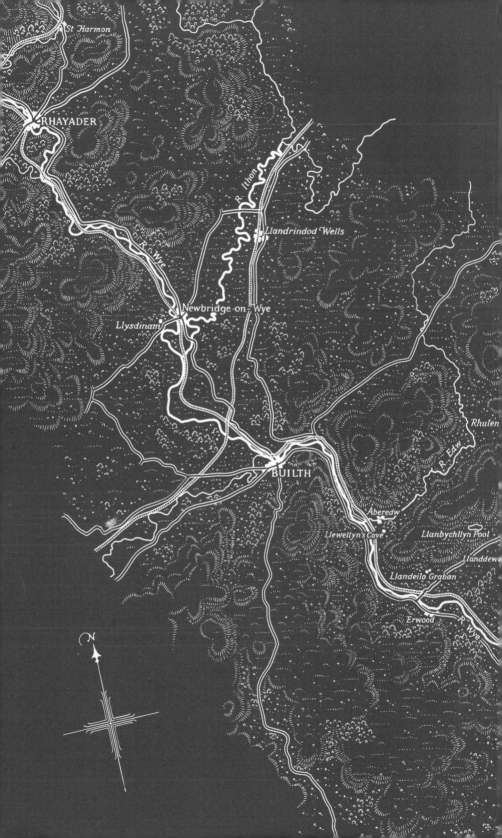